Praise for Ben Lesser's Memoir

"Ben Lesser, Living a Life that Matter is classic in structure: Before, During and After. His life before the Holocaust was a life of privilege in two of the most important Jewish cities of Eastern Europe Krakow and Munkacs, in Poland and Hungary. His life during the Holocaust includes ghetto-ization and escape into Hungary where in 1944 he is transported to Auschwitz-Birkenau. His life after the Holocaust includes a sojourn in Germany and then training for aliyah to Israel and finally life in the United States.

As many survivors, his first years in the golden medina were marked by hard work and beginning a family. It is a important rags to riches story, but his last years have been his most significant for Ben, as many survivors, has become a teacher, bearing witness to the past and teaching students of all ages from elementary school to college the important values of tolerance, democracy, respect for human dignity and decency. He has truly lived a life that matters and has shown us all that while suffering may not confer meaning, how one deals with suffering can make all the difference in the world, conferring meaning on the life of the witness and in the lives of those of us who have become witnesses to the witness. One is privileged to know such a man and honored to read his work."

Michael Berenbaum
American Jewish University
American scholar, professor, rabbi, writer, and filmmaker
Los Angeles, California

NAZI HOLOCAUST SURVIVOR'S MEMOIR:

LIVING A LIFE THAT MATTERS:
from Nazi Nightmare to American Dream
by Ben Lesser

Comes to Canada's Northwest Territories!

A Book Review by Michael Botermans,
Chief Jimmy Bruneau Regional High School,
Behchoko, Northwest Territories, Canada

After reading Ben Lesser's powerful memoir, **LIVING A LIFE THAT MATTERS:** *from Nazi Nightmare to American Dream*, my life seems utterly changed. It was as if each character of each event became a part of my own life, my own family. It is a poignant reminder that our *lives are worth living* — and that "living a life that matters" can change the face of the world around us — and beyond. It makes clear that it isn't so much the unique hardships we each face, but how we respond to them, and endure them.

As Ben shows us, we all are accountable for our own choices. Therefore, we each must "live a life that matters," and embrace others' ethnic backgrounds, cultures and creeds. In our world, there is just no place for intolerance, racism, injustice and indifference. **LIVING A LIFE THAT MATTERS** helps to move the world one step closer to peaceful resolve and harmony.

LIVING A LIFE THAT MATTERS: *from Nazi Nightmare to American Dream* is an easy read. Each page overflows with vivid sketches of The Holocaust, of Ben's boyhood and adolescence, along with the history of the Jewish People. Ben's life, with all its sorrow and success, has been one miracle after another, a marathon of hope, and sheer bravery in the face of evil during the darkest chapter of human history. From beginning to end, we are immersed in The Holocaust and challenged to search deep within ourselves for answers to some of history's simplest yet meaningful questions: How could man do such unspeakable acts to man? And even today, how has the whole world not learned from crimes against the humanity we all belong to? What is my role today to ensure history not repeat itself? How can I prevent bullying, discrimination, and segregation from happening in my school or workplace or neighborhood?

How can I reach out to someone who is being victimized? How can I teach, tell, and re-tell the story of The Holocaust in a meaningful way so our young people can learn—and remember?

The theme of Ben's memoir—and of his life—is "Zachor." This means, "remember," and it shows us that we cannot remain indifferent or complacent—we must prevent the world from "acquiring amnesia." Ben's story helps me "remember" not only the pain man inflicted on man, but also man's resilience and resistance, and finally, man's determination to live, "to live a life that matters" as he so eloquently has proven.

After reading Ben Lesser's *Living A Life That Matters: from Nazi Nightmare to American Dream,* I am even more determined to live what years I have left with stronger purpose and in the hope of helping others attain that same conclusion. How honored I am, and blessed, that Ben's life, in his 83rd year, has met up with mine in the Canadian Arctic!

More Praise for Ben Lesser's Memoir

"Here is a most unusual book by a most unusual person that leads us to change our thinking about the Holocaust with its millions killed not as a matter of statistics but as the fates of individual human beings who might, like the author, have lived meaningful, and productive lives; and who deserve to be remembered lest there be a repetition."

Gerhard L. Weinberg
Professor Emeritus of the University of North Carolina at Chapel Hill
Author of "A World at Arms: A Global History of World War II"

"In any culture, it is critical to acknowledge and understand the past, as it helps build the foundation of our future. In the Northwest Territories, the legacy of residential schools remains, but we are on a path of reconciliation and healing. We are teaching our youth that this is important if we want to move forward to a stronger, brighter future for our residents and territory.

Mr. Lesser is an incredible role model for people of any culture. His resilience and courage to acknowledge the past and share his vision for a brighter future after his time in concentration camps is empowering. His dedication to ensuring the world never forgets these dark periods in our collective history is a testament to his strength and character." thanks for making a difference and sharing the history."

Masi Cho Jackson Lafferty
Deputy Premier Minister of Education, Culture and Employment, Legislative Assembly of the Northwest Territories

"Among the myriad of Holocaust autobiographies currently available, Living a Life that Matters by Ben Lesser is especially well suited to K-12 age pupils for several reasons. First, like many such autobiographies it tells an important and compelling life story.

Second, it includes enough general historical material that the reader can consider Lesser's experiences in an appropriate historical context without outside research.

Third, unlike many Holocaust autobiographies, Lesser writes prose in a conversational tone that neither puts off young readers with strident overtones nor sends them scampering to a dictionary. It is appropriate for adults as well, but it is especially useful for introducing middle and high school pupils to Holocaust studies."

Dr. Nancy E,. Rupprecht
Chair MTSU Holocaust Studies Program
Holocaust and World War II, In History and In Memory.
Co-Author , Nancy E. Rupprecht

"Ben Lesser's book is a haunting journey which takes the reader from an idyllic childhood in Poland through the horrors of Dachau and Auschwitz to a new life in America. This bittersweet memoir is filled with personal stories within a historical context written in the authors' own voice. It explores both the discovery of hope and the depths of evil and is about reinventing a life in America. This book is not just a Holocaust story. It is about growing up in a war torn place, about survival and ultimately about adoring a family and living a life to inspire and remember. Ben's optimism and courage embody the best of the human spirit."
Nancy N.

"Lesser's book has made a positive and profound impact on my life . . . it is a poignant reminder that we are all an important member of broken humanity, that our lives are worth living and 'living a life that matters' can change the face of the world around us--and beyond. "

"Ben's life resonates "hope", and in that hope he endured the barbarism of the Nazis with all its tragedy and trauma and, in the end, realized the American Dream."

"Ben Lesser's amazing and lasting gift to humanity shines on every page of his book. He lights our way from the darkest pages of a child's sudden plunge into the despairs of Nazi Germany to his stunning transformation (rebirth) to new life in America."

"Lesser's intimate story is a page-turner with a unique gift for every reader. He gives us rare insights into how we can overcome the worst of circumstances."

"Ben Lesser's love story with his soul-mate touches our hearts and his success as a professional business man touches our minds."

"Ben has been given the talent to orchestrate the story of his life wherein the reader can "taste" the atrocities that were thrust upon him at such a young age . . . few people can begin to imagine the strength of his human spirit that allowed him to survive and ultimately thrive!"

"This book serves as a precious gift, making us question who we are, who we can become, and how we can live a meaningful life – all against the backdrop of a man who survived the Holocaust and found the American Dream- and so much more."

"Ben's life wasn't just the Holocaust – because he chose to live a meaningful life, there was also love, joy, humor and success . . ."

"It really is an extraordinary story and an excellent learning tool for young adults and everyone else, Ben's tenacity, strength and ambitions are to be admired and are a great example for our children to give of their best and they will receive the best."

Praise for Ben Lesser's Presentations

". . . It is easy for people in this day and age to take everything for granted but you are living proof of someone who is constantly aware of the blessings around them . . . after your beautiful speech all I wanted to do was hug and kiss them (my family) *and voice my love for them."*
~ **Student**

". . . I must say that for every person you move as much as you did my son, they will make sure the world never forgets!"
~ **Parent**

"They were so touched by your story and experiences of the holocaust, it affected them deeply. They continue to wear the pins that you gave them daily and are proud to share your story with all who inquire about the pins.
~ **Teacher**

". . . Looking back, the hour or two that I spent with you along with my class was the most impactful and educational time I've ever had. I wanted to give you my thanks for sharing your story with me 5 years ago . . ."
~ **Student**

"I cannot begin to thank you enough for giving my students the gift of hearing your testimony. In all of my years of teaching . . . I have never seen a single event have such a tremendous impact on a group of students."
~**Teacher**

"From the day I heard your story, I will always ZACHOR!
~ **Student**

". . . I have already begun to spread your message and will continue to make sure the words of hate do not spread to actions."
~ Student

"You didn't let the controlling attempts of others take over your life. Instead, you fought to survive. And after you were liberated, you fought out into the world . . . Your words stuck with me; "This is America! I believe that hard work, studying, will allow you to get where you want. . . ."
~ Student

". . . telling his story with a magic that kept even the most restless of us still. We knew that something was happening; something was changing, changing as the man in front of us brought what had previously been just text on a page to life . . ."
~ Student

"I have worn the pin a few times and see it almost every day in my jewelry box. I just have to hold it and touch it and your story stays with me. With the pin, I feel as I can remember every word. . . It is almost as if all of those stories, of everyone who was murdered, are held within that tiny pin, begging to be told . . ."
~ Student

"If enough people remember the stories of genocide survivors, we could avoid future genocides. I, for one, will do my best to speak out in the face of injustice."
~ Student

"My favorite thing I learned from your speech is that anyone can become successful."
~ Student

"Again and again he told his story with such powerful details and eloquence, that afterward audiences refused to leave, but stayed on to ask questions. His host of "thank you letters" from students and adult audiences alike would fill suitcases. The intense Interest also made him realize how much the world needed this information, and how much they valued it."
~ **Holocaust Survivor, Educator**

"... One of the things that I learned was that words filled with hate can change a nation ... The Holocaust was caused by hateful words. Those words soon led to violence. I made a promise to myself that I will not say anything hateful..."
~ **Student**

"I know that I will face tough situations in my life but none like yours ... I do not ever want to give up because now I know that anything is possible."
~ **Student**

"You've changed how I see things in life and in the world. You impacted my life a whole lot by letting me know not to take my life for granted."
~ **Student**

"Thank you so much for sharing your experiences, motivating us to never give up and empowering us to teach others."
~ **Student**

"Each student walks away from you a changed person, not only in themselves, but with their friends, goals and families."
~ **Teacher**

LIVING A LIFE THAT MATTERS:

from Nazi Nightmare to American Dream

by

Ben Lesser

Copyright © 2012 Ben Lesser.

All rights reserved. No part of this book may be used or reproduced by any means, graphic, electronic, or mechanical, including photocopying, recording, taping or by any information storage retrieval system without the written permission of the publisher except in the case of brief quotations embodied in critical articles and reviews.

Abbott Press books may be ordered through booksellers or by contacting:

Abbott Press
1663 Liberty Drive
Bloomington, IN 47403
www.abbottpress.com
Phone: 1 (866) 697-5310

Because of the dynamic nature of the Internet, any web addresses or links contained in this book may have changed since publication and may no longer be valid. The views expressed in this work are solely those of the author and do not necessarily reflect the views of the publisher, and the publisher hereby disclaims any responsibility for them.

Any people depicted in stock imagery provided by Thinkstock are models, and such images are being used for illustrative purposes only. Certain stock imagery © Thinkstock.

ISBN: 978-1-4582-0272-7 (sc)
ISBN: 978-1-4582-0274-1 (hc)
ISBN: 978-1-4582-0273-4 (e)

Library of Congress Control Number: 2012904211

Print information available on the last page.

Abbott Press rev. date: 12/28/2015

*"Life is the sum
of all your choices."*

~ Albert Camus

Acknowledgements

Anyone who has attempted to be a writer, whether of newsletters, novels or memoirs, knows that his or her success depends upon the help of many people. Such has certainly been the case with my memoir. In addition to my wonderful family, I'd like to acknowledge the generous support of the many students, teachers, parents and Survivors who have shared their questions, comments and encouragement in the creation of this book. My profound appreciation goes to my son-in-law, Michael Gerber, for inspiring the title of my memoir.

It was also my good fortune to have my book edited by talented Editor, Researcher, Educator and Personal Historian, Joanne D. Gilbert, M. Ed, who believed in me and this memoir from the start. I thank her for helping to make my story become **LIVING A LIFE THAT MATTERS:** *from Nazi Nightmare to American Dream*.

Editor's Note

If an editor is very lucky, that rare project will come along that not only combines occupation with vocation, but one that also is profoundly moving on a personal level. Such has been the case with **LIVING A LIFE THAT MATTERS:** *from Nazi Nightmare to American Dream*. Ben Lesser is a natural story-teller with an eye for facts and details. Combined with his passion and commitment, his story makes audiences of all ages sit-up, listen, remember — and take action. Working with him to transform his manuscript, presentations, and correspondence into this memoir has been a joyful honor. I am grateful to have had the opportunity to help preserve Ben Lesser's personal contribution to the history of the Jewish People.

Dedication

I dedicate this book with love to my family: past, present, and future. First, to my young, loving and courageous parents, Shaindel and Lazar Leser. How I wish they could have lived to see their beautiful descendants. They would have been so proud. Also to my two brave brothers, Moishe and Tuli; and my beautiful sister, Goldie, who all were so brutally slaughtered by the Nazis.

And then to the love of my life, my dear wife, Jean, who with love and devotion for over 60 wonderful years has shared in all my dreams, and chased away the nightmares. She has also deciphered my illegible handwriting, tirelessly typed my memoirs, and enthusiastically supported all my ventures. Jean, you have always been, and always will be my best friend.

This book is also dedicated to my devoted daughters, Sherry and Gail, and my sons-in-law, Michael Gerber and Larry Kramer, who are more like the sons I never had. And to my precious grandchildren: Robyn, Jenica, Adam and Cindy.

And to my life-long inspiration, my only surviving sister Lola, who I've always looked up to with love, respect and admiration.

I am so blessed to have you all in my life. It is for you all that I have tried to live . . .

"A Life That Matters."

Table of Contents

PART I: THE NAZI NIGHTMARE

1. Dear Reader. 3
2. 2006: Dear *Mammiko* and *Tattiko* 9
3. The Nightmare and the Dream 13
4. What's in a Name?. 17
5. 1928-1939: The Early Years 21
6. How Could *The Holocaust* Happen? 35
7. Summers in Munkács 45
8. 1939: Autumn in Kraków. 51
9. 9/1/1939: The Germans Occupy Poland. 57
10. 1941: Escape from Kraków. 67
11. 1943: Escape from Niepolomice 75
12. A Modern-Day Queen Esther 87
13. 1943: Escape from Bochnia 95
14. A Happy Munkács Reunion 99
15. 1944: The Nazis Invade Hungary. 105
16. Auschwitz-Birkenau and Durnhau. 111
17. The Death March. 131
18. The Death Train to Dachau. 135
19. April 29, 1945: Liberation!. 139

PART II: SURVIVOR!

20. Holocaust Survivor. 145
21. A Purim in July!. 149
22. The *Chalutzim*. 153
23. A Joyous Reunion!. 163
24. Life in Post-War Germany. 169
25. Leaving the Old World. 177

PART III: THE AMERICAN DREAM

26. America!. 183
27. True Love. 199
28. Achieving the American Dream. 205
29. A New Career. .223
30. An American Citizen. 229
31. American Adventures. 235
32. Ben Lesser and Associates. 249

PART IV: ZACHOR!

33. Retirement and a New Challenge. 263
34. 2006: Transported to the Past. 269
35. 2009: *ZACHOR!*. 281
36. 2010: The March of the Living. 291
37. 2010: Dear *Mammiko* and *Tattiko*. 297
38. Dear Reader. 299

APPENDIX

Dear Ben. 305
Timeline. 321
List of Major Concentration Camps 330
Reader's Guide & Selected Vocabulary. 331
A Thank You to MOTL - 2010. 339
About Lola. 345
Resources. 347

PART I

"The Nazi Nightmare"

Part I: The Nazi Nightmare

Poland: Summer, 1939

1. DEAR READER

My name is Ben Lesser, and I am a Holocaust Survivor. What this means is that for some reason, unlike more than six million other innocent Jewish people, I did *not* die during Hitler Germany's Third Reich. These lives were eliminated from the face of the earth as if they didn't have any value. *As if they didn't matter.*

It also means that throughout the over 66 years since I was liberated from the Dachau *Concentration Camp*,* I have never stopped wondering why my life was spared. And I have never stopped grieving for those who were lost. The Hebrew word *Zachor* means remember, and we remaining Survivors are determined to make sure the world never forgets that every life matters.

While I was lucky enough to survive the camps, come to America, live in freedom, fall in love, marry and raise a beautiful family, work hard and achieve the *"American Dream,"*** my heart and soul have at the same time, inhabited a world shadowed by sorrow. And in my mind there are questions that have never been answered. You might be surprised to learn that my first unanswered question is not, Why did that *insane* Hitler try to destroy the Jewish People? Instead, my first unanswered question

---

*Concentration Camps were squalid, savagely inhumane prisons designed to torture and destroy anyone considered alien to Hitler's Aryan Master Race. Opening in 1933, Dachau Concentration Camp, near Munich, was the first Nazi concentration camp in Germany.
**The concept of the *American Dream* is based on the second sentence of the Declaration of Independence, and tells us that "All men are created equal . . . endowed by their Creator with certain unalienable rights . . . including . . . Life, Liberty and the Pursuit of Happiness." As a result, America has always been considered an oasis of freedom for oppressed people from all over the world.

Part I: The Nazi Nightmare

is, Why did the so-called *sane* world stand by and let this *Genocide** happen?

Having experienced the savagery of genocide first-hand as a child, while living in a supposedly modern, cultured, European country, I also have two additional questions: One: What are the circumstances and choices that led up to this and other genocides? And two: What must we do to prevent it from happening again? Anywhere. Because, sadly, as the old saying tells us,

> *"The more things change, the more they stay the same."*

This means that no matter how much progress the human race makes intellectually and technologically, human emotions never change. This is just as valid today as it has been throughout history. And if you look around, you will see that there are *genocides* taking place today — in Darfur, Sudan, the Congo, Uganda, and Ethiopia, just to name a few. As we Holocaust Survivors enter our eighties and nineties, we are the last remaining people who can bring the authenticity of real life experience to these questions. We, therefore, have both the responsibility and the honor to share our experiences with others before our time runs out.

And because of this, for the last 16 years since retiring from my real estate business, I have dedicated myself to learning and teaching about how the Holocaust could have happened, and its impact on humanity. In this sometimes painful but always enlightening process, I have learned a great deal both about human nature, and about myself. I have come to understand that so much of what happens in life is the result of seemingly simple human choices. A

---

*Genocide is the deliberate, often government sponsored extermination of an entire group/race of people.

1. Dear Reader

person can choose not to hate. A person can choose not to use hateful speech. Hitler did not start with weapons. He started with hate. And then he proceeded to use hateful speech. A person can choose to not become a perpetrator or a bystander, an oppressor cannot succeed on his or her own. When someone is being victimized—whether by a school-yard bully or a maniacal national leader—those who are not victims make the choice to join the bully or to become the bystander who does nothing.

I am grateful that I have the opportunity to not only speak up about what happened, but also to inspire others to recognize the conditions—and choices—that might lead up to—or hopefully prevent—genocide. As a result of my many presentations to schools, religious organizations and community groups, I have seen that on a historical level, far too many people of all ages have no real idea about what happened to the Jewish people of Europe before, during, and after the Third Reich (1933-1945). And despite those who would deny the existence of the Holocaust, there are many people who are hungry to know the truth about this savage time. I realized that many people do not understand that they have the power to make choices that will determine the course of their lives. In response to their questions, heartfelt interest, and commitment to take action, I decided to put my experiences in writing so that after I am gone, my stories, my choices, and the lessons they teach, will continue.

> *... thou shalt not be a perpetrator,*
> *but, above all, thou shalt not be a bystander."*
> ~ Yehuda Bauer (1926-)
> Jewish-Czech-born Author,
> Historian, Holocaust Scholar

Part I: The Nazi Nightmare

We Survivors are often asked how accurate our Holocaust memories are. It's a good question, because in a unique way, our memories are quite different from what most people think of as memories. Since each event was permanently burned into our minds, bodies and souls, when we talk or even think about them, it's more like actually reliving the experience—rather than just remembering it. And although these details remain painfully clear, mere facts alone cannot tell the story. In order to truly learn the lessons of the Holocaust, it is also necessary to understand the human emotions that accompany the details and the facts. And just like the facts, these emotions are also just as real today as they were then.

Communicating the reality, both factual and emotional, can sometimes be a real challenge because there is no *human* language that can possibly convey the *inhuman* events of the *Shoah*.* So we can sometimes be heard to say, "*I have no words to describe . . . .*" And since an old saying or proverb can sometimes add to the understanding of the essence of an experience, I hope you will indulge my occasional use of well-known quotations throughout my story. My recollections have been aided by the many notes that I've made throughout the years. As I look them over, these notes almost seem to be "letters" to my parents—letting them know about my life—and letting them know that they will always remain a part of it.

These notes, along with the answers to questions I've been asked at my numerous presentations, have formed

---

*Shoah is derived from the Hebrew *HaShoah*, meaning "catastrophe." It specifically applies to the Nazi Holocaust (1933-1945), when 2/3 of the European Jewish population was murdered under the directive of the German government.

1. Dear Reader

the basis of this book. While I never dreamed that I would be able to visit my parents' gravesite and speak to them directly, I have been privileged on three occasions, in 1995, 2006, and in 2010, to visit their memorial in the old Jewish Cemetery in Bochnia, Poland. On each of these occasions, in order to avoid being overcome by emotion, I read aloud from "letters" that I had prepared in advance. It is in my parents' honor, therefore, that I will begin my story—as I began my life—with them.

Sincerely,

Ben Lesser
Las Vegas, NV
2012

Part I: The Nazi Nightmare

Jewish Cemetery
Bochnia, Poland (2006)
Lesser Family Collection

2. 2006: DEAR MAMMIKO & TATTIKO*

Old Jewish Cemetery of Bochnia, Poland
July, 2006

Dearest Mammiko and Tattiko,

It's me, your middle son, Baynish. Can you imagine that your curly-haired boy is now 77 years old? Not once in the ten years since my wife, Jean, and I were last able to visit here with you, did I ever dream that I would stand in this God-forsaken place again. To tell the truth, that visit was so traumatic for us that we never wanted to come back to this Jewish-blood-soaked country. However, as you know, sometimes fate steps in and changes our plans. And so I am grateful to be here again with you today — blessed by the presence of family members who carry you in their hearts even though they've never met you.

In the almost 70 years since that terrible night when little Tuli and I had to leave you behind in Bochnia, I have often held silent conversations with you in my heart and in my soul. Today, surrounded by your descendants, I am grateful to be able to give voice to my words. Standing here I am overwhelmed with joy to have survived the Nazis and to be blessed with such a family. At the same time, I am flooded with pain that your lives were so brutally extinguished — never to experience the life you had earned and so richly deserved. That you were never allowed to see your own beloved children grow up and live lives that we hope would make you proud.

Mammiko, I am stunned as I realize that my beautiful, strong, talented and loving daughters are just about the same age that you were when you and Tattiko were discovered and executed

---

*Mammiko and *Tattiko* are Hungarian terms of endearment for mother and father.

Part I: The Nazi Nightmare

while trying to escape from Nazi Poland. As I look at your granddaughters, who now have grown children of their own, I am filled with gratitude that they all were able to grow up as free Americans, never having to face the horrors of the Nazis. Never having to feel like despised outsiders in the country of their birth. I know how pleased you would be to see that all of your grand- and great-grandchildren have consciously made choices that would allow them to live meaningful lives. And they all are leading "lives that matter." I also know that this could never have happened without the selfless and careful choices you both made throughout your own too short lives.

As you know Moishe, Goldie, and little Tulika were brutally murdered by the Nazis. Lola and I were the only two of your five cherished children to survive the Holocaust. In the short time that we were able to live as a family, we learned from you how to lead lives that matter. We have both striven to lead lives that would make you proud. Remember how Lola used her artistic talent to help forge the Hungarian citizenship documents that allowed many Jews to escape certain death in the Bochnia **Ghetto**?* After the war ended, Lola became an accomplished and well-known fine artist. Remember the last time we were all together in 1941 at her brave little wedding to Mechel in our gray and barren backyard in Niepolomice? The courage and determination that Mechel displayed in saving our lives and the lives of so many others remained with him after the war, as he fought the cancer that would succeed where the Nazis had failed in taking his life.

Today, while wandering through this spirit-filled cemetery, we stopped at the burial site of five members of Mechel's family. With grief-filled hearts, we stood lost in our thoughts about that night over 66 years ago in Bochnia when these innocent, loving

---

*A *Ghetto* was a squalid, dangerous, and usually deadly section of town where the Jewish people were forced to live.

2. 2006: Dear *Mammiko* and *Tattiko*

people were murdered in a vicious Pogrom.* *We said* Kaddish, *the Jewish prayer for the dead, for them. And then your great-granddaughter, Robyn, motioned for us all to look up to the sky. It was with great astonishment that we saw above us the five protective branches of a sheltering oak. And now, as we stand at your memorial, almost as if we were given a signal, we again all turn our eyes upward to the heavens. It is with profound awe that we see that you, and the nine others who perished with you, are protected by eleven branches of another ancient, majestic oak. As we looked at each other again, we knew that we were in the presence of not just one, but two miracles.*

Dearest Mammiko and Tattiko, this visit with you has been yet another miracle. You would be proud to know that two of your beautiful great-grandchildren organized this whole trip! And because they have asked me to tell them about our family's history, together we will be transported to the past. We will visit places of infinite happiness and unspeakable horror. I will tell them the story of my life and that of the Leser/Lesser family. In this way, they will also learn about their own place in the ongoing story of the Jewish people. They will learn about the choices that all people must make in order to live lives that matter.

Now as we say our loving farewells, I want you to know that no matter where I am, I will continue to have conversations with you in my heart and in my soul. I will continue to write "letters" to you. And I will continue to live a life that matters. Maybe one day if God is willing, I will be able to visit you again, and once more speak my words aloud. ZACHOR!

May you always rest in peace.

Your loving son,

Baynish

---

*A *Pogrom* is a violent, usually government-sanctioned anti-Semitic riot that includes massive destruction, instant execution of those found in hiding, deportations to concentration camps or other unknown locations, and death.

Part I: The Nazi Nightmare

**Reading a "letter" to my parents
Bochnia's Jewish Cemetery, Poland (2006)**
Lesser Family Collection

3. THE NIGHTMARE AND THE DREAM

> *"You might leave the concentration camps, but the concentration camps will never leave you."*
> ~ Holocaust Survivor

As I leave the Bochnia Jewish Cemetery with my family, I am flooded with so many mixed emotions about the present and the past that it's almost impossible to differentiate between them. Gazing at the shining faces of my daughters and their children—so eager to know about their family's past—I see reflections of my parents and siblings. And I wonder... where can I begin to tell the story of my life? There isn't a whimsical, "Once upon a time..." beginning, or a "Happily ever after..." ending to neatly sum it all up. It all just circles around again and again. And with each circle, with every new fact, insight and lesson, it gains more power, so that the remains of the past flow through the present and on into to the future.

And so it is that on each and every day of the 66 years spanning the distance between my liberation from the Nazi Nightmare of the Dachau Concentration Camp in 1945, and the subsequent American Dream that I've been blessed to live in the United States, I thank God. At the same time, as a Holocaust Survivor, not a single day of those years has gone by without my soul being thrust back into that nightmare. It may be something as obvious as a 21st century nightly news broadcast showing an Iranian dictator denying the existence of the Holocaust. Sometimes it's as subtle as a faded number tattoo on the withered wrist of an elderly woman slowly pushing a grocery cart. For a Holocaust

Part I: The Nazi Nightmare

Survivor, there is no experience today that doesn't also have its own echo. Every current experience has a shadow.

We Holocaust Survivors are the keepers of a history that is both heinous and heroic. We cannot, and will not, allow this history to be distorted, denied, or forgotten. This is a sacred promise we made to the ones who were lost. It is also a sacred promise we make to our children, their children, and those who will follow. Without this vigilance, once we are gone, there will be nothing to stop the coming of another Nightmare. It is essential, therefore, that we heed the wisdom of another wise old saying:

> *"Those who do not learn from history are doomed to repeat it."*
> ~ George Santayana (1863-1952)
> Spanish-born Philosopher,
> Author, Scholar

In order to avoid repeating our tragic history, it is necessary to learn the human choices from which these events developed. Now, in memory of those who were doomed, and to ensure the freedom and safety of future generations, we must work diligently to bring people together in mutual understanding, respect and responsibility. To paraphrase the great ancient Jewish religious leader, Hillel the Elder (c.110 BCE-10 CE):

> *"If not me...Who?*
> *"If not now ... When?"*

Clearly the answer to Hillel's question is that WE must do it. And we must do it *now*.

Part I: The Nazi Nightmare

WHAT'S IN A NAME?

S U R V I V O R

4. WHAT'S IN A NAME?

> *"For in our name lies our soul and self."*
> ~ Rabbi Berel Wein (1934-)
> American Scholar, Historian

You may have heard the question, "What's in a name?" Well, now as I look back in order to look forward, I am reminded of the many names—good and bad—by which I have been known throughout my long and eventful life. I can tell you that something as simple as a name can contain the history of a single person—and if you care to look further, the history of an entire people. How interesting it is that something as seemingly simple as a person's name can contain such a world of memories.

For example, today in America, I am known as Ben Lesser. To Jean, my beloved wife of over sixty years, I am known as Sweetheart. To my precious grown children I am still Daddy. To my adored grandchildren, I am Papa Ben. And depending upon my age, who was addressing me, and what country I was in at that time, I have also been known as Benyameen (Hebrew) Baynish (Yiddish), Benek (Polish), Benesz (Czech), Bundy (Hungarian), and Benku—(Little Ben), the affectionate nickname that my big sister, Lola, still calls me. While these names bring a sense of warmth, comfort and life, there are other "names," that represent cold, brutal dehumanization and death.

An honored name that I once shared reverently with all Jewish People now slices like a butcher knife through my own heart and soul. That name is: *JUDE*. And despite its innocent original meaning: a Jewish person—when it was screamed by the murderous Nazis, or smeared across

Part I: The Nazi Nightmare

the windows of a destroyed Jewish shop, this name came to symbolize an indescribably brutal time in history that changed our lives and the world forever. There was also yet another name, one that signified contempt rather than reverence, by which I personally was known from May, 1944 through the end of April, 1945. But, of course, it wasn't really a "name" at all. During that year, I was known only as a number. And that number: *41212* — so innocent as long as its hideous meaning is not known — was forced upon me in exchange for my identity and dignity as a human being in the Nazi Concentration Camp known as *Auschwitz-Birkenau.**

All these names — and their many variations — are me. And there are memories that go with each one. As these names might indicate, I have lived in many different places — some were wonderful, and some were unspeakably horrific. There were two very different reasons for these circumstances. The first reason, while challenging, was very positive: Our large, extended family resided in two homes, in two different countries! This was because our father needed to run his two successful businesses in Kraków, Poland, while my mother's large, closely-knit family had lived in Munkács, Hungary (sometimes Czechoslovakia) for generations. So we alternated residences depending upon the season. During the school-year, we lived in Kraków. During the summers, we lived in Munkács.

The second reason why I had lived in so many different places was very different, and defies description and comprehension. The "name" of this reason was the Holocaust, which comes from the Greek word, *holokauston*

---

*Established in 1940 near the Polish village of Oœwiêcim, *Auschwitz-Birkenau* was the largest network of Nazi labor and extermination camps. Almost 1 million Jews were murdered there.

4. What's in a Name?

(*olos* = all, *caust* = burned), and means totally consumed by fire. For the Jewish People in Europe, especially in Poland, The Holocaust was Hitler's "Final Solution" to the "Jewish Problem," a government-sponsored, carefully organized campaign whose only goal was to wipe the Jewish People from the face of the earth. It resulted in the demonization, savage torture and brutal deaths of millions of innocent victims. Those who managed somehow to survive would face the future, valiantly determined to create new lives. They would live "lives that matter" in honor of the millions whose lives had been taken.

5. 1928-1939: THE EARLY YEARS

> *"With each child, the world begins anew."*
> ~ Ancient Jewish Proverb

I know that my childhood was happy, but hard as I try, I can't remember much other than occasional, unexpected flashbacks, or what my sister, Lola, tells me. I have no memories of school, but I must have had some education, because to this day, I know how to read and write Hebrew.* I can read and translate some *Chumash* — the Five Books of Moses also known as the *Torah*, the Hebrew Bible. And I can still read and write *Yiddish*.** Unfortunately, lack of use over the years has caused my Polish, Hungarian, and German to fade. The interruption of my education at the beginning of sixth grade left me with a life-long hunger for learning. Education, more than anything else, allows us to evaluate circumstances, make good choices, and take effective action. It's our best weapon against ignorance and hate. As a result, after the war, even though I worked full-time, I attended night-school whenever possible.

On a deep level, I feel guilt about forgetting most of my early life with my childhood family — it's as if I've somehow abandoned them. But on another level, I know that it was the Nazi brutality that burned huge holes in the fabric of my memory, destroying the beauty, innocence

---

*Hebrew has been considered the official language of the Jewish people for over 2,000 years.
**The *Yiddish* language, originated by Eastern European (Ashkenazi) Jews, comes from German, and is still spoken throughout the world. For a wonderful, true story of how Yiddish is being saved, read, *Outwitting History: The Amazing Adventures of a Man Who Rescued a Million Yiddish Books*, by Aaron Lansky. http://www.yiddishbookcenter.org/people

Part I: The Nazi Nightmare

and joy of everything that had happened in the years before. It may also be that blacking out my early happy life actually worked as a survival strategy for me in the camps. Whatever it was, my mind and emotions shut down. I just got up every morning, and did whatever I had to do in order to live another hour. I couldn't expend emotional time and energy on remembering what had been stolen from me. I needed to focus mind, heart and body on the immediate tasks of survival. I learned that even when I had to make difficult choices, I should try to determine what the right thing to do was, and then do it. Maybe this pragmatism was already in me, and I was able to draw upon it when needed. Wherever it came from, I have continued to draw upon it to this day.

Shaindel (Shari) Leser
Poland (1939)
Lesser Family Collection

I do remember some good things about my childhood in Kraków, Poland, the charming, ancient city where I was born on October 18, 1928 to Shaindel (Shari) and Lazar Leser. For generations, my beautiful young mother's family had been very prominent and highly respected members of Czechoslovakia's Munkács community. As Orthodox Jews, they lived their lives in strict accordance with the religious laws contained in the *Talmud*. As one of seven siblings, she loved being part of a big family, and adored her husband and five children. Slender and graceful, she had a real flair for fashion.

As was the custom for Orthodox Jewish women, she also owned numerous wigs. When the wigs needed cleaning

5. 1928-1939: The Early Years

and styling, she would place them outside the front door where the hairdresser would pick them up and then bring them back all clean and shiny. Wigs were very important because an ancient tradition required Jewish women to observe modesty by covering their hair after they were married. This tradition is carried on to this day.

My brilliant and artistic older brother, Moishe, was a *"Belzer Hasid."* This means that he had been selected to study with the famous Rabbi Aharon Rokeach, in the nearby town of Belz. A dedicated scholar, Moishe was away studying in the Belzer *Yeshiva* (religious school) most of the time before the war broke out, so I didn't see him often. I remember seeing an amazing scale-model of a street scene which he had constructed. It looked like it was made out of the finest silver, but he'd probably made it out of polished pewter. He'd hand-carved this intricate miniature scene and put it on a large display board. He didn't miss a detail—

Moishe Leser
Poland (1943)
Lesser Family Collection

there were streets with horses and carts, automobiles, streetcars on tracks, buildings, shops, landscaped parks with benches and duck-ponds. There were even men, women and children having picnics, playing ball and walking their dogs on sidewalks. He really surprised the whole family with this skill, which until then no one knew he possessed. This great artistic talent and eye for the smallest detail would play an important role in saving many Jewish lives during the coming German Occupation, when Poland would become part of the German General

Part I: The Nazi Nightmare

Government, and no longer its own independent country. And my religious, scholarly, artistic brother, Moishe, would become part of the underground resistance, working as a forger and courier.

My soft-spoken, tender-hearted sister, Goldie, had the face of an angel. It was more than just her physical beauty — she actually seemed to have an inner glow. She was highly intelligent and an accomplished violinist. She practiced all the time, and always got excited when groups of travelling musicians, both men and women, wearing colorful big aprons and swirling skirts, danced through the streets, and came to our house in Munkács. In fact, they sometimes came right *in* the house — whether we wanted them to or not! They would perform on our big verandah, singing and playing their beautifully haunting tunes while we children tried to sing and dance right along with them! Their violin music, somehow both sad and joyous, was especially lovely. Enjoyable as their entertainment was, however, we had to watch them carefully because they would sneak into the house and steal whatever valuables they could find.

Goldie Leser
Munkács **(1943)**
Lesser Family Collection

One day, when Goldie commented on the extraordinary sound of a particular violin, she was surprised and

5. 1928-1939: The Early Years

delighted that they offered to sell it to her on the spot. For an unusually good price. For weeks afterwards, she loved practicing on that violin, and we loved to listen. She thought it must be a *Stradivarius*, an exceedingly rare and valuable instrument, because of its unusually brilliant tone. A few weeks later, after another visit from the musicians, Goldie was devastated to realize that her precious violin was missing. We finally figured out that these exotic "entertainers" would sell the same violin over and over to the various neighborhood families, and then, just as often, steal it back again.

Sadly, I have very few memories of my little brother, Naftali, whom we called Tuli. He was a few years younger than I and very handsome. In fact, people would look at him, smile, and say that he was much too pretty for a boy. I know he looked up to me and even though I was a child myself, whenever we two were on our own, I always tried to take good care of him. Tragically, I wasn't able to take care of him at the moment when it mattered the most. The last time I saw my little brother was when he and our sister, Goldie, were torn away from me upon our arrival at Auschwitz-Birkenau. Although we couldn't have known it then,

Tuli Leser
Munkács **(1939)**
Lesser Family Collection

Part I: The Nazi Nightmare

they were sent directly to the line that led to immediate death.

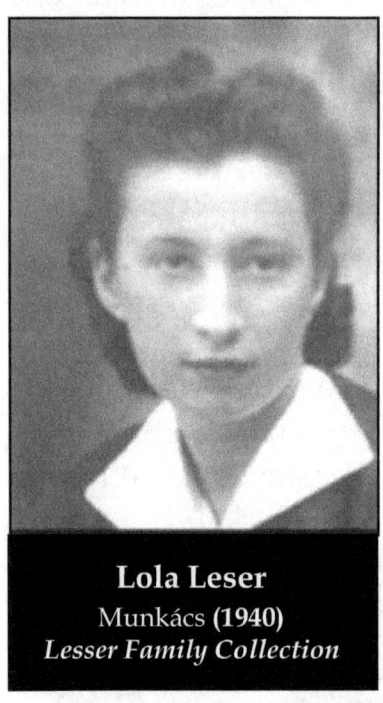

Lola Leser
Munkács **(1940)**
Lesser Family Collection

My surviving elder sister Lola, whom I love and admire very much, has always been a hero, not only to me, but to the many people whose lives she helped to save, and their families. To this day she still possesses the great beauty, elegance, intelligence and artistic talents that were so evident when she was a young teenager. Lola lived in Munkács with our grandparents. She loved drawing pictures and painting, and always won first prize in school art exhibitions. In fact, she even won a fully-paid scholarship to a prestigious art school in Amsterdam, which sadly, she never got to use.

After the war, however, Lola became a renowned artist in America. One of her first projects was to paint a series of hauntingly beautiful paintings to memorialize the lives of those who were lost. Her work has been exhibited in many galleries across the USA, is part of many private collections, and is in the permanent collections of both the San Francisco Museum of Art and the Yad Vashem Museum in Jerusalem. She is listed in "Who's Who in American Art," and as I write this memoir she still runs her own art gallery, Lola's Art Gallery, in Brooklyn. Now in her late 80s, she recently

5. 1928-1939: The Early Years

published her own very moving memoir, A WORLD AFTER THIS: *A Memoir of Loss & Redemption*, which tells the love story of a courageous and devoted young couple: my sister Lola and her husband, Mechel. Their strength, courage, and commitment to each other, their religion, and their families, could not be defeated by all of Hitler's evil power.

Of paramount importance to the five of us children and our mother was the beloved head of our family, my carefully-groomed and always tastefully-dressed father, Lazar. We children lovingly called him Tattiko. One of twelve siblings from a very prominent Orthodox Jewish family, he was extremely religious and industrious. As a very learned individual, it was particularly appropriate that his name, Lazar, means "scholar." He was a soft-spoken, no-nonsense man who was devoted to his family's well-being. He took his responsibility as the family provider very seriously, working long and hard to take good care of us. He was very active in our synagogue, owned two flourishing businesses in Kraków, and was a well-known and highly-respected member of the community. He had a *kosher** wine and fruit-syrup manufacturing business named *Sklad* (Store) *Wino* (Wine) *i* (and) *soki* (syrup) *Owotsowe* (Fruit).

I remember that the wine factory was made up of several very large rooms in a basement containing huge vats filled with fermenting wines. There were also large fruit-presses, bottling-machines, and separate labeling and packing rooms. This very extensive operation was entirely subterranean, with its entrance off a back alley. The factory was on Starowislna Street (which means "Old River"). It was a very busy and beautiful major thorough-fare that wound all the way through the city and across the Vistula

---

*Kosher items are made in accordance with strict Jewish dietary laws.

Part I: The Nazi Nightmare

Lazar Leser
Poland (1940)
Lesser Family Collection

River into Podgórze. This was the poor industrial district with train tracks that would gain great significance later, when the Nazis invaded.

In another Kraków location, my father had a wonderful chocolate factory, named Pischinger's. The company specialized in chocolate-covered wafers, similar to American Kit Kat Bars. These were made in the shapes of various animals — dogs, rabbits, bears — all kinds of animals — and covered in foil. We were told that our father was the first to manufacture this cookie in Poland. To this day, whenever I see a Kit Kat Bar, I think of my father and how we children raced each other to search his pockets when he came home from work!

While we were very fortunate that our father was such an excellent businessman, it was at the same time, also unfortunate because it created a logistical problem. This was because my mother was from Munkács, which was about 300 miles away. Today, 300 miles might not seem like such a big distance, but back then, it was a very big deal because the trains were slow and made numerous stops. Additionally, the train had to make its way through the winding mountains, and cross the borders of different countries. So depending on the frequently changing government circumstances, Munkács could sometimes be in Austria, Czechoslovakia, Poland or Hungary. Today it's part of Ukraine, and known as Mukachevo.

5. 1928-1939: The Early Years

Because of the distance between these two cities, we would spend the school-year in Kraków, and the summers in Munkács. Being separated from my maternal grandparents' loving family during the school year was very difficult for all of us. And so my father felt a lot of pressure to build a business in Munkács. But much as he tried, he couldn't make a success of it there because he lacked the language skills and business contacts. And as a foreigner, he couldn't get a business license. So while we children thought that living in two different countries was normal and fun, it was stressful for our parents and grandparents. We all made the best of the challenging situation, however, and enjoyed our two different homes, in two different countries.

And in an unexpected way, we benefitted from the constantly changing boundaries and governments of these countries. Because as a result, we all grew up able to understand several different cultures and languages. And we became highly adaptable—a quality that would become very important to our survival. We were fluent in Yiddish, Polish, Czech, Hungarian, and Hebrew. Of all the languages we spoke, however, we focused on perfecting our German. Spoken by a people whose country had such a rich history of achievement in science, architecture, art, music and literature, German was considered the language of sophistication and achievement. It was the universal language of members of the European cultural and business aristocracy, much as English is today. So there was no question that we would also become fluent. My mother insisted that my sister Lola become not just fluent, but expert in the German language. This fluency would later allow her to survive and help many others during the coming years of Nazi oppression.

Part I: The Nazi Nightmare

Our home in Kraków was a lovely, spacious ground-floor apartment in a large and beautiful, three-story French-Normandy style building at #23 Starowislna Street. It was conveniently located just a few blocks away from my father's wine and syrup factory. There were two apartments per floor, and across the hall from us lived the only other Jewish family. They had two little girls and an infant boy. The younger girl was around my age and we used to play together in the yard after school. But more about them later...

To this day, despite the horror, I do have happy memories relating to the religious traditions of my childhood. For example, I remember standing with my father on a Saturday evening in a *shtiebel* — a room in a store-front which was used for a synagogue. The room was crowded with men drinking beer and bidding the Sabbath farewell by singing traditional *Z'miroth* songs. In another happy memory, I am standing in a synagogue, when during a priestly blessing, my father covered my head with his *talith*, the prayer shawl. I was not supposed to look, because all eyes were supposed to be averted out of respect, but I peeked anyway. I always wanted to know what was going on around me — another habit which contributed to my later survival, and has benefited me throughout my life.

In addition to the *talith*, other religious items that are worn during prayer include, a *yarmulke*, and *tefillin*.* Throughout the years, whenever I have put these on to pray, I am reminded of those happy moments with my father.

We also always looked forward to celebrating Chanukah at my Grandfather Leser's house. This joyous Festival

---

*Tefillin consist of a set of leather straps and boxes containing scrolls inscribed with Torah passages.

5. 1928-1939: The Early Years

Here I am wearing a *yarmulke*, *tefillin*, and a *talith* as I pray at Jerusalem's Western Wall.
Israel (1971)
Lesser Family Collection

Part I: The Nazi Nightmare

of Lights commemorates the miracle of a container of consecrated oil which lasted for eight nights when there'd only been enough oil for one night. This is why we light a single candle of the nine-branch *Chanukah menorah* (candelabra)*, for each of eight nights. My grandfather had this huge, ornately decorated, gleaming silver Chanukah menorah. The members of our family would gather around it while he lit the *Shammash* — the ninth or special "helper" candle. This candle would be used to light a wick for each night, and it then was placed in its elevated place of honor. Then we would all sing songs and recite Chanukah prayers. Finally, *Zaydie* (Grandfather) would hand out the customary Chanukah *gelt* (coins) to all of us delighted children. I've been just as delighted to carry on this joyous custom with my own children and grandchildren.

Erte's bronze "Tree of Life" Chanukah menorah
Photo courtesy of The Greg Lane Fine Arts Gallery

Our family especially enjoyed the joyous *Festival of Purim*. As told in the Bible's *Book of Esther***, this holiday celebrates the escape of the Jews from the evil Haman's campaign

---

*The nine-branch *Chanukah menorah* differs from a traditional seven-branched menorah, which since ancient times has been a symbol of Judaism. Today, one of our faily's most precious possessions is a beautiful bronze Menorah that was designed by the artist, Erté.
**Queen Esther influenced the king to free the Jewish People and to execute Haman.

5. 1928-1939: The Early Years

to destroy them. Traditional customs consist of very lively public celebrations, including carnivals with rides, games and entertainers. Everyone can be seen in the street enthusiastically eating—and, all too often overeating—sweets and delicacies, drinking wine, wearing fanciful masks and exotic costumes! One of the highlights of *Purim* is exchanging fancy gift packages, known as *Shelachmones*, with family and friends. These packages contained wines and home-baked sweets, including the popular poppy-seed, fruit or nut-filled *Hamantashen*. This special, three-cornered, cookie is said to represent either the pockets, hats, or severed ears of the evil Haman! Our family always looked forward to the *Shelachmones* sent by our father's brother David, who had immigrated years before to New York City. We eagerly devoured exotic pineapples and other "American" treats. I never could have dreamed that one day Uncle David's generosity would change my life.

Whether Haman's pockets, ears or hats, Hamantashen are delicious!
Photo: Joanne D. Gilbert

I have another memory of what usually would have been the very joyous Jewish *Festival of Purim*. But instead, this *Purim* didn't bring any happy memories. On that particular day, I was delivering gifts to our relatives and friends. While I crossed Krakówska Boulevard, a busy major thoroughfare that ran through the historic Jewish District of

Part I: The Nazi Nightmare

Kazimierz, I enjoyed watching the carefree people having fun at the *Purim Carnival*. Suddenly, some masked thugs came out of nowhere, beat me up, and took everything away from me. These hooligans must have had quite a field-day stealing the treats that had been so lovingly made in Jewish kitchens that day — treats that celebrated the Jews' escape from another ancient hooligan that they'd probably never even heard of!

Other than an occasional bully, though, I think that my life as a young Jewish boy probably had not been much different from children in other middle-class families. We were privileged to have a wonderful family, two beautiful homes, opportunities to practice our religion, pursue education and participate in an abundant cultural life that included summer and winter vacations at lovely resorts. We were an extremely close family whose strong religious beliefs were deeply embedded in our intellects, our souls, relationships and daily activities.

And while we were aware of the *anti-Semitism*, the hatred of Jews, that had existed throughout Europe for centuries, we were for the most part untouched by it, and could never have imagined what horror was to befall us. And if we could have imagined it, we would not have believed it. Even now, over 73 years since it all began, those of us who experienced it first-hand, still cannot believe that human beings could be capable of such unspeakable evil.

6. HOW COULD THE HOLOCAUST HAPPEN?

> *"Monsters exist, but they are too few in numbers to be truly dangerous. More dangerous are ... the functionaries ready to believe and act without asking questions."*
>
> ~ Primo Levi (1919-1987)
> Jewish-Italian Writer, Chemist,
> Holocaust Survivor

Although Hitler was the first to turn anti-Semitism into an actual state-sponsored Industry of Death, the virulent, irrational hatred of the Jewish People did not just spring up with the Nazis in the 1930s. The events that led up to World War II and the Holocaust had their roots in human nature, ancient history, and a deadly combination of religion and economics. When there are desperate economic times, it is often the case that people who don't understand basic economics look for a scapegoat to blame. Why? Why were the Jewish People so often singled out to be persecuted and exiled?

Well, if you look at European history going all the way back at least to 8th–6th Century BCE (*before the common era*, approximately 3000 years ago, when the numbering of years starts at year one), you will see that the Jewish People lost a series of wars with the Romans. As a result, the Jews were exiled from their homeland which was in what are now the Middle Eastern countries of Jordan, Israel, and parts of Lebanon. This exile was called the *Diaspora*. Being exiled from their own homeland resulted in them usually being unwelcome minorities in the various countries where they then had to live. As foreigners, whose religion, language, customs and dress seemed strange to non-Jews, they were often targeted for scorn, abuse and persecution. Being subjected to punitive restrictions, blamed for any alleged infraction, and murdered when problems occurred were all routine daily events. One frequent problem involved money.

In the early days, the Christian religion prohibited its followers from lending money—a practice that was, and remains today, essential to doing business. Being prohibited from lending, however, didn't stop Christians from needing to borrow and invest. So by the late Middle Ages (1066–1485 AD), the Jews, who as "undesirable outsiders" were usually prevented from owning land and businesses, found a business that they would be allowed to do: moneylending. They filled the need to provide the necessary funds for Christians to do business. Since this activity was so distasteful for Christians, it was very convenient to delegate this activity to the Jews who were prohibited from most other professions.

So the socially despised foreigners now performed a socially despised, but necessary and valuable function. Ironically, this necessary enterprise significantly benefitted the economies of the very countries where the Jewish People lived. But as they grew successful, becoming bankers and business owners, they were often criticized for their economic power—despite the fortunes that they helped non-Jews also amass. And so the very welcome function that Jews provided others paradoxically became the very reason that they were often held in contempt. It was easy for uninformed people to believe that Jews influenced, if not controlled, the economies first of the communities, and then countries where they lived. So in spite of the economic benefits that the Jewish money-lenders brought to their communities, human nature being what it always has been, a dangerous level of jealousy developed, often leading to great hostility, special taxes, restrictions, exclusion, expulsion, and death.

6. How Could *The Holocaust* Happen?

Let's take a look at Poland, for example, where my family had lived and thrived for generations. Going all the way back at least to the 11th century, there have been many large, flourishing Jewish communities in Poland, complete with their own separate language, culture, education and social institutions. This was due to the several periods of time where Jews were tolerated and sometimes even welcomed because of their many valuable skills — including the ability to read and write. In fact, Poland was once known as the spiritual center of Europe's Jewish People, and for a long time, was home to the largest and most important Jewish community in the world.

My hometown of Kraków, which is the second largest city in Poland after Warsaw, goes all the way back to the 7th century. It was one of the leading centers of Polish academic, cultural, artistic and economic life, and was even the capital of Poland from 1038 to 1596. The Jewish district in Kraków, founded in 1335 on the Vistula River, was originally known as Kazimierz, after its founder, *Kazimierz III the Great.** Anyway, legend has it that Kazimierz had a beautiful Jewish lover named Esterka (Esther). Since he wanted her to live conveniently close — but not actually in — his home at the historic *Wawel Castle*,** he just went ahead and created an entire Jewish community nearby where she could live. Who knows the real reasons, but it is true that he created a community for Jews, and also gave them unheard of freedom and rights throughout Poland. Previously they'd been subjected to extreme restrictions and

---

*Its spelling, like so many other things, depended upon who was in charge, so sometimes "Cs" were used instead of "Ks." And sometimes "Ss" were used instead of "Zs." That's why you will sometimes see his name spelled "Cazimir."

**It's interesting to note that ancient *Wawel Castle* would again become historically prominent when it became the luxurious headquarters of the Nazi Government of the country that had once been Poland.

Part I: The Nazi Nightmare

persecution. As could be expected, however, immediately after Kazimierz' death, Polish Jews were once again cruelly victimized by anti-Semitism.

Despite this setback, however, the Jewish population and cultural life of Kraków-Kazimierz managed to grow, becoming a renowned center of Jewish culture and learning. By 1900, Kraków had a Jewish population of almost 26,000 — over a quarter of the total. Despite the innumerable contributions of the Jewish people, however, Poland's cultural and religion-based anti-Semitism was deeply rooted. And Poland wasn't alone in hating the Jews. Vicious anti-Semitic propaganda had spread throughout Europe and was particularly prevalent in Russia. This propaganda, which blamed Jews for all of Russia's problems, including the Russian Revolution, contributed to waves of deadly anti-Jewish pogroms throughout the *Pale of Settlement*.

The "Pale" was the area where Russian Jews had been sent to live when they were expelled from Russia in the late 1700s. The Pale, meaning "boundary," was located along the western Russian border between present-day countries such as Lithuania, Hungary, Poland and Ukraine. From 1791 until the fall of the Russian Empire in 1917, the boundaries of the Pale changed frequently, so Jews never knew where they'd be allowed to live and work. They could be expelled at any time, often having to move with no notice. Sometimes they were not allowed to live in cities. Other times they couldn't live on farms. Many ended up creating their own little out of the way villages, called *shtetls*,* where they

---

*Renowned author Sholom Aleichem's stories of *shtetl* life became famous in the 1964 award-winning Broadway musical, *Fiddler on the Roof* and the 1971 film version, which also won many awards. A wonderful documentary, *Sholem Aleichem: Laughing in the Darkness*, was released in 2011.

6. How Could *The Holocaust* Happen?

lived in poverty and constant fear of attack. Jewish men and even boys—as young as 12 years old—were subject to being drafted to fight in Russia's wars, and the length of their service could last 25 years.

The concentration of Jews in certain areas made them easy targets for pogroms—and ironically also set a precedent for Hitler's ghettos and concentration camps. In 1917, with the fall of the Russian Empire, most of the Pale became part of Poland. The sudden influx of almost five million impoverished Jews added immeasurably to Poland's historic anti-Semitism. This situation provided an advantage to Hitler because it allowed him to combine his hatred for Poles* with his hatred of Jews. And eventually, he would make the Occupation of Poland an essential step in his "Final Solution to the Jewish Problem."

In the late 1930s, because of its history, culture, economy and geography, Poland, was a very convenient place for Hitler's barbarous Industry of Death to thrive. By the autumn of 1939, almost 70,000 of Kraków's approximately 240,000 residents were Jewish. As rabbis, doctors, lawyers, bankers, teachers, business-owners, merchants, political activists, artists, writers, entertainers, and even athletes, they were a very important part of this bustling, sophisticated city. Their importance, however, instantly evaporated when the Germans invaded on September 1, 1939. The German Occupation was an essential part of Hitler's *Stufenplan* (step-by-step plan). Would you believe that the details of this heinous campaign had been meticulously written while Hitler was in a Landsberg, Germany prison following his conviction for an attempted government *coup d'etat* (illegal

---

*Germany's hatred of Poland goes back to a border dispute in the 1700s, and was intensified in 1918, when The Versailles Treaty following World War I allowed Poland to become an independent country again.

Part I: The Nazi Nightmare

overthrow of government power)? He carefully laid out his plan for all to see in 1925-26 with the publication of his two-volume *Mein Kampf*. Since his plan was so readily available all over the world, it still is a source of amazement to me that the world neither protested his intentions, nor the unspeakably monstrous events that ensued. There is an old saying that perfectly summarizes the tragic truth of this human behavior:

> *"All that is necessary for the triumph of evil is that good men do nothing."*
>
> ~ Edmund Burke (1729-1797)
> Statesman, Author, Orator,
> Political theorist, Philosopher

And nowhere has the devastating result of the silence of "good people" been more apparent than in Hitler's Holocaust. One man, no matter how evil, could not have created the Holocaust all by himself. It required the tacit, and sometimes even active, complicity of all the "good people" not just in Germany, but in the whole world who preferred to avert their eyes, block their ears, close their hearts, remain silent, and in some cases, to develop a kind of collective amnesia.

Although throughout history there have been countless exterminations of entire groups of people, it's interesting to note that the word "genocide" didn't even exist until the Holocaust. This was because never before had there been such a massive, systematic, government-sponsored machine of death. Historically, genocides were really the expected results of wars, the losers of which were traditionally enslaved or murdered. In fact, genocides were seen by many as being a function of "Survival of the

6. How Could *The Holocaust* Happen?

Fittest," the newly popular *Darwinian Theory* * that helped to justify the belief that the superior race would prevail, ultimately ruling the world — all others should be enslaved or eliminated. Many other highly "civilized" European countries of that time, including England, Holland, France, Spain, and Portugal, had followed the path of *Imperialism*. This means to conquer and then turn less-developed countries into their colonies. This corresponded to the traditional German philosophy of *Lebensraum*: the belief that Germans have the right to expand into other countries whenever they needed more land to accommodate their increasing population. This policy justified their ruthless annexations in 1938-39 of Austria, Czechoslovakia, and Poland, among others.

While this brutal process was clearly inhumane, at least it was predictable and understood by the participants. It wasn't personal. What made the Nazi extermination of the Jewish People so different was that it was not the result of warring factions or the need for land. Indeed, the Nazis simply believed that the Jewish People should cease to exist — for no reason other than that they were Jews. Needless to say, *this was very personal*.

The amazing electronic and technological advances in communication, transportation, photography, manufacturing, and weapons that resulted from the *Industrial Revolution** also had a negative outcome, because they allowed the Nazi war-machine to differ even further from history's previous perpetrators of ethnic-cleansing. These industrial innovations provided the Nazis with the infra-

---

* Darwin's theory suggests that there is a natural process resulting in survival of those who can adapt most successfully to their environment. Hitler amended this to mean that only those who were physically and mentally superior should have rights.

Part I: The Nazi Nightmare

structure that was needed to implement its infamous, government-sponsored industrialization of death. The advances in chemistry, mining and transportation, plus the ability to build roads, communicate instantly via telephones and radios, use newly available computers to keep and organize data on prisoners, expedited Hitler's campaign against the Jewish People. Nazis not only used their own new technology, but also were experts at adapting the advanced technology of major western corporations. It has been only in the past few years that declassified documents have shown the extent to which the Nazis copied the newest American technological and manufacturing processes.

And for economic rather than environmental reasons, death camps were required to be profitable as well as efficient. In fact, the camps competed with each other to be the most efficient — requiring that increasing numbers of Jewish corpses needed to be processed within shorter amounts of time. And the "by-products" of these corpses were put to good use. Literally tons of Jewish hair were recycled into heavy duty felt, mattresses, blankets and clothing. Bones were ground down to be used as fertilizer. Shoes, eyeglasses, and even artificial limbs were mended, cleaned and then sent to be used by German military and civilians. Through the years, many sources have reported that gold taken from teeth was recycled into money through foreign banks and then later used to underwrite — or pay the costs of the Holocaust. Even America's decade-long *Great Depression*, which started when the New York Stock Market crashed in 1929, provided

---

*During the 1700s and 1800s, the *Industrial Revolution* changed the European economy from agrarian (farming) to manufacturing. This brought a new level of power to those who owned the factories, and a new level of poverty and frustration to those who worked in them.

6. How Could *The Holocaust* Happen?

Hitler with an advantage. He used this international calamity to scapegoat Jews for Germany's economic problems, and made outlandish promises of German economic recovery once the Jews were eliminated.

Another event that helped to pave the way for Hitler to implement his Final Solution was the infamous 1942 *Wannsee Conference*, which was held at a luxurious lakeside villa in the Berlin suburb of Wannsee. Unlike the thugs who were Hitler's original supporters in the 1920s and 1930s, the fifteen senior Nazi officials attending this Conference were highly educated scholars and professional men, including attorneys and military leaders. The goal of this conference was to actually assign each participant with his specific responsibilities for implementing Hitler's campaign to exterminate the Jewish People of Europe.

Back in the early 1930s, however, we Leser children were growing up comfortably in Kraków and Munkács. It wouldn't have occurred to us to question the safety of our cozy little lives. . .

Part I: The Nazi Nightmare

7. SUMMERS IN MUNKÁCS*

> *"And even if you were in some prison . . .*
> *would you not then still have your childhood . . .*
> *that treasure-house of memories?*
>
> ~ Rainer Maria Rilke (1875-1926)
> Austro-Hungarian Poet

At the end of every school year, my mother would take us children to Munkács, where my siblings were born, to spend the summers with her family. This beautiful town was over one-half Jewish, and everyone got along with each other, so we were very comfortable there. The large family home was located on *Cukor Utca* (Sugar Street) — such an appropriate name for a place that holds such sweet memories! This was a major street that started in the town square and ended at the train station, with our family's house in between. From the street, we would walk through an impressive, huge ornamental iron gate to gain entrance to the property on which stood my grandparents' stately home. I remember staying cool on hot summer days by running barefoot up and down the elaborately tiled veranda that ran the entire length of the building. And there were many beautifully furnished rooms, each with its own separate entrance, so that when we or guests came to visit, there was complete privacy, just like separate little apartments. My grandparents' family had built the

---

*There's an interesting film clip on Google Videos, *Jewish Life in Munkatch-March 1933*. http://video.google.com/videoplay?docid=1622609518319953327#. Recently a wonderful movie was released about Munkács: *A Man from Munkács: Gypsy Klezmer* (2005). For information, see: http://www.yalestrom.com/films.html

Part I: The Nazi Nightmare

house, so it had always been ours. It was actually more of a compound with several structures in addition to the large, beautiful home. The property was not very wide, but it was extremely deep. In the very rear of the property, there was a small house where the coachman and the caretaker lived. Just behind the main house you entered a luxurious rose garden with manicured hedges.

Within this rose garden there was an exquisitely constructed gazebo that had a unique roof which opened in summer and closed in winter. There were beautiful shutters in front of the gazebo's colorful stained-glass windows. The walls were constructed of brightly-hued glass bottles which were carefully laid top to bottom between strips of mortar. So when you looked at the wall, you'd see the round bottoms of bottles alternating with the round tops surrounded by the mortar — and of course it was just the opposite on the other side. It was truly a work of art — an amazing, brilliantly hued, glass mosaic. I don't think that there was anything like that anywhere! When the sun beams streamed through the windows and lit up the walls, they would sparkle with all the brilliant colors of a prism — like a technicolor crystal palace.

When we opened the roof, the gazebo could also function as a *sukkah*, which is a kind of hut, used during the week-long festival of *Sukkot*. We would create a traditional roof of *schach* (branches) and make colorful paper chains with birds to decorate the ceiling and imaginative pictures to cover the walls. Originally a celebration of the harvest, *Sukkot* later came to celebrate the temporary shelters used by the Jews during the 40 years that they wandered in the wilderness after being freed from Egyptian slavery. During this holiday it is traditional for Jewish people to eat, sleep and otherwise spend many happy hours in the *sukkah*.

7. Summers in Munkács

Behind the roses a berry garden provided us with many varieties of seasonal berries. Then came the huge orchard where almost every fruit imaginable grew in abundance. Running down the center of the orchard there was a trellised walkway covered with grapevines and multicolored clusters of hanging grapes. We often sat on the redwood benches along this walkway. There were always delicious fruits, grapes and berries for us children to pick and enjoy. I remember playing hide and seek in the gardens with my two female cousins, Bobbiko and Alisko. In addition to the usual games that children played, we also picked pears, wrapped them in tissue paper and then formed a chain-line, handing them individually from one person to the next to be placed up in the attic for ripening. All of these years later, I remember our little assembly-line whenever I gather the delicious pears from the tree in my backyard.

And the busy woman who ran this entire compound with style and grace was my amazing grandmother. She was affectionately called *Bubbiko* by her adoring grandchildren and *Mimeh Rosheh* (Auntie Rose) by people outside of the family. She was tall, slender, and always neatly dressed — never a hair out of place. She was respected and loved by all who knew her — which was just about everyone because she was involved with so many activities! She was President of the Ladies Auxiliary, and along with her life-long best friend, Mrs. Spiegel, who lived across the street, was always busy organizing charitable parties and fundraising functions. So rarely was one seen without the other that they sometimes were referred to as "Spiegel and Segal"! Their dedication to helping others was widely known and greatly appreciated in the community. Since they travelled a lot for charitable purposes, they needed an efficient means of transportation. So they joined forces to purchase a horse and carriage, and also hired a steady coachman. The horse

Part I: The Nazi Nightmare

and buggy stayed at the Spiegels' house, and the coachman lived in our caretaker's house.

Always industrious, my grandmother also had a little side-line business packaging and selling delicate jeweled brooches that were intricately designed in the shapes of small butterflies, animals and insects. She set a powerful example of a meaningful life that was creative, productive and helpful to others. My grandfather, Yosef Segel, the revered patriarch of my mother's side of the family, seemed ancient to us because of his beautiful long white beard. He was very prominent in the community and ran several successful enterprises. In particular, I remember that he had a Slivovitz factory, where he manufactured popular alcohol drinks from prunes or plums. People said that once they tasted his Slivovitz, they could never drink any other. He also functioned as the *gabbai* of the synagogue, which means he had been elected to represent the congregation and make sure that various needs and details of the synagogue, including prayer services were properly organized and carried out.

Grandfather Yosef Segal
Munkács **(1939)**
Lesser Family Collection

Our summers in Munkács were filled with love, security, religion, laughter,

7. Summers in Munkács

outdoor games, wonderful food, and an innocence that would soon be obliterated.

Part I: The Nazi Nightmare

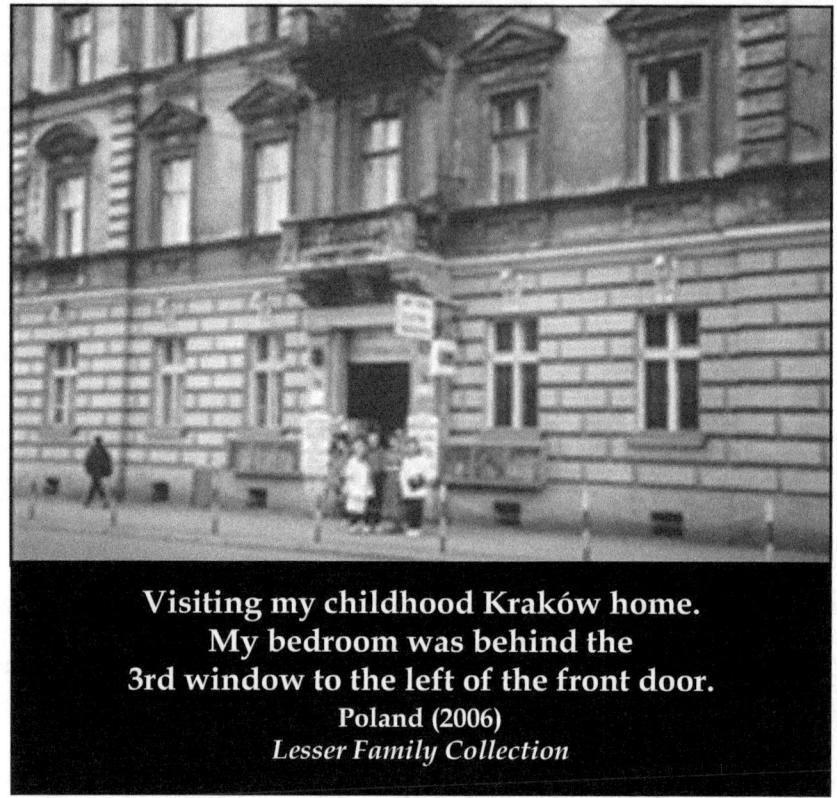

Visiting my childhood Kraków home.
My bedroom was behind the
3rd window to the left of the front door.
Poland (2006)
Lesser Family Collection

8. 1939: AUTUMN IN KRAKÓW

> "Where books are burned, in the end, people will be burned."
> ~ Heinrich Heine (1797-1856)
> German Writer, Poet

In November 1938, in accordance with the *Munich Conference Agreement*, Germany took over much of Czechoslovakia, while Hungary annexed Munkács. This set into motion some political events that wouldn't affect us until the end of the summer of 1939, when as usual, my mother brought my brother Tuli, Lola and me back to Kraków. This time, however, we had to leave abruptly because the governments of Poland and Hungary were not getting along. And since Mammiko's Polish passport included us younger children, we had to leave what was now Hungary within 24 hours or we would be considered illegal aliens — a very dangerous situation. Fortunately, Goldie's Czechoslovakian passport still allowed her to stay in Munkács, where she had lived with our grandparents and gone to school for several years.

Unfortunately, because of the short notice, our new Kraków home wasn't ready for us yet, so we stayed in my paternal grandparents' tiny apartment. Our father would join us after he had finished making all the details for the move. And since there wasn't room for all of us, my parents had arranged for Lola to spend a couple of weeks at a resort in Krynica, a beautiful spa town, before joining us.

My grandparents' apartment was very small, so Mammiko, Tuli and I slept together in one bed that was pushed into a corner of my grandfather's study. This little

Part I: The Nazi Nightmare

sleeping area was partitioned off with only a bedsheet. Getting any sleep was a real challenge because my grandfather would keep his light on into the late hours of the night in order to study *Talmud*. We were relieved to move into our large Kraków apartment just in time for the Fall-1939 school year. Always eager to learn, I was excited about my new teachers and classes. Sadly, my academic education would come to an unexpected halt just a few days after the school year started. But on that bright and shiny first day of school in 1939, so full of promise, we kids could not have known that the deadly changes that had been taking place in Germany since 1933, were only days away from our beautiful home in Poland.

The adults, of course, knew that life for Jews throughout Europe was becoming more and more precarious. They had heard about the brutal Nazi persecutions that began with Hitler's takeover of Germany in 1933, when the *Reichstag Fire Decree and Enabling Acts** were implemented. They knew about the Nazi Government's official anti-Semitic *Nuremberg Laws*** which had been enacted in 1935, limiting every aspect of German Jewish lives, including the right to work. Jewish-owned homes, businesses, bank accounts, valuables and properties had been immediately transferred to German ownership. Jewish people throughout Europe also had heard about the infamous *Kristallnacht* — the Night of Broken Glass: November 9-10, 1938. On this night of horror, Jewish books were looted from homes and

---

*The *Reichstag Fire Decree and Enabling Acts* legally allowed the Hitler-controlled Cabinet to enact laws and appoint the next Chancellor: Adolph Hitler.

**In 1935, the *Nuremberg Laws* legally stripped the citizenship of all German residents who weren't considered pure Germans. The presence of "one drop" of Jewish blood eliminated any possibility of German citizenship.

8. 1939: Autumn in Kraków

synagogues and burned in huge piles on the streets. So many Jewish homes, synagogues and shops were ransacked and destroyed that night that the sound of the broken glass has been described as sounding like a "hailstorm of crystal shards."

Many Jews were murdered, and 25,000 to 30,000 were arrested and sent immediately to concentration camps. More than 250 synagogues, some of them centuries' old and containing priceless artifacts, were destroyed. Much of this carnage was carried out by rampaging members of the *Hitler Youth*, a military-training organization for teenage boys that had been founded in 1922 and remained active until the end of the war in 1945.

Additional butchery was carried out by the *Gestapo*, (*GE-heime STA-ats PO-lizei*), Hitler's secret police, and his infamous *Schutzstaffel*, or SS, which means, "protective shield." So by 1939, it was no secret anywhere that the Nazis were on a campaign to persecute Jews. The monstrous goal and scope of this persecution, however, would exceed anything in both human history — and human imagination. What still remains a secret today is why the whole world stood by and let it happen.

When it became obvious that the Nazis were about to invade Poland, the Jewish residents began to make whatever preparations they could. They hid money, clothes, jewelry, and non-perishable medicines and food in places where they might have later access. They created secret hiding places behind their homes' walls, beneath trap-doors, underground, and even in the forest. I often wonder how much of this priceless treasure is still hidden throughout Europe. The men knew that they were particularly vulnerable, having heard that the Nazis were rounding up Jewish men for forced labor. So my father, along with

Part I: The Nazi Nightmare

many other Jewish men, had tried to go to Russia, where they thought that they could wait it out until the German Occupation ended, and they could come back home.

It was inconceivable that this latest wave of anti-Jewish oppression might be more than temporary. The men knew that if they stayed in Poland that they would become part of the Nazis' forced-labor groups which usually led to death. So going to the Soviet Union—or *Rusland* (Russia) as we called it in Yiddish—was a fairly common survival strategy, and was not considered to be an abandonment of their families. It seemed like the pragmatic thing to do under the circumstances. Sadly, of those who did get into Russia, some were immediately killed, while others were sent to Siberia where few survived the brutal conditions there. Anyway, a few days after my father had left home to try to get to Russia, he was forced to return because the Nazis had already closed the border. At the time, we all felt relief that he had been able to elude them, and return to us unhurt. But before anyone could comprehend what was happening, on September 1, 1939, without even declaring war, the Germans invaded Poland. And the civilized world as we had known it had ended.

Part I: The Nazi Nightmare

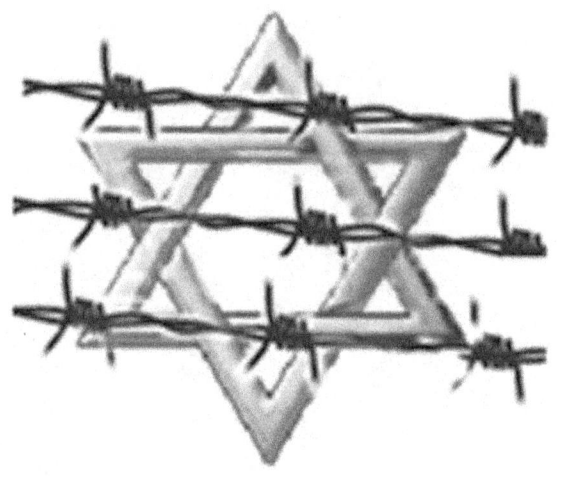

9. 9/1/1939: THE GERMANS OCCUPY POLAND

> **"BLITZKRIEG!"**
> 9/1/1939 Newspaper Headline
> across Europe & USA

As if it happened yesterday, I remember that it was around five in the morning of what would otherwise have become just another beautiful, crisp, sunny autumn day. Our entire solidly-built apartment building suddenly started to shake and rumble—I thought it must be an earthquake. I jumped out of bed, rushed to the window, and saw an unbelievable sight: huge military tanks rolling right down our beautiful street! These tanks were followed by half-tracks, which had regular wheels on the front, and caterpillar tracks on the back, and were filled with soldiers. Every few feet one of the soldiers would jump out of the half-track with his weapon and stand menacingly on the sidewalk.

With their stiff, robotic posture and vacant expressions, they looked more like machines than humans. And of course that's exactly what they were: machines of death. Following the half-tracks, came the *Wehrmacht*, the foot-soldiers, noisily goose-step marching with their tall shiny black leather boots. Horrifying as it was, that morning's arrival of the Germans was not really a total surprise since they'd already occupied Austria, and Czechoslovakia in 1938. Even in our serene little neighborhood, there'd been a few bombs. But since we couldn't have imagined what was in store for us, we'd just adapted to the changes on a daily basis. We tried to live as normally as possible until it was over. This wasn't such an unusual response, because

Part I: The Nazi Nightmare

throughout history, the Jewish People had always adapted to oppression, and as a result, they had survived. This adapting behavior had been reinforced so many times by survival, that to many, it seemed like the logical course of action. Unbeknownst to us, however, the world had changed. So this centuries-old, once-successful strategy of adaptation now became the basis for a very deadly modern delusion. And despite each new adaptation, each new degradation, and every shocking death, this was the delusion we clung to: If we remained calm, followed directions, lived as normally as possible, then we would survive this latest campaign against us.

So it was on this beautiful morning, that the Germans came to occupy Poland. Years later I would learn that this Occupation was called the "*Blitzkreig!*" because it was so fast and so overwhelming that it was like a "lightning war." For a ten-year-old boy, it was just too overwhelmingly surreal to understand. I didn't have the intellectual or emotional sophistication to process the events that bombarded us. What did I know about one country swallowing up and enslaving another whole country? So the most terrifying thing for me was the terror I saw in my parents' eyes — even as they tried to maintain a sense of normalcy around the house. There was an almost electrical current of anxiety.

After a few days, despite his fears, my father risked going to his business. When he got there, he was confronted by the unmoving, unresponsive armed guards who blocked the entrance. It was as if they just looked right through him. To his great shock and sorrow, his business, so selflessly developed over the years with his tireless, dedicated work, had been confiscated. Just like that. A man of achievement and dignity was cut off from his thriving livelihood by uniformed, unthinking thugs. When he slowly came

9. 9/1/1939: The Germans Occupy Poland

through our front door he didn't look like our *Tattiko*. How could we have understood the transformation that had just taken place? Instead of running to greet him, we quickly averted our eyes and hoped that our mother would make everything better.

In the next few weeks, the ordinances against the Jewish People started to come in, fast and furious. All Jews had to register with the authorities; each received a new identity card with a large red "J" imprinted on it for *JUDE*. The public schools banned Jewish kids, and we all had to wear armbands with the six-pointed Jewish Star of David imprinted on them. If a Nazi caught us without our armband, he would shoot us on the spot. Can you imagine  shooting a child because he'd lost his armband? There were no judges, no juries for Jews. If we seemed to be disobeying any of those new ordinances, even if we hadn't heard about them yet, the Gestapo would simply execute us right then and there.

Soon after the Occupation, the Leser family had our very first personal taste of Nazi brutality. At around five in the morning, a military truck thundered up to the front of our building. Nazis jumped out and started banging on our gate for the building caretaker. When he ran out to the gate, tucking in his shirt-tails, they ordered him to open up and tell them where the Jewish people lived. He was very quick to oblige, pointing to our apartment and the other Jewish family's apartment across the hall. Then the Nazis kicked down our door and came in shouting, *"Schnell!*

Part I: The Nazi Nightmare

Schnell! Jûdische Schwein! (Hurry up – move it, Jewish pigs!)," while hitting us furiously with their pistols. One minute we had been a normal family sleeping safely in our beds. The next minute we and our suddenly helpless parents were being beaten up. The Nazis carried burlap sacks, which they filled as they ransacked our home, shouting that we must give them all of our valuables, such as gold, silver, cash and furs. They even ripped the rings from my mother and sister's trembling fingers.

Amidst this violent chaos, we heard terrible, almost inhuman, shrieks from the apartment across the hall. The infant boy had awakened during all the yelling and commotion. Both my sister and I ran over to see what was happening, and we saw a Nazi holding the baby by his legs and swinging him, bellowing at the mother to make him stop screaming. Of course, the parents screamed, "My baby, my baby!" and then with a hideous smirk on his face, this barbarian swung the baby with full-force headfirst into the door-post, cracking his tiny skull open and killing him instantly. Of course, both parents jumped on this monster which resulted in them being brutally pistol-whipped and kicked until, and even after, they were both unconscious.

One minute they'd been a normal, happy, loving family living in their apartment, and the next minute their lives were hideously destroyed. We were all in complete shock – there was no way to comprehend this. Suddenly it ended. It almost seemed as if the Nazis might have been shocked by their own barbarism – they just turned and left. Maybe the adrenaline-rush from their initial burst of brutal enthusiasm had worn off. Who knows why such things begin and end? In the eerie silence, my shaken family huddled together in our wrecked living room, trying to gain comfort from each other. Today, as a parent and grandparent, I feel physically ill at the thought of my

9. 9/1/1939: The Germans Occupy Poland

parents having to watch helplessly while their children were being beaten. And I can't let myself think about the parents across the hall.

Soon, throughout Kraków, the authorities closed all the synagogues and confiscated all their sacred artifacts and valuables. We'd heard that the Nazis were stabling their horses in the temples. Then there came a new directive ordering all Jewish males over the age of fourteen to report to a government building that the Nazis had taken over. The Nazis then would march the Jewish men around town, making them do all kinds of menial work such as digging ditches and shoveling snow. When this work was finished, the men were then forced to clean the sidewalks with various little brushes — sometimes even toothbrushes. The Nazis were having their fun — laughing and taking pictures and kicking the Jews at the same time. The only purpose of this was to degrade and demoralize the Jewish men and their loving families — just to let everyone know that we were completely helpless.

Another activity that the Nazis thought was great fun was holding Jewish men down and slashing off their long beards. Sometimes they would try to be "artistic" and cut the beards into what they thought were funny shapes. To say the least, they weren't particularly careful about their "artistry." One evening, my father came home all bruised and bloody; they had cut his face while slashing off his beard at a weird angle. This was spiritually as well as physically brutal because a beard is very important to an Orthodox Jewish man. The Bible instructs:

> *"Ye shall not round the corners of your heads, neither shalt thou mar the corners of thy beard."*
> ~ Leviticus 19:27

Part I: The Nazi Nightmare

This means that an actual razor cannot be used in certain places on the face or head. Of course the Nazis also found it necessary to beat my father, so his whole body was black and blue from the blows he had received. After this incident, he sadly shaved off his beard. It seemed as if our father was gone. Some sad, silent shadow of a man had taken his place.

Soon after, there came yet another new ordinance informing all Jewish people that they were no longer permitted to live in their own homes in Kraków. Many of these homes had been in their families for generations. The Nazis gave us two immediate choices: either we could move across the river to a newly created ghetto in the impoverished old Podgórze District, or we could move to small villages on the outskirts of Kraków. Either way, the Jewish People were forced to leave their homes, businesses and belongings behind. Of course their former Polish neighbors eagerly moved into these suddenly vacant homes, assuming ownership of everything that had been left behind. How interesting it is that Jews were too dirty to be considered human beings, yet their homes and belongings weren't too dirty to steal. Still to this day, there are Poles living in homes that had been owned by their Jewish neighbors. How is it that something so unimaginable could happen in a civilized, 20th century world?

The earliest stage of Hitler's Final Solution included the use of frequent, conspicuous, random harassment and brutality. Examples of this Nazi persecution included: immediate execution of any Jew caught without the required identity documents; the German take-over of all Jewish business licenses, bank accounts and pensions; the prohibition of employing Jews, including Jewish physicians who were no longer allowed to treat their non-Jewish patients; and the banishment of Jewish lawyers from the courts. In some cases, non-Jewish spouses would lose their

9. 9/1/1939: The Germans Occupy Poland

jobs if they did not divorce their Jewish husbands or wives. Robberies — often violent — of Jewish homes and businesses were common, and not subject to prosecution. Jews were required to pay various fines and hand in their valuables. Spontaneous round-ups for forced labor became frequent, and unprovoked killings became commonplace. This arbitrariness was part of the deliberate plan of psychological terror — since there was no logic to it, there was never any safety anywhere.

The next stage of the Final Solution was the establishment of five major Jewish ghettos in Poland, where the Jews from all over Europe would be sent. Once concentrated in a ghetto, the Jews would then be subjected to the highly efficient *Selektion* process which would determine who would remain alive as slave labor, who would be sent to labor or death camps, and who would be killed immediately. These five major ghettos were located in Warsaw, Lodz, Lublin, Lvov, and our beautiful home-town of Kraków.

Created on March 3, 1941, the Kraków Ghetto was located on the south side of the Vistula River, in the town's poor, run-down, pre-war industrial zone near the train tracks. It was separated from the rest of the town by the river, huge limestone boulders — many of which resembled grave stones — and concrete walls. We learned that all windows and doors that faced the *Aryan,** or non-Jewish, side were bricked over. The guarded entrances allowed only authorized traffic to pass in and out. Approximately 17,000 Jews were given the "option" to leave their homes

---

*According to Hitler, this German *"Aryan Master Race,"* was characterized by being tall, and having blond hair and blue eyes. It was supposedly descended from the "Nordic" region of Europe which includes Denmark, Finland, Iceland, Norway, and Sweden. It's interesting to note that the Austrian-born Hitler possessed none of these characteristics himself.

Part I: The Nazi Nightmare

and belongings behind and move into this ghetto, an area which had previously housed 3,000 in squalid conditions. Many people were squeezed into small spaces, sometimes two or more families in one single small room, sleeping on floors, sharing foul and inadequate plumbing facilities. Crime, starvation and disease were rampant. And in the winter, it was freezing cold, so people actually starved or froze to death right on the streets. Sometimes their twisted bodies wouldn't be found until the snow melted.

In March 1942, the first group of Kraków Ghetto Jews was sent to the newly constructed Belzec Death Camp. This hellish place had the distinction of being the first official extermination camp, where almost 434,500 Jews were murdered. The facilities included gas chambers and large rectangular burial pits, which were dug by inmates to become mass graves. It has been said that only two people survived Belzec because the Nazis were so careful not to leave any witnesses to tell about the horrors that were perpetrated there. Years later, I learned that the new arrivals at Belzec were "welcomed" by a Jewish orchestra from Kraków, playing German marches. Most of the musicians were later exterminated.*

By 1942, Poland was the Nazis' official "dumping ground" for all of Europe's Jews. Many more ghettos had been created, each with a Town Square or *Umschlagplatz*. In the Kraków Ghetto, the name of this place was, Zgody Square. This would be where the decisions were made about which of our families and friends would live and which would die. It was all very systematic and organized in order to create maximum terror. Adding to the surrealism

---

*For more information on concentration camp musicians, see, *Bach in Auschwitz and Birkenau*: www.cympm.com/orkest.html

9. 9/1/1939: The Germans Occupy Poland

was the fact that many of the vicious Nazi orders had to be carried out by the *Judenrat*, a special Nazi-appointed committee of Jews who had no choice but to enforce the Nazi-imposed rules, all too often even against their own families and friends.

One particularly strange event that I heard about years later involved the Nazis organizing a staged "deportation." This was conducted for the benefit of the world press, and had photographers placed around the square to take pictures documenting the "humane" living conditions in the ghetto and the "respectful" Jewish relocation process. Jewish ghetto residents carefully cleaned and decorated the Square with flowers. Everyone was ordered to look happy and relaxed. The "selected" Jews, carrying neatly packed suitcases, calmly filled the horse-drawn wagons — assisted by conspicuously courteous drivers. After the photographers left, however, the Jews were chased off the wagons, beaten and relieved of their possessions. The drivers, and now empty horse-carts, hurried off on their way without any passengers.* It was all just a publicity set-up designed to make it comfortable for the world to believe the Nazi lies.

---

*The 2010 documentary, *A Film Unfinished*, shows how Nazi propaganda movies were used to spread anti-Semitic propaganda. For info: http://www/afilmunfinished.com/

10. *1941: ESCAPE FROM KRAKÓW*

> *"Giving your son a skill is better than giving him one thousand pieces of gold."*
> ~ Old Proverb

By an unexpectedly happy twist of fate, my immediate family avoided ending up in the Kraków Ghetto. Most of our relatives, including my grandparents, uncles, aunts, and cousins, ended up there and eventually perished. Despite the horror surrounding us, however, it's interesting that the most basic, hopeful human instincts sometimes can still manage to emerge. And this was the case with my sister Lola, whose brilliant young suitor, Mechel Lieber, was madly in love with her—a feeling that was clearly mutual. He declared his intention to marry Lola, and said to my father, "Mr. Leser, do me a favor—you know how I feel about Lola. My family is not going to go into the ghetto. We are leaving Kraków, please move with us to Niepolomice (which means "indestructible"), I'll make all the arrangements." The young couple urgently begged my father to move out of town, rather than going into the ghetto. And given our so-called "choices," my father agreed to go to Niepolomice. And so in a time of horror, because of a young couple in love, we were spared from the certain death of the Kraków Ghetto.

Before leaving, and unbeknownst to us, our father had gathered all the money he possessed—having carefully saved it over the years for a "rainy day." It was around $1,000 in American money, which was a fortune in those days. He had carefully pasted each bill between the pages of a *sefer*, an important book of Hebrew religious commentary.

Part I: The Nazi Nightmare

He placed this book along with many others in a sack, which we loaded onto the wagon that Mechel had arranged for us. After adding as many of our personal belongings as possible, we left Kraków, along with all the other Jewish families who now embarked on similar journeys. This "evacuation" was carefully planned and expected by the Nazis, so at least we didn't have to steal away in the night.

Our greatest fears were realized when, just as we left the city, we were surrounded by Nazis. Of course they knew that the Jews would be leaving, so they were waiting for us. On the side of the road, there was this huge mound of books, which to me seemed as big as a house. When the Nazis jumped up onto our wagon, we held on to each other tightly, thinking that they would kill us right then and there.

However, all they wanted to know was if we had any Jewish books. Of course, they knew we would have Jewish books — all Jewish families had precious collections of Jewish books. They are the foundation of our religion. Taking them was part of the Nazi plan to destroy our culture and our spirit. They quickly grabbed and tore open our sacks and heaved the precious contents up on the top their ever-growing pile — eventually to be burned.

While we watched in horror, waiting to be killed, my lovely sister, Lola gracefully walked up to a young soldier. She begged him in her flawless German, which of course, impressed him: "My father is a writer, he wrote his autobiography in one book, please let him keep it." We were frozen in helpless terror — what would happen to her? Surprisingly, he agreed, giving us five minutes to find the book. Of course he knew that it would be impossible, and enjoyed our frenzied struggle. We kids desperately tried to find this book, but unfortunately, all of the black and brown leather-bound volumes looked alike. And hard as we tried to scramble up the unstable mountain of books,

10. 1941: Escape from Kraków

we kept sliding down. After about five minutes of this frenzy, the soldier got tired of his little game, and chased us away. Back on our wagon, our once happy, respected middle-class family, with strong business, cultural, social and familial roots in Kraków, was now totally destitute. Dazed, but determined, we journeyed toward our next "home" in Niepolomice.

Under ordinary circumstances, a trip to beautiful, historic Niepolomice would have been a special treat. Twenty-five miles east of Kraków, the Royal Niepolomice Castle was built in the 1300s in the center of a lush ancient forest. As in other areas of Poland, a strong Jewish community had thrived in the nearby village since the latter part of the Middle Ages. On that terrifying night, however, we weren't interested in history or beautiful scenery—all we cared about was that our lives depended upon reaching our destination. And eventually we did get there—totally exhausted and completely penniless. And our father was without even the hope of a job, since no one was allowed to hire Jews.

The two-room "house" where Mechel had arranged for us to live, was a small, very old clay structure, topped by a thatched straw roof. It came equipped with an outhouse, since there was no indoor plumbing. The Polish landlord, an apple-orchard farmer, and his wife lived in the other room. They weren't doing us any particular favors by renting to us, because at that point, the Poles were still allowed to rent to Jews. Unfortunately Jews weren't allowed to work, so they had to sell off the remaining little bits of their valuables in order to pay the rent. The Nazis figured that the Jews would come up with the money somehow. Although it didn't last long, this arrangement was a real benefit to the Poles. Our family lived all together in one

Part I: The Nazi Nightmare

room. It had a window, a small stove for heat, and some very basic furniture. Fortunately for us, there was a large stone baking-oven situated in the hall between the two rooms. This ancient oven would become very important to the Leser family.

The traditional Jewish "housewarming" gifts for moving into a new home are bread and salt—symbolizing the abundance that is wished for the family. And when we arrived, in keeping with both tradition and necessity, my very thoughtful future brother-in-law, Mechel, gave my father a 100-pound sack of flour and a supply of salt. He figured that at least father would be able to bake some bread to feed his family. At this point, we could almost see my father's spirit return. Always a resourceful businessman, he decided he could do something more beneficial with the flour and salt. So, instead of just baking bread for us, and eventually using up all the precious flour, he set about making pretzels to sell to the neighboring bars. At that time pretzels were a local novelty, and really went over well with the villagers. And that is how my father started to earn some money.

While this little enterprise was developing, we were so hungry that my mother had to beg the landlord's wife to let us have the husks from the wheat after her own flour was ground. This would normally have been considered unfit for human consumption and fed to the pigs. It was terrible to eat, but it was food. Little by little, as the demand for pretzels grew, my father would add small amounts of his precious flour to this mush that we called *kasha*. He was always careful not to use too much because it had to go for the pretzels. Naturally, everyone in the family pitched in with the baking. And once the pretzels had caught on, my father expanded his little business and added more

10. 1941: Escape from Kraków

products: *challahs* (braided Jewish breads), *matzos*, cakes and his very special *mandelbroyt*,* all of which he would deliver throughout the village. Before we knew it, he had become the town's baker! And with each new customer we were able to eat better—at least for a while.

To this day, my memories of baking with my father are so real, it's as if I can just step back in time, into that warm, fragrant old room with him again—sifting the flour, mixing in sugar, dusting with cinnamon—and especially baking the *mandelbroyt* twice so it would be extra crispy. Making sure to do everything the right way—no short-cuts! At 80-plus years of age, baking *mandelbroyt* is still an important part of my life. I bake it often, and each time I do, I still feel like that young boy. I can still sense my father's pride in my youthful determination to help, and my step-by-step mastery of this life-giving little baking business.

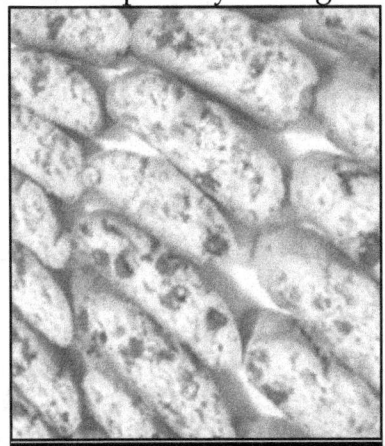

My *mandelbroyt*— fresh from the Papa Ben's Kitchen oven!
Lesser Family Collection

One day, just as if our lives were perfectly normal, my little brother and I went outside to a nearby field to search

---

*Mandelbroyt, or "Almond Bread," is a delicious sugar-dusted biscuit, often including nuts, chocolate chips & dried fruit. It is similar to the Italian biscotti, but richer and denser.

Part I: The Nazi Nightmare

for a special plant that grew wild. We needed this weed because its root was *Chrayn* (horseradish), an essential ingredient for our *Pesach* dinner, the Jewish holiday known as *Passover*. This celebrates the escape of the Jewish People from enslavement in Egypt, and is known in the Bible as the Exodus. We needed horseradish for the traditional *Maror*, the bitter herbs that are eaten to remind us of the bitterness of the Jewish slavery in Egypt.

While Tuli and I were digging, I suddenly saw something that sparkled. Wondering what it could be, I worked furiously to dig it up. Needless to say, we were surprised to see that of all things, it was an upper plate of gold false teeth! Naturally we raced with great excitement to show it to our parents, who were thrilled by our valuable discovery. My father was able to sell it, and with some of the money, he bought shoes for me and a bicycle for us to share. What joy it must have given him to be able to provide these otherwise normal, but now exotic, gifts for his sons. My father was an extraordinary man, so totally dedicated to his family. He never gave up. I wish I could have had more years with him. I wish he could have seen the families that his surviving son and daughter were able to create after the war. He would have been so proud of the lives that all of his grandchildren and great-grandchildren are leading.

Well, for further proof that life goes on no matter what else is happening, in a few months my older brother, Moishe, married his beloved Frieda, and they moved to their own apartment. Soon after, my sister Lola and Mechel were married in a brave little wedding ceremony in our little backyard in Niepolomice. It was illegal for us to go to *shul*, the synagogue. In fact, for us, just gathering in the backyard was illegal, and therefore extremely dangerous.

Adding even further to the danger was our determination that Lola would have a few photographs of her wedding

10. 1941: Escape from Kraków

day. So we were profoundly grateful to one of the guests, who not only took the photos, but also somehow got them printed. And today, as I look at each frightened face in that last photo of our loving family, some managing to show brave smiles for Lola's sake, I am overwhelmed to think that only three of us would survive the coming horror.

Mr. and Mrs. Mechel Lieber
Niepolomice, Poland (1941)
Lesser Family Collection

So now Tuli and I were the only children still living in our little cottage. And although we had more room and more food, we sorely missed our big brother and sister. It seemed as if pieces of our hearts had gone with them. But we all did our best to act as though everything was normal, and life seemed to settle down into a routine. For the next two years, other than the fact that Jewish kids, just like the adults, had to wear the yellow Star of David arm band, and weren't allowed to go to school, our lives were uneventful. This was, however, just a temporary existence. *Even as young as we were, we felt in our bones that it was the calm before the storm. . .*

Part I: The Nazi Nightmare

Leser family at Lola and Mechel's wedding.
I am in 1st row, 3rd from left.
Niepolomice, Poland (1941)
Lesser Family Collection

11. 1943: ESCAPE FROM NIEPOLOMICE

> "... What can man do to me?"
> ~ Hebrews: 13:5-6

And all too soon the storm came. One night, Mechel's father, Herschel Lieber, along with many other Jewish men, were rounded up by the Nazis and taken out into the woods. They had been given shovels and told that they would be working. We never saw him again. We later learned that the men had been forced to dig their own mass grave. They were then shot, and fell or were kicked into the pit. A traumatized witness who had been hiding in the woods, said that the ground had kept moving for days after the Nazis had left—almost as if it were breathing—because many of the victims hadn't been dead when they were buried.

One day Mechel was told by his friendly landlord, who was also the mayor of the town, that something very bad was brewing. He had been informed that there was going to be a pogrom, where Nazis and their local collaborators would destroy Jewish homes and load any Jews who could work into trucks for deportation to labor camps. Others, especially those who were found in hiding, would be killed on the spot. The mayor told Mechel to have the family leave town immediately. So that very night we dressed as peasants, loaded as much as we could into our horse-drawn cart, and slipped out of town. The closest town was Bochnia, a midsize city, known throughout history for its salt mines. It also was known for the anti-Jewish brutality inside its ghetto. Bochnia was particularly notorious for its atrocities against Jewish children, so we really didn't want to go there, but at that point we had no choice.

Part I: The Nazi Nightmare

Since the Nazis' ultimate goal was to make the world *Judenrein* — cleaned of Jews — they saw no reason for a younger generation to even exist. They also felt that children were not productive, and that their existence diminished the productivity of their parents. Nazi actions against Jewish children were particularly systematic in Bochnia. During a series of *Aktions* (deadly pre-planned anti-Jewish pogroms and deportations) in August 1942, the Nazis had eliminated as many Jewish children in Bochnia as possible. For maximum terror, these pogroms were specifically targeted against children and would take place in the middle of the night. First big dump-trucks would rumble slowly down each street in the ghetto. The Nazis then went from house to house breaking down the doors, pulling the innocent sleeping children from their warm beds and throwing them into the trucks. Just like garbage.

When the trucks were filled beyond any imaginable capacity, they would then speed out of town. In front of the children's eyes, the Nazis used machine guns to mow down the frenzied parents who ran screaming in agony behind them. Of course these children were never heard from again. It was said that they were taken to the forest, shot and then thrown into a massive burial pit. Those who didn't die from the bullets were buried alive. This horror resonated profoundly all over Europe. From major cities to small villages, everyone heard about it. Bochnia was a place to be avoided at all costs.

Our "choice" that hellish night, however, was the possibility of a few more days of some kind of life in Bochnia, or certain, immediate death in Niepolomice. And it was "good" that we left when we did, because that very night all the Jews that could be found in Niepolomice were rounded up, never to be seen again. They too were taken into the forest, shot and buried in the huge pits that they'd

11. 1943: Escape from Niepolomice

had to dig themselves. So once again, we were saved by Mechel's friend, the kind mayor of Niepolomice. We also felt fortunate that Mechel had somehow gotten word to friends of his in Bochnia, who had given him the address of an apartment where we could stay. We headed there in our horse and cart with no idea what our reception or accommodations would be like. All we could hope for was the possibility of living for a few more days.

Having ridden silently huddled together through the night, we finally reached the Bochnia Ghetto. When we found the squalid apartment building that Mechel's friend had directed us to, we were shocked by the deplorable living conditions. The four of us joined eight other people who were already crowded into one small eerily empty room. In the middle of this emptiness, however, there was one piece of real furniture—a large, ornately carved, wooden armoire that stood against a wall. It seemed strange there, so out of place all by itself. It was a lonely reminder of the beautiful furnishings that used to fill the room and the people whose tasteful home it had once been. As a fourteen-year old boy, however, I didn't give much more thought to it other than it was where we hung our coats. This piece of furniture, however, would soon become very important to us.

At night, we slept on blankets that were thrown over straw on the floor. During the day, we all went out to work—the men did manual labor such as digging ditches, and the women sewed clothing for the German military.

Part I: The Nazi Nightmare

The only food we had consisted of the barely edible rations provided by the Nazis. With twelve people sharing one room, obviously there was no privacy. And no modesty.

We heard every conversation and every personal noise, no matter how intimate. The only sanitary facility was an outhouse, which emitted a horrendous odor in the summer and was difficult to get to and use in the frigid winter. It still amazes me that despite these unbearable circumstances, we all got along with each other. We understood the stress that each of us was under, and how important it was to try to keep our spirits up. Being self-centered or falling into a depression would have been disastrous for all of us, so we worked hard to always be understanding and supportive of each other.

Each day was much like every other day in Bochnia, which just goes to show you how even the unimaginable can become routine. Every morning we had to report to the authorities, and if we were physically able to work, we were given rations — otherwise we had to scavenge or deal with black-marketers who snuck out through hidden holes in the fences to obtain food and supplies. Sometimes — rarely — friendly Poles would risk their lives to bring food to the fences in the middle of the night.

Luckily, Mechel had been able to find his old friend, Mr. Farber, who put himself in danger in order to help us. The Nazis had forced Farber to become a *kapo,* a Jewish enforcer of Nazi rules. Having had no choice, he was therefore required to carry out certain functions in the ghetto — the most important of which was to keep his fellow Jews under control. He carried no weapons, and was in an extremely precarious position because he had to do whatever the Nazis told him to do — no matter how horrifying. Sometimes *kapos* were cruel and therefore hated by their own people as much as they were hated by the Nazis. But some of them

11. 1943: Escape from Niepolomice

actually did their best to help their people. Especially when they had access to information that might save Jewish lives.

One day, at great personal risk, Farber told Mechel that something very bad was going to happened in the ghetto that night, and that everyone should hide. As a result of what the Nazis had done previously with the town's Jewish children, most people had created hiding places, like bunkers, in or near their homes. Some were under floors; some were between walls or even outside, under dog-houses or chicken-coops. These hiding places were supplied with food, clothes, blankets, some books, small toys, and whatever medical supplies that could be gathered. I was surprised to find out that the secret hiding place in our house was located right behind that big armoire. It turns out that there was an opening in the wall behind the cabinet's secret back panel. The twelve of us could just barely squeeze through this hole into a small outdoor hiding space between the walls of our building and the building next door. Since this outside space was closed off at both ends, it couldn't be seen from the streets. It was, however, open to the sky, so we could clearly hear what was going on. We also were very cold.

Sure enough, that night, the Nazis and their murderous dogs came in rumbling trucks, and surrounded the ghetto. They then went house-to-house and told everyone just to come out and climb into their trucks. Can you imagine that? In the middle of the night, families were forced to leave their homes and get into these trucks, going God knows where. Anyone who refused was shot on the spot. Then the Nazis went into each house. By stomping with their big black boots, they were able to detect hollow flooring, and their dogs were able to sniff out people cowering in bunkers and attic spaces, so most of the people in hiding were quickly found, pulled out, and shot. Worrying desperately about

Part I: The Nazi Nightmare

our own fate, we stood silently all night, body to body, trembling together in our cramped hiding space. We were afraid that even our breathing might betray us to the Nazi murderers. We had to stifle cries of terror at each eruption of machine guns, the barking of killer-dogs, and the agonized screams of innocent Jews. As the only children, little Tuli and I were really under pressure because we had to be just as careful as the adults. There was no margin for error. If either of us made a noise, everyone would die. Quite a responsibility for a fourteen-year-old and his little brother.

Toward morning, it became ghostly quiet. We carefully moved our stiffened arms and legs, and risked crawling back into the apartment. Once we had confirmed that, other than our thirst and hunger, we all were alright, we fearfully ventured outside. A grisly sight and complete pandemonium awaited us. Dead bodies and pieces of dead bodies that had been torn to shreds by the dogs were scattered all over the place. You couldn't even tell that they had once been human beings. Just yesterday they'd been our friends and neighbors.

Heartbroken survivors embraced and wept over the corpses that they weren't allowed to bury properly. They would have been shot if they tried to take the bodies away. Adding to horror, other Jewish people were ordered by the *Judenrat* to go around and pick up the mangled bodies, and body-parts, pile them into push-carts and then take them to the square, where they were then hurled onto an ever-growing heap. Finally, the Nazis poured gasoline all over the mound of corpses, and ignited it, eventually incinerating all the remains. The result was a massive human bonfire, created by Nazis in the civilized 20th century, right in the ghetto's town square. Amid the screams, the smoke, the stench, and the ashes, the murderers then went about the routine activities of their day.

11. 1943: Escape from Niepolomice

Of course we were worried sick about Lola and Mechel. Had they survived? We knew that they had prepared a bunker with Mechel's family out in a field and under the floor of a chicken coop. This floor could be removed, and a ladder led down into a hole that had previously been dug. Seven people could hide there. Lola later told us that just before the *pogrom*, they walked over to the bunker along with Mechel's mother, three sisters and a niece. They were suddenly confronted by Moishe Schiller, who was accompanied by his mother and sister. He came right up to the Liebers and told them that unless they took his mother and sister in, he would turn them in to the authorities.

Whenever Lola tells about this night of horror, we wonder—how could Schiller have known? This was an impossible situation. What could the Liebers do? There was barely enough room for seven. After all that work, how could two loved-ones be sacrificed? When Lola later told us about the heart-wrenching decision about who would go into the shelter, I was awed by her selfless determination to protect others.* Mechel's widowed mother and older, unmarried sister had insisted that they would give up their places in the bunker so that the young couple could be saved. But Lola and Mechel wouldn't hear of it. So these beautiful young newly-weds, with everything to live for, had nowhere to go. As the daylight dwindled, and the dreaded night grew closer, they wandered the streets with nowhere to hide. Knowing that they would not live to see another day. By sheer chance, the kind *kapo*, Mr. Farber, saw them and asked with surprise, why they weren't hiding in some safe place. Mechel told him about Schiller's betrayal. Farber told them not to worry, and then

---

*For the searing details about this night of terror, please read Lola's memoir, A WORLD AFTER THIS: *A Memoir of Loss & Redemption.*

Part I: The Nazi Nightmare

gave them directions to the location where his sister and her two children were hiding.

Lola and Mechel then trudged through the ice and snow to a leather-tanning factory that had been owned by Farber's family. On the roof stood a large, metal water-tank that supplied the water needed to clean the animal hides. Farber's sister, her young daughter and baby were hiding in this tank. Farber had told Mechel and Lola that they should climb up the ladder, go over the top edge and then slide down a rope into the tank. Following his directions, they carefully let themselves down into the tank and ended up in filthy, ice-cold water up to their knees. They cringed when they felt the slimy fur of water-rats swimming around them, nibbling at their legs. For hours, the weak and tired mother had held both her baby and her toddler. Lola immediately reached for the infant, and Mechel took the older child, who would have drowned if she had fallen into the water.

All night long, gunfire, terrified screams, vicious shouts and the barking of murderous dogs punctuated the silence. At one point, the harsh voices of several soldiers could be heard on the ground outside debating about whether they should check the tank to see if anyone was hiding there. One finally said "No, it's cold and getting late, there's no one in there. Come on, let's go." Could that soldier have known that he was saving lives that night?

Eventually it was morning, and with great relief, they heard Mr. Farber's "all-clear" knock. Stiff, wet, cold and exhausted, they helped each other out of the tank and down the ladder to the ground. Mechel and Lola immediately headed to the Liebers' chicken coop bunker to see what had happened to Mechel's family. That's when they saw the most unspeakably horrific sight: each of the seven people had been shot dead. And with a bullet-hole precisely in the middle of her sweet forehead lay Mechel's precious

11. 1943: Escape from Niepolomice

little three-year-old niece, Marilka, still holding onto her tiny doll.

Lola collapsed to the ground, her face contorted by a silent shriek. Mechel rushed to her begging, "Please Lola, we must be quiet or the Nazis will hear us. We have work to do." Together, they somehow mustered all their self-control, held each other close, and softly sobbed. At that time, my sister was not yet eighteen years old! To this day, I am still awed by Lola's self-discipline and ability to focus on the task at hand. Despite their misery and grief, she knew that Jewish law requires burials as soon as possible, preferably within 24-hours. So my sister and brother-in-law proceeded to do what they had to do. They found a rusty and battered old wheelbarrow, which Mechel shakily balanced on the ice and snow. Then, terrified that they'd be seen, they

"Aftermath of the Pogrom" (1950)
Painting by and courtesy of Lola Lieber
Lieber Family Collection

Part I: The Nazi Nightmare

"To the Cemetery" (1950)
Painting by and courtesy of Lola Lieber
Lieber Family Collection

proceeded to load the stiff, broken and bloodied bodies of their murdered loved-ones onto the rickety wheelbarrow. Lola placed her hand protectively on top of the bodies to keep them from falling as they began their tragic journey. Slipping and sliding, they pushed the old wheelbarrow as quickly as they could, up the icy hill to Bochnia's Jewish cemetery. Mechel found a shovel, and without the benefit of gloves, they took turns digging through the frozen ground. After many hours, in that bitterly cold night, they managed to excavate a grave. Just as they finished this grueling, heartbreaking work, they were stunned and disgusted to see Schiller suddenly appear. They knew he would not be bringing good news. And so they were not surprised when he cried to them that it wasn't his fault.

11. 1943: Escape from Niepolomice

He told them that the Nazis' dogs had found the bunker and discovered the terrified trapped people. He continued, "How could it be my fault? They murdered my own mother and sister." Then, after sobbing about his own misery, he got to the point, saying, "This grave that you have just dug is now going to be for my mother and sister. Give it to me — or else!"

Forced once again into an impossible situation, Mechel stepped aside and motioned Lola towards the cemetery's fence. He whispered to her once more, that they couldn't give up. That they had no alternative but to be strong, and start all over again.

And so, ignoring the bitter cold, their grief, their exhaustion, aches, and bloody blistered hands, they had no choice but to start all over in another spot. At last, their

"Burying Our Murdered Family" (1950)
Painting by and courtesy of Lola Lieber
Lieber Family Collection

Part I: The Nazi Nightmare

faces stiff with frozen tears, they were able to reverently lower the remains of their loved ones into the grave.

When this heartbreaking task was completed, they glanced back to see Schiller busily burying his dead. Just as he had replaced the last handful of soil, they heard a Nazi jeep coming up the hill toward cemetery, so they quickly hid themselves behind a bush. Then they heard the Nazis shouting, "Schiller!" To which he quickly responded, "*Jawohl!* ("Yes Sir!")," while running dutifully to his masters. They pulled out their pistols, and a moment later two shots rang out. Then silence.

It wasn't until Lola and Mechel heard the receding sound of the jeep's engine that they risked emerging from the bushes. They saw Schiller dead on the ground. Such was the fate of Jewish collaborators who the Nazis no longer needed.

Physically, mentally, and emotionally numb, Mechel and Lola somehow found the strength to finish burying their family. Then, they slowly trudged back to their apartment in the ghetto. Once inside, they held each other close, and wept uncontrollably. *And tried not to think about what new horror would befall them. . .*

12. *A MODERN-DAY QUEEN ESTHER*

> "... but Esther had not revealed her nationality and family background..."
> ~ Esther 2:20

Early the next morning, the pile of bodies still smoldered in the town-square, and the stench-filled air was dark with smoke and ashes. Horrified survivors crept slowly out of hiding. They heard announcements blaring from a truck with a loud-speaker, and saw newly-printed Nazi signs directing everyone to report to the Judenrat to receive their new IDs. The Nazis wanted to know how many of us had survived. Anyone who didn't report would miss out on food rations. If we wanted to eat, we had no choice but to go.

So, hungry, cold, and frightened, our family stood in a slowly progressing line. My sister Lola, whose once beautiful eyes were now haunted, was first. The clerk asked her many questions: her age, where she lived, where she was born. She answered that she had been born in Munkács — which at that time was in Hungary. Behind this clerk stood the new Chief of the local Gestapo, Captain Schomburg, who had been silently and closely observing the whole process. This Nazi official who had just been assigned to Bochnia would have an unexpectedly powerful impact on not only the Leser family, but on many other Jewish families as well. Hearing Lola say that she had been born in Munkács, his face lit up and we were then shocked to hear him tell the clerk, "Don't give this Lola a new ID. I want her in my office at 10 am tomorrow. You be sure to bring her." None of us could breathe. You can imagine why he wanted her.

All night long we held a vigil, holding each other and crying. No one could sleep. Early the next morning, as

Part I: The Nazi Nightmare

ordered, a *kapo* reluctantly came for Lola. We tearfully followed them, telling her to be brave, that we were all praying for her. As they walked through the gate of the ghetto, my father called out to his precious daughter that if necessary, she should die *"al Kiddush Hashem,"* which means that if she had to die, she should die as an honored martyr to her faith—without breaking sacred Jewish laws. As we watched from the gate, they left the ghetto and went to a beautiful, formerly Jewish, home that now housed the Gestapo office.

Later, we were stunned as Lola told us what had happened. When Schomburg's door opened, Lola forced her knees to stop shaking, and walked in with quiet dignity. The formally uniformed Schomburg sat behind a big desk at the far end of a huge office. Seeing Lola, he did something that was totally out of character—he acted like a human being instead of a Nazi. He stepped out from behind his desk and pulled out the chair for her to sit down. This gentlemanly courtesy was absolutely unimaginable. In fact, in those days, if a Nazi was walking on a sidewalk, an approaching Jew would have to get off the sidewalk and walk in the street. At this point Lola was white as a sheet, shaking and scared stiff. He gently told her, "Sit down and be calm."

Next, just as if they were having a normal conversation, he asked, "Were you really born in Munkács?" When she answered in perfect German, *"Ja,"* he asked, "Can you also speak Hungarian?" Since she spoke perfect Hungarian, she responded, *"Igen."* Things got even stranger as he started talking conversationally about Hungarian music and even kidded with her about Hungarian foods, like *goulash*, a popular beef stew. She couldn't understand the purpose of this conversation. Was it some Nazi trick? He then lifted

12. A Modern-Day Queen Esther

up her arm and gently pulled her arm-band off. Terrified to think of what would happen next, she was stunned to hear him say, "You are one lucky young lady—you are an *Auslanderin*, a foreigner. Munkács is now in Hungary We have no quarrel with Hungary; they are our allies. We have no jurisdiction over you—you shouldn't even be in the ghetto. You have the right to live wherever you want."

Despite the conflicting emotions that were threatening to overwhelm her, Lola had the presence of mind to quickly reply, "But what about my husband and my family?" Schomburg thought a moment, and then asked, "Where were they born?" Without missing a beat, Lola told him, "Munkács"—and held her breath. He then ordered his secretary to make out papers for everyone in the family. So just like that, thanks to Lola's courage, and quick thinking, all of us were now considered to be Hungarian citizens! We all now would have permission to leave the ghetto. He then turned to the *kapo*, who had witnessed the entire scene in stunned silence, and told him, "Bring this young woman's relatives to me tomorrow morning at 9." It seemed to Lola as if Schomburg actually was ashamed of what the Nazis were doing to the Jews. Who knows? Maybe despite being a Nazi, he still had a human conscience. Trembling, she softly repeated, "*Danke Schoen* (Thank you)," and even kissed his hand. No one had ever heard of, much less survived, such a thing. A Jewish woman kissing a Nazi's hand? Weeping, Lola whispered a final "*Danke Schoen*," and staggered out. The whole ordeal had taken less than twenty minutes.*
(Years later, we learned that Captain Schomburg had been executed by the Nazis.)

The astonished *kapo* then escorted Lola back to the ghetto, where they found everyone—even the revered

---

* Read more about this event in Lola's memoir, A WORLD AFTER THIS: *A Memoir of Loss & Redemption.*

Part I: The Nazi Nightmare

Bobover Rabbi, Shlomo Halberstam—standing pressed against the gate and along the adjacent walls. They had been there prepared to wait as long as necessary for her return. When we saw her, we couldn't believe our eyes! She wasn't bruised or battered. Her clothes were in perfect condition. In fact, she looked good—almost as if she was happy! How could this be? We'd thought we'd never see her again. After she breathlessly told us all what had happened, we picked her up and danced with her over our heads! We were so honored when the Rabbi joined us in walking her home. The Rabbi, who was a learned man with a warm personality, and well-known for his story-telling, had often risked his life to help Jews escape the ghetto. On more than one occasion, he had dressed up as a nun in order to rescue other Jews. That day, as we cheered Lola, he told her that she was a modern-day "Queen Esther."

At first she didn't understand what he was saying to her. Always, modest, she felt that whatever she'd accomplished had been only with God's help. With his soft voice and powers of persuasion, the Rabbi then spoke carefully to my sister: "Lola, just as Queen Esther saved the Jews from the evil Haman, your actions today will save many Jewish lives." We all listened closely as he further explained what he meant. He told her that she and Queen Esther had both used their wits and courage to gain freedom for their people.

The Rabbi had quickly realized that the Hungarian citizenship papers that our family had just received thanks to Lola could also be used as templates to make many additional citizenship papers. And since he possessed a typewriter and some high-quality paper, a document-forgery operation could begin immediately. This would allow many more Jews to be released from the ghetto. They could then make their way to Hungary, which was still a free country.

12. A Modern-Day Queen Esther

And so thanks to a creative Rabbi who refused to be a victim, the bravery of my teenaged sister Lola, plus the business acumen of her husband Mechel, and the artistic talents of my brother Moishe, an extraordinary escape operation was created for many Bochnian Jews. This dangerously daring exploit would have a profound impact on generations to follow. It involved the detailed falsification of birth-certificates and citizenship documents. Using a rubber ball carefully carved with special engravings that worked as an official "stamp," along with meticulously forged signatures, Moishe and Mechel set up an assembly-line creating the life-giving papers that would allow Jews to leave the ghetto.

This process eventually included everyone in the family. Lola helped with the artwork, and even my mother had an important job—staining the paper with tea to make the documents look old and well-used. Of course everyone in the community clamored for these priceless papers, and although they offered large sums of money, Moishe and Mechel refused to take any payment. The entire enterprise was conducted on the basis of a handshake. Their goal was to save Jewish lives, not enrich themselves. The first four families that received documents agreed to take one or two members of our family with them when they escaped.

Thanks to this family enterprise, many escaped. These included our beloved Bobover Rabbi Shlomo Halberstam and his family. They were first able to get to Hungary, then to England. Tragically, despite all of his efforts, Rabbi Halberstam was not able to save his own parents, Rabbi and Mrs. Ben Zion Halberstam, or many other relatives who were murdered along with thousands of others in the forest outside of Lvov, Poland—now Lviv, Ukraine. Finally able to immigrate to the United States, the Rabbi worked tirelessly

Part I: The Nazi Nightmare

to re-establish the historic *Bobover Dynasty** in Borough Park, Brooklyn. Throughout the rest of his long and fulfilling life, until his passing in 2000, Rabbi Halberstam made a point of publicly thanking Lola for the efforts she and her family made on behalf of the Jewish people of Bochnia, and the Bobover Dynasty.

At this point, thanks to Lola, we all had been able to move into a small apartment outside of the ghetto. We didn't have to wear the yellow Star of David armbands, so we were able to come and go more freely. This made it possible for Mechel and Lola to arrange for our escape to Hungary. Mechel had found a coal-truck driver, and offered to pay him whatever price necessary to add a false bottom to his truck and smuggle us out in small groups. When the first group of ten escapees was ready to leave Bochnia, as previously agreed, they included Mechel and Lola. They had wanted to go first in case the driver could not be trusted. This was a particularly dangerous process because the Nazis paid *Gentiles* (non-Jews) to betray escapees and their helpers. So, of course, all Gentiles were potential bounty hunters. It was a real challenge to find a driver who not only could elude spies, but who wouldn't end up taking the money, only to then betray his hidden passengers.

That non-Jews would even consider doing this was nothing short of a miracle. They put their lives and the lives of their families on the line to do the right thing. I've often wondered what qualities allowed them to do the righteous thing when so many others didn't. And all too many of them paid for their actions with their lives. These Heroes

---

*The *Bobover Dynasty* is a *Hasidic* (a branch of Orthodox Judaism) group that originated in the late 1600s in Southern Poland. It has been headquartered in the neighborhood of Borough Park in Brooklyn (where Lola still lives) since the end of WWII.

12. A Modern-Day Queen Esther

have become known and honored as *Righteous Gentiles*,* and are honored for their self-sacrifices on behalf of the Jewish People.

In order to confirm that an escape had succeeded, it was necessary to create a secret password that would be given to the driver upon the completion of the trip. When he returned, the driver would then communicate this password to a member of our family. This would mean that all had gone well. On the night that Lola and Mechel were to leave, we clung to them, telling them we loved them and that we would pray for them. We tearfully bid them to, "Go with God." No one slept that night. The next day, you can imagine our joy when the driver came back with the correct secret password! For once, all was well! We even dared to have a little hope that our lives would be saved.

---

*For more information on *Righteous Gentiles*, see "Yad Vashem — Righteous Gentiles," http://www1.yadvashem.org/righteous_new/index.html; and, "The International Raul Wallenberg Foundation," www.raoulwallenberg.net/

13. ESCAPE FROM BOCHNIA

> *"When you have no choice, mobilize the spirit of courage."*
> ~ Old Jewish Proverb

Now it was time for the second load of escapees, and little Tuli and I were chosen to go along. Here we were at the young ages of fourteen and seven, no longer able to remember what it had been like to be safe, secure children. Wondering if we'd ever live to become men. We were embarking without our parents, upon a dangerous escape to freedom. The rickety old coal truck pulled into a nearby barn that night. Just before daybreak, along with the eight other frightened travelers, we slid into the secret compartment. We crawled in and lay on our backs, squeezed together like sardines. Then, at the usual time, the truck pulled out in the morning to make its rounds of coal deliveries.

About an hour later, as we reached the outskirts of Bochnia, we heard, "Halt!" The terrified truck-driver had no choice but to follow this order. In our cramped, dusty hiding place, our hearts seemed to have stopped beating. Between the cracks in the sides of the truck, we could see the German soldiers with their rifles. We were surprised and relieved when we began moving again. This relief didn't last long, however, as we soon became aware that the soldiers were coming right along with us on the truck. Since I was closest to the front of the truck I actually could see one of the soldiers, standing on the running board — a narrow step under the vehicle's doors — just inches away from me. He was so close I could have touched him. We could hear the others talking with the driver. We could tell that another

Part I: The Nazi Nightmare

soldier was riding along on the driver's running board. Because of the roar of the engine, we could not make out what they were saying, but we were certain someone had turned us in, and that the soldiers would be taking us to either a forest or cemetery to be shot. Others were walking on top of the coal — and dust filtered on down to us. I saw that Tuli was about to sneeze and fortunately I was able to hold my hand over his small face, preventing this from happening and exposing us. We all held our breath and prayed until the truck lurched to a sudden stop and the soldiers started saying friendly goodbyes to the driver. And then, just like that — they were gone, and we were still alive. Apparently, they were only hitch-hiking. In the meanwhile, we had all aged about ten years.

The truck then took us all the way to the forest near the top of the mountain at the border of Poland and Czechoslovakia, where the nervous driver let us out on a desolate road. We were all black with the dust, and our legs shook from being cooped up for so long in one position. The driver gave us directions to climb to a spot where a Forest Ranger, who also smuggled escapees, would be waiting for us. At that time, being a "smuggler" was a good thing! After an exhausting climb, we somehow found him, and he took us to his cabin in the forest. His kind wife showed us where we could wash-up, and then led us to a beautiful table where she had prepared a wonderful hot meal for us.

Around three in the morning, after getting a little restless sleep, we left this warm, safe-house, for the next stage of our escape to freedom. We moved silently through the forest until we could see the guards at the Czech border. There were also patrol dogs, barbed-wire, and powerful searchlights sweeping the terrain. On our hands and knees, we climbed closer and closer, waiting for a break in the sweep of those merciless searchlights. Luckily, the Forest

13. 1943: Escape from Bochnia

Ranger knew that when the guards changed shifts, they'd have a little guard-changing ceremony. And during one of those breaks, we were able to shinny our way up the hill, squeeze through the barbed wire, and crawl over to the other side.

The Forest Ranger had told us that there was a big ravine on the other side of the hill. But he said not to worry, that if we were careful and rolled down, with our heads, arms and legs tucked in, we wouldn't get hurt. At that point the night was pitch-black — no moon, no stars, which meant we wouldn't be seen, but it also meant that we couldn't see a thing. It looked like we were going to roll off the edge of the earth. This clearly would be a leap of faith in more ways than one. I took my brother's hand and we slid down the ravine as quietly as we could, getting scraped on rocks and branches. When we finally rolled to a stop, we tried to catch our breath, bring our heartbeats back to normal, and figure out what to do next. Suddenly from nowhere, I felt a gentle tap on my shoulder. Even though I had been trained not to make any noise, I nearly jumped out of my skin. When a deep, soft, caring voice asked, "Binesh?" I felt my body relax. It had seemed like forever since I had heard a soft, caring voice.

It was my mother's brother, our Uncle Belo. He had known where to find us because he'd been in close contact with Lola and Mechel, who had ended up in the very same spot! He then smuggled us across the border into what was known in 1943, as Slovakia. His brother, our Uncle Beri had recently moved there deliberately in order to help escaping Jews. We were welcomed warmly at his house, where we cleaned up, ate, and stayed only one night. The next day we went by train to the city of Košice, and prepared to cross yet another border into Hungary — and freedom.

Part I: The Nazi Nightmare

Compared to what we'd been through so far, this final border-crossing was relatively easy. This time we were lucky enough to have a guide who knew a place where there weren't any guards. And although we did see some of the Hungarian soldiers wearing their bright red jackets and helmets with ostrich feathers, we were able to bypass them completely. You can imagine how overwhelmed with relief we were when we made it across to Hungary.

We brushed ourselves off and tried to look presentable. And then, just as if it was all completely normal, just as if we'd been out for a little stroll instead of sneaking through the night across borders, we walked casually into a little town. We found the train station, and took the train to Budapest. As soon as we arrived, a very strange thing happened. My Uncle Belo took us to the police station, where we were put in jail. It turns out that it was just a bureaucratic process requiring that "guardians" come get their kids out of jail. When Uncle Belo "came" to get us, he had to sign some papers declaring that he was our guardian.

It didn't take much time, since he was already there. It was all just a charade. But even though he had explained in advance that this was going to happen, it was still very frightening. Once that jail-cell's door had closed on us, I'd had a flash of fear that something bad would happen to my uncle, and that Tuli and I would be stuck there forever. So when the door opened and we were released after only about 15 minutes, I breathed a big sigh of relief. And soon, with great excitement, we rushed into Lola and Mechel's apartment, where they were waiting for us with tears, hugs, kisses and a lot of lovingly prepared food!

14. A HAPPY MUNKÁCS REUNION!

> *"The great enemy of the truth*
> *is very often not the lie,*
> *deliberate, contrived and dishonest,*
> *but the myth,*
> *persistent, persuasive and unrealistic."*
>
> ~ John F. Kennedy (1917-1963)
> American World War II Hero,
> Statesman & US President (1961-1963)

Wonderful as this reunion in Budapest was, we needed to be on our way to Munkács, so we couldn't even stay the night. Again, we took the train, just as if we were two typical young boys on an adventure with their uncle! We could barely contain our excitement until we were reunited at our safe and loving family home with my sister Goldie, our grandparents, aunts, uncles, and cousins; the whole family from my mother's side. It was easy to think that our lives would almost be normal.

Munkács seemed to be untouched by the horror that was consuming its neighbors. But much to my surprise, adjusting to the "normal" life that still existed there was a real challenge for me. After what we'd seen and been through, this carefree normalcy seemed very strange. Almost insulting. My brother and I moved in with my Uncle Hershel, who owned a very successful fabric store. I'd always looked up to his son, my cousin Isaac, who was a few years older than I. He was very knowledgeable and sophisticated, but he still made time for his younger cousins. I appreciated that I didn't have to be the responsible older brother. All around us, life was going on as if the

Part I: The Nazi Nightmare

Holocaust were some imaginary horror story instead of the unimaginable reality just a few miles away. It was hard to reconcile what we'd just been through with what we were seeing. One night we had been hidden in the bottom of a coal truck, and a few days later, here we were out among seemingly carefree people, enjoying a stroll on a beautiful busy street. Lively Jewish kids played outside and went to *Cheder*—school. Mothers gathered in parks with their little children and pets. Bearded Jewish men in full Orthodox attire, engaged in profound discussions, safely walked to and from various places of worship. People dressed up and went to movies, theaters, restaurants, and drank coffee at outdoor cafes. Typical teenagers who were still rabidly interested in the latest styles, sports, celebrities and movie stars, flirted with each other and went to fancy Proms.

Everywhere we looked, there was business as usual—which was highly unusual for us. In fact, I hadn't seen such a sight in the last four years. When I told the people about the atrocities which were going on in Poland, many thought I was just a kid with a wild and morbid imagination. Even those who did believe me, smugly felt that this could never happen in Hungary; not to them. The Hungarian Jewish People were highly assimilated, meaning they were absorbed in into every aspect of Hungarian culture. And most importantly, Germany and Hungary were allies. It was unthinkable that Germany would turn on its own ally. No, the Hungarian Jews had nothing to worry about.

Finally safe and settled in with our family, Tuli and I eagerly waited for our parents to arrive in the next transport. Of course they had insisted on being the last members of the family to escape. We were so anxious to see them, to hold them, and to resume our normal family life in this bustling little city. It seemed, however, like we were waiting forever.

14. A Happy Munkács Reunion

One month. Two months. We heard nothing from or about them. We became more and more worried. Unbeknownst to us, the worst thing imaginable had happened.

We eventually learned that my brother Moishe had been discovered and captured by the Nazis. Apparently, someone had called the authorities and informed on him. So the Nazis learned that he was responsible for falsifying documents. They arrested him and sent him to *Plashov** Concentration Camp, a place that was well-known for the unspeakable atrocities and murders committed there. We never saw my brother again. Years later we learned that he had miraculously escaped from two concentration camps, only to be killed by Allied bombs. Today, since the camp was bulldozed after the war, there is nothing left except for a small monument. Despite hearing the devastating news about Moishe, we still held on to the hope that our parents would manage to join us. Week after week we waited, forcing ourselves to live as normally as possible despite our fears.

Two months later, we met an acquaintance from Bochnia who had just been smuggled across the borders, and he sadly told us the terrible truth. The night that our parents climbed into the secret compartment in the bottom of the coal truck, some neighboring farmer saw what was going on and called the authorities. Since informers were paid to turn in their neighbors, this was always a danger. The Gestapo immediately came down, bringing a terrified *kapo*, Mr. Roth, to watch. They lined up all the people, including the courageous gentile driver, and shot them.

---

*It's interesting to note that since Oscar Schindler's factory was near the *Plashov* Concentration Camp, many events from the camp's history formed the basis of the movie, *Schindler's List*. Schindler was able to save 1000 Jews from Plashov.

Part I: The Nazi Nightmare

"A Failed Escape" (1950)
Painting by and courtesy of Lola Lieber
Lieber Family Collection

The Nazis then ordered Mr. Roth and a few other men to bury the eleven bodies. They took them to Bochnia's Jewish Cemetery, where they carefully buried them in a mass grave. Mr. Roth was an extraordinary human being, who deserves to be honored. At great risk of certain torture and death, he consistently chose to do the right thing. His kindness and actions not only saved countless lives, he went even further than that by also caring for the bodies and souls of those who couldn't be saved. He never lost his humanity.

Somehow, Mr. Roth survived the war, and since he knew, respected and cared deeply about Mechel and Lola, he was determined to find out if they had survived. When he finally tracked them down, it was a bittersweet reunion. They were all so happy to see each other alive and Lola and Mechel's gratitude for all Roth had done for them was

14. A Happy Munkács Reunion

profound. But the news was heartbreaking. He told them about the executions, and the following mass burial. And then Roth performed yet another *mitzvah* (worthy deed) for the Leser family. He carefully described the location of their burial site. Lola took detailed notes, and drew a primitive map. She and Mechel promised him and each other that someday they would return to Bochnia and build a memorial on the burial site.

Twenty years later, Lola and Mechel did return to Poland and made good on this promise. Lola's notes from Mr. Roth enabled them to describe the burial site to the cemetery's caretaker who was then able to help them find it. Although Jean and I were unable to join them, the entire family contributed to the creation of a beautiful memorial on which all the names were listed.

Despite the horrific capture of my brother and the devastating, brutal deaths of my parents, I had no time for grieving. It seemed as if that my experience with the Nazis

Leser Memorial, Bochnia Jewish Cemetery
Bochnia, Poland (2006)
Lesser Family Collection

had somehow made me older than my cousin, Isaac. My responsibility for my own survival and that of my brother Tuli had become even more profound than before. And now

Part I: The Nazi Nightmare

that our survival depended upon the safety of my Uncle's family, I also felt a sense of responsibility for them.

Since I had seen and experienced what had happened to the Jewish people in Poland, I urged my Uncle to convert some of his assets into diamonds. I pointed out to him that if something drastic should happen, the diamonds would be small enough to hide in the lining of his clothes. That way, at least his assets would be portable rather than stationary. I was honored that he listened to me as if I were an adult. Unlike many disbelieving Hungarian Jews, my uncle understood the reality of what I had gone through, and respected my suggestion. *This respect would be seen again under the most terrifying circumstances. . .*

15. 1944: THE NAZIS INVADE HUNGARY

> *"A great deal of intelligence can be invested in ignorance when the need for illusion is deep."*
> ~ Saul Bellow (1915-2005)
> Canadian–born Jewish-American Writer,
> Pulitzer & Nobel Prize Winner

One day in the early spring of 1944, Uncle Herschel came home from work with boxes of brand new, sturdy black leather shoes for every member of the family. This was a very welcome surprise! Then he told us that hidden within the heels of the shoes were diamonds. He had taken my advice about making most of his assets portable. Those precious stones were, of course, only to be used in case of deportation, or other emergency. Sure enough, a couple of weeks later, in March, the Germans invaded Hungary. Since Hungary was an ally of Germany, there was no fighting; it seemed as though Hungary had invited the Nazis in. And of course, according to their well-practiced routine, the first order of the new regime was to make Hungary *Judenfrei*, free of Jews.

In retrospect, it's clear that Hitler must have already known that Germany was on the brink of losing the war. So it's still a mystery why he chose to siphon off desperately needed resources from his own military in order to occupy a friendly ally like Hungary. The tragically obvious answer is that Hitler's obsession to kill as many as possible of Hungary's 750,000 Jewish inhabitants was more important than his desire to fight a losing war. He was willing to sacrifice his own military, his own country, in order to satisfy his sick obsession. I've heard that he even said that

Part I: The Nazi Nightmare

"the German people deserved to lose the war because they hadn't worked hard enough to win it." To Hitler, killing defenseless Jews was more important than winning the war. Looking back, I sometimes wonder if the war itself wasn't just a part of his grandiose and depraved Final Solution.

By the time they got to Hungary, the Nazis had had so much practice occupying other countries that it was almost like the final performance of a well-rehearsed show. Thanks to newly developing computer technology, the Nazis were meticulously organized, and quickly coded the entire Jewish population of Hungary. With tremendous speed and precision they set up *Judenrate* almost as if they were franchises in each neighborhood. They knew the routine — immediately confiscating all Jewish businesses, issuing new identification papers with the large "J" for "Jew," and ordering everyone to wear armbands with a Star of David. Bank accounts were frozen, travel for the Jewish people was forbidden. There was no need to confiscate businesses or homes, because very soon, their Jewish owners and inhabitants would cease to exist. In fact, the next morning, with the assistance of local Hungarian policemen, the "SS" began the process of evicting the entire Jewish community. We had received our orders. Everyone seemed to move in a shocked daze. After a sleepless night, and without much conversation, we got dressed and put on our new shoes. We then assembled, as ordered, with all the other Jews outside our houses.

Such a sight. Imagine a beautiful residential neighborhood very early on a crisp April morning. The trees lining the street showing the first innocent buds of spring. And outside of their well-tended homes, all along the sidewalks where children had so recently played with marbles and ridden tricycles, lined-up speechless with terror and disbelief, stood an impossible sight: All the Jewish families. From the

15. 1944: The Nazis Invade Hungary

aged to the newborn. From the sick and handicapped to the healthy and strong. It was another event that couldn't be believed even by the people living through it. And only the few people who had believed our desperate warnings had made preparations.

The Nazis reassured us that we were going to a labor camp, and that we should definitely bring our valuables. We were allowed to take only what we could carry — everything else had to be left behind. So we layered on our clothes, and stuffed pockets and hidden pouches with valuables. Very soon everyone, loaded down with their valises, bundles, suitcases, and even some food, was ordered to fall in step with the terrified marching crowd. Our destination was the brick factory. Its large yard, conveniently located next to the train tracks, became a staging area for a journey that unbeknownst to us, few would survive.

We saw the long line of filthy cattle cars awaiting us, but instead of terror, we were actually hopeful. We believed that we were being deported to a German labor camp, where the whole family would stay together. The able-bodied men and women would work at various jobs, and the children would be cared for and go to school. This seemed to make sense since the German military needed workers. Why is it that it is sometimes easier to believe a lie than the truth? At that time, since the actual truth was unbelievable, it was easier to believe the lie.

The Nazis quickly divided us into groups of eighty per car. I stood there with my brother Tuli, my aunt, my uncle, and my cousin Isaac. We didn't know where our other relatives were. While calmly waiting to be loaded, I saw two men carrying a stretcher with a horribly beaten person on it. They set this stretcher down carefully at our feet. When I looked closer, I was shocked to see that it was my beautiful sister Goldie. Her blood-soaked clothes were

Part I: The Nazi Nightmare

in tatters, she was black and blue, and her swollen face was battered almost beyond recognition. I bent down and tearfully asked her, "Goldie, what happened to you?"

Through cracked lips that could barely form words, she whispered that she'd tried to escape, but had been spotted by a former schoolmate who informed on her. The Nazis easily caught her, beating and kicking her until she lost consciousness.

Soon, the authorities ordered us all to climb into those cattle cars. We knew we had to make it look as if Goldie could walk on her own, so we struggled to hold her upright between us. The Nazis brutally pushed and screamed at all of us—men, women carrying babies, teenagers, grandparents—everyone. When those heavy doors slammed closed, it sounded and felt as if we were being entombed alive. And we all wondered about the two buckets of water that stood under a small barbed-wire air vent. As the rickety train slowly began to move, we were too afraid to think about what lay ahead.

These cattle cars had never been intended for human passengers. The conditions during what turned out to be a three-day journey were so inhumane, that I cannot find enough adjectives in all of the languages I speak to describe them. Because of the many bundles of belongings, it was too crowded for everyone to even sit down at the same time. If someone needed to sit down, someone else had to stand up. The only food and water we possessed were what we had brought with us. You can imagine the tension and aggression that developed when some people who had already finished their food watched the others who had been more careful with their own portions. Human nature being what it is, some people would do anything to eat or feed their hungry children. And people who were naturally generous learned quickly to protect their own

15. 1944: The Nazis Invade Hungary

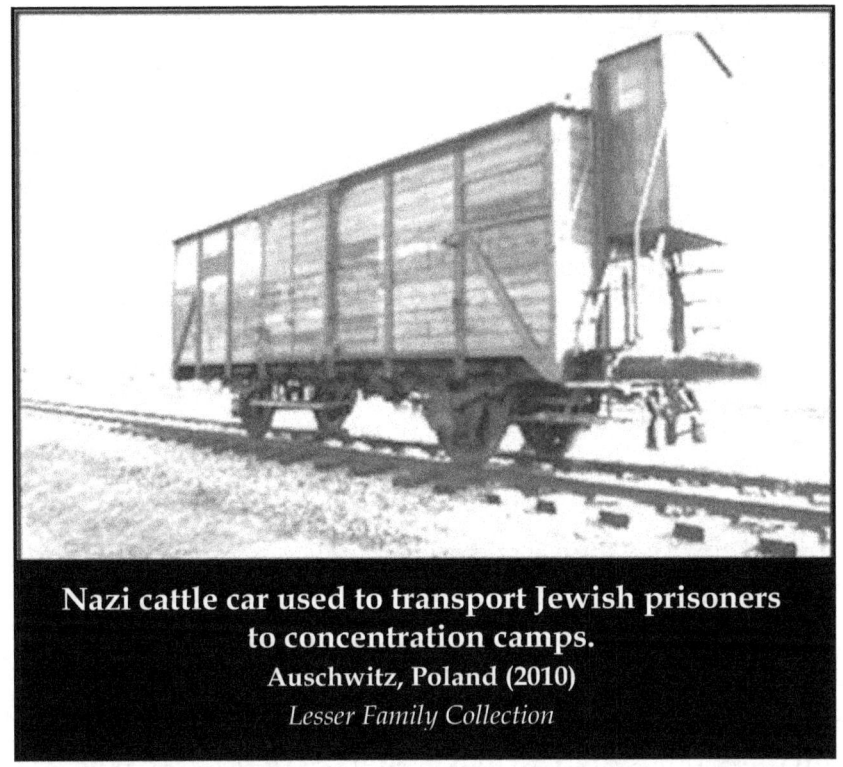

Nazi cattle car used to transport Jewish prisoners to concentration camps.
Auschwitz, Poland (2010)
Lesser Family Collection

food by moving little bits secretly to their mouths. Naturally hostilities broke out. We had to huddle together to protect ourselves from our own people.

Making the situation even more unbearable was the complete lack of sanitary facilities. One day we had been living in our own comfortable rooms in lovely homes with modern plumbing, and the next day we were crowded into box-cars, where the only plumbing consisted of those two buckets. These buckets had originally been filled with water. Once the buckets were emptied of water, they were then used for human waste. Needless to say, these buckets very quickly filled and overflowed. Soon the entire floor was covered with urine, excrement, and vomit. There was no way to avoid getting splashed and covered in the filth.

Part I: The Nazi Nightmare

No one was safe from it. Now we actually appreciated our bulky bundles, because sitting on them kept us elevated a bit above the mess. The stench, the noise, and the chaos increased by the minute. Men, women, children, infants, the elderly—everyone got sick. And of course this only added to the problem. Along with the constant sounds and smells of bodily functions, there were the agonized prayers, moans, cries and shrieks of people in unspeakable physical and emotional pain. It was hard to breathe without choking on the foul air.

Three hellish days later, when we passed through a town, someone was able to see through the small, barbed-wire covered air-vent that the name of the train station was Oœwiêcim (Auschwitz), so we knew we were in Poland. We finally pulled into a railroad siding, and someone saw the sign over the gates that said, "*Arbeit Macht Frei*" (Work makes you free). This seemed to make sense for a labor camp. At that time we didn't know that Auschwitz was anything other than a village, so most of us were relieved that we would finally be getting out of the cattle cars, settling in and getting to work. We also saw some barracks, and figured that we would be housed in them. After a while, however, when the doors didn't open, our fragile spirits fell. The train then pulled away slowly and rumbled on for what seemed like another couple of kilometers. That night, when it finally stopped, we still believed that this would be the place that we were going to reside and work. As I look back now, it seems as if once we believed the big lie, we just interpreted everything else to fit in with it. *And we hung on to that lie as if it were life itself. . .*

16. AUSCHWITZ-BIRKENAU & DURNHAU

> *"Arbeit Macht Frei"*
> Sign over entrance gate of
> Auschwitz Concentration Camp.

Eventually, very late that night, the doors were abruptly flung open to a scene of utter pandemonium. We were ordered to leave our belongings on the train. Gasping for fresh air, holding on to our loved ones, we all tried to squeeze through the doors. As we tumbled down, we were "greeted" by shrieking, gun-waving Nazis and their vicious barking dogs. We were also greeted by other prisoners who were later forced to pick through our bundles. They were looking for the valuables we had been told to bring. Whatever they found that was of value—clothing, shoes, eyeglasses, jewelry, pots and pans, canned food—would be taken to giant warehouses.* These prisoners also became our interpreters. Just in case someone didn't get the message or just didn't get it fast enough, they told us in many different languages what the Germans were yelling. Instead of giving us orders, the Nazis clubbed us viciously while screaming at us to move fast. "*Raus! Schnell, Schnell!* (Get out! Fast! Fast!)."

Women and children were roughly directed to the right, and men to the left. One minute I was holding on tightly to my little brother and to my sister Goldie. And then suddenly—the next minute—they were gone. We were just torn apart. Never to see each other again. I am still filled with sadness and guilt when I think about not being able

---

*These warehouses were located in an area of the camp which was known as *Kanada*, because everyone thought that Canada was a place of great wealth.

Part I: The Nazi Nightmare

to protect Goldie and Tuli. It was at that moment that I lost my faith. How could a God let this happen to us?

My Uncle Hershel, Cousin Isaac and I were then lined-up with the other male prisoners. As we looked around, we were shocked by what we saw. This camp, which by then we had discovered was named *Birkenau,* was a strange, completely alien world. Almost like science fiction. And as we stood quietly lined up in the eerie darkness, we were almost overcome by an indescribably sickening stench. We saw four huge chimneys with flames rising above them. Constantly erupting from these chimneys, as if from belching volcanoes, were dense clouds of ashes. Like a snow storm, these ashes rained down on us, completely covering the ground with a strange white dust. Whenever we moved, we left ghostly footprints in this dust. We couldn't have known that we were walking on the dust of our loved ones. Since there was no way we could have guessed the truth, most people believed that the flaming chimneys were part of smelting factories, where we probably would soon be working. So we stood quietly in our ghostly line, calmly waiting to be directed to our new "home."

Once again, officials decided who would go to the left and who would go to the right. We had no idea what this meant. Always alert and observant, however, I noticed that at the head of the line stood a man, who looked like a medical doctor, wearing a bright white lab-coat and spotless white gloves. We wondered if we would be receiving medical attention. He just stood there, expressionless, motioning with his index finger for people to go to the left or to the right.

Occasionally he would ask someone a question. As I came closer I could hear him ask various men whether they could run five kilometers (3.10685 miles) or whether they rather go by truck. When he asked this of a seemingly

16. Auschwitz-Birkenau and Durnhau

young, healthy man, the frightened guy looked almost relieved and told him he was having trouble with his knees. The "doctor" quickly pointed to the right. The poor soul didn't realize that this meant certain death. At that point, I didn't know it either, but I figured that since we were in a labor camp, they would have no use for people who couldn't do the work. I had already learned an important lesson that would stay with me for the rest of my life: If you want to succeed at an assignment, first find out what is necessary to succeed, and then just do it. Of course, I didn't dream that instead of making us free, the "work" we would be assigned, was designed to kill us.

As we got closer to the head of the line, I began to realize that it was important to be directed to the left. Maybe on some unconscious level, I had an idea that this monstrous doctor was asking certain questions in order to separate the weak from the strong people. I told my uncle, "Whatever he asks you, be sure to take the hard part; say yes, you can run if he asks you that." At that time, I was just 15 ½ years old, and not very tall. I wasn't quite a man, and it had been a long time since I'd been a child. I had always been very observant, however, and knew from what I saw going on around me, that my survival depended upon my being useful to the Nazis. And strong men would be much more useful than boys.

So, when it was my turn, I stretched myself out as tall as I could, and saluted the man in the white lab coat before he even asked me a question. And in the deepest voice I could manage, I said, "*Achtzen yahr alt, gezunt, und arbeitsfahig* (I am eighteen years old, I am healthy, and I can work)." Then he asked me if I could run five kilometers, and I quickly said, "*Jawohl!*" So he sent me to the left. My uncle and my cousin, both gave the correct answer, and followed me in

Part I: The Nazi Nightmare

the same direction. Later on, I found out that this "doctor," was Dr. Mengele, the "Angel of Death," who was notorious for conducting horrific medical experiments, particularly on twins. With a slight motion of that pristine, white-gloved index finger, he decided who would live and who would die. Of course, we had no idea then what lay ahead for us. We couldn't have known. No one could have imagined. And still today, some people don't believe.

In fact, we couldn't have been more stunned if we'd been transported to another planet. No one had any idea what this Hell on earth was all about. After a while, the Nazis marched us into a huge one-story cinder-block building and then into a very large room, the size of a high-school gymnasium. They told everyone to get undressed, and leave all our belongings right there—our clothes, and of course, our shoes, and then get in the line leading to "barbers" (other prisoners who'd been assigned to the job) with clippers who were waiting for us.

Well, I got undressed, and left what little I still owned on the floor. Everything, that is, except my beautiful black shoes with the diamonds in the heels. Of course, both my uncle and cousin did exactly what they were told and left their shoes, but I decided to risk keeping mine. Trying to look inconspicuous, I walked right up to those barbers, and immediately found out that this would be no ordinary haircut. Apparently they were trying to rid us of the lice that carried the deadly typhus fever, so they cut the hair from all over our heads and then our entire bodies. Everywhere.

And they weren't particularly gentle with the clipping. You could probably have seen my heart furiously pounding in my skinny young teenage chest, as I held my breath during the entire process. I don't know what was more terrifying, the degrading clippers or the chance that my

16. Auschwitz-Birkenau and Durnhau

shoes would be discovered. By some miracle, however, nothing was said to me about the shoes. I still can't understand how this miracle — or the others that came later — happened. So I followed the others into the showers — still with my shoes on! After the showers, we got in yet another line where other inmates sprayed us all over with *DDT* (dichlorodiphenyltrichloroethane), a powerful pesticide that would kill the deadly disease-carrying lice. This made the air thick and hard to breathe. And still no one said anything about my shoes. So there I was amidst hundreds of terrified, exhausted, completely hairless, naked men and boys, and no one noticed my black shoes! Only now as I think about it, I realize that everyone must have worked hard to keep their eyes averted from my feet. I can only explain it as another miracle — for which I am still grateful.

We were soon directed to yet another line, at the head of which was a clerk, who was also a prisoner. He shoved a bundle of those striped concentration camp clothes into my hands. They were not new, but they were clean, and therefore an improvement over what I had been wearing, and I put them on quickly. Mine were way too big for me, however, so just as if I was shopping at a men's clothing shop, I asked for a different size. Would you believe that the clerk accommodated my request?

Along with the clothing, we were given some wooden clogs with canvas tops. I put on the clogs and hid the soaked, but still priceless, black shoes under my arms where they were covered by my jacket. We obediently walked out of the building, and still no one said a word about the shoes. It was then that the guards finalized our dehumanization process by handing each of us a round wooden disc on a string. We were ordered to wear this "necklace" at all times. Like a dog collar. On this disc was the number that would

Part I: The Nazi Nightmare

become my new, non-human identity.* My number was *41212*. I no longer had a name.

Next, we were led into our barracks where I saw three-tiered rows of bunks against the two long side walls. These really weren't "bunks" in the usual sense of the word. They were just rough wooden platforms, thinly covered with filthy, moldy, vermin-infested straw and rags. The three of us took an upper bunk together, thinking that with no one above us, we'd have more air. In the center of the room was a small, pot-bellied stove. This stove turned out to be more useful for killing lice than providing warmth. Every morning we would take off our infested clothes and stretch them around the outside of the rounded stove as if we were ironing them. But ironing was the last thing on our minds. This process was our only way to remove lice. We would actually see them bounce, crackle, and then explode from the heat—it sounded just like popping corn.

Our so-called "sanitary facility," or latrine, was also primitive. It was located in its own building, and shared by all the barracks. It consisted of rows of long, cement boxes with crude holes cut into them. At that point we were like animals—we no longer had the luxury of being embarrassed. Our daily existence had been reduced to mindless, emotionless, bodily functions. Soon the *Stubenälteste* (the prisoner in charge of our barracks), self-importantly gave

---

*Unlike previous transports of prisoners, by the time the Hungarian Jews were rounded up, the Nazis no longer had time to tattoo our numbers on our arms, so they gave us the numbered discs.

16. Auschwitz-Birkenau and Durnhau

us gruesome news. He announced in uneducated German, "You big-shot Hungarian Jews think you are here on a vacation? Well, think again. You see those chimneys? Do you see those smoke-stacks constantly billowing smoke? That is the smoke of your burning grandparents, mothers, fathers, brothers, sisters and children."

He then told us about the electrified barbed-wire surrounding the camp, the gas chambers, crematoria, killing-fields, and fire-pits. "If you don't behave, if you don't do exactly as you are told, this is exactly where you will wind up: ashes coming out from all those chimneys." We heard the words he spoke, but we just couldn't comprehend their horrific meaning. Was he taunting us with a cruel joke? How could these ashes erupting from the chimneys and falling under our feet be our precious families?

Despite the horrors we had already seen and endured, this information absolutely paralyzed our brains. We still couldn't grasp that a civilized, cultured people like the Germans were capable of actually running death factories. It was just something that could not quite sink in. But, all too soon, there would be more evidence of the monstrous acts that were being committed. What was the world thinking?

That night we heard strangely muffled screaming in the distance, almost like demonic background music. As we peeked through the cracks in the wall, we could see just beyond our barracks that the dark night air was flooded with a strangely flickering, orange glow. The unnerving shrieks and the orange-tinged black night air made it seem as if we actually on the edge of Hell. Still trying to make sense of this surreal situation, I walked up to the *Stubenälteste*, and in Polish, asked him what was going on. "Hah! You ignorant Hungarian Jews don't know anything. They were expecting you! Before they even invaded Hungary, they

Part I: The Nazi Nightmare

were busy preparing. They dug the fire pits especially for you so that no time would be wasted taking your corpses to a crematorium. By the time the Nazis started transporting you here, they were expected to process at least 12,000-15,000 a day." He never missed an opportunity to show his disgust for Hungarian Jews. I had no clue what he meant by "process." The real meaning was all too quickly clarified. It meant that at Auschwitz-Birkenau, the Nazis tried to kill up to 15,000 Jewish human beings per day.

In fact, like all good manufacturing businesses, they actually had a quota to meet. And this obscene quota had increased from 600 a day, in the original gas chambers, to 2,000, and then, ultimately, 15,000 per day in the newly built, more spacious gas chambers. The death camps even competed with each other to see who could "process" the most Jews. The elimination of the Jewish People was now the winning goal for the teams in this competitive league of monsters. I learned later that these death-merchants were proud that they had figured out how to increase the murderous capacity of their original gas chambers. They were able to make use of an innovative I. G. Farben* product, a deadly gas known as *Zyklon B*.

Depending upon where the prisoner stood in relation to the ceiling vents into which the pellets were poured, this gas could take from five to twenty minutes to actually kill a person. And then the chamber's air had to clear for fifteen

---

*I.G.Farben was one of Germany's largest and most successful corporations. It's been said that The Holocaust could not have happened without Farben's mutually beneficial partnership with Hitler. Its deadly *Zyklon B* (hydrogen cyanide) gas not only speeded up Hitler's "Final Solution," but by using 1000s of slave laborers, gained massive profits. After the war, several Farben executives were convicted of War Crimes at the Nuremberg Trials. For info: www.ushmm.org/wlc/en/article.php?ModuleId=10007135

16. Auschwitz-Birkenau and Durnhau

minutes before the workers could go in and remove the bodies. Always striving for improved efficiency, and since the new transports from Hungary were now coming in without a break in the action, the Nazis decided that they no longer had the luxury of wasting a half an hour per group. So in order to process more, they squeezed more people in by ordering the prisoners to raise their arms high over their heads. And in order to process them still faster, they shortened the amount of time that the victims would be in the gas chambers. As the Jews struggled to breathe, the Nazi guards watched this grotesque death dance comfortably from their observation booth. When they saw all the bodies lying quietly on the floor, they sent in the special units of Jewish Sonderkommandos to do the "dirty work" of pulling the bodies out. Some of these "bodies" were still alive.

It didn't matter how these corpses were handled, because to the Nazis they were just garbage. Other prisoners were assigned to cut off the hair, pull out the gold teeth and check body orifices for concealed valuables. Then they would pile five or six corpses on a cart, rope them together like logs so they wouldn't roll off, and finally take them to the crematorium. Always striving to increase "productivity," and realizing that even this process took too much time, they soon began to just throw bodies into dump trucks. These trucks took this human cargo to a huge fiery pit not too far away from our barracks. This pit was the source of those constant eerie screams and the orange glow that never went out. Curious, I asked the *Stubenälteste*, who seemed to enjoy being such an important source of information, "What is this strange screaming?"

He laughed and replied, "*Kleinkind*" (Babies).

Apparently the Nazis couldn't be bothered with babies taking up space in the gas chambers. Baby hair was worthless and they didn't have gold teeth. So these inmates would just

Part I: The Nazi Nightmare

hurl these precious little living beings into the dump-trucks along with the gassed bodies, and then dump all of them all into the fire pits. This news was incomprehensible to my 15½-year-old mind. While I never saw these pits, I was always aware of them—and will never forget the sound, sight and smell of hell on earth.

They kept us in Birkenau for approximately two weeks, in the most squalid conditions imaginable. In spite of having been sprayed that one time with DDT, we were practically being eaten alive by the lice, parasites and bugs that lived on and in our bodies. Twice daily, when we heard the order for roll call, "*Zum Appell!*" we rushed to stand in line—sometimes for hours in the scorching summer and bitter winter. I guess this was one of the ways they could weed out the weak from the stronger.* Anyone who couldn't keep up by standing perfectly at attention would be pulled out and disposed of. If we sneezed, looked sideways, or even for no particular reason at all, we would be shot. The Nazis seemed to particularly enjoy a little game that involved ordering us to take off our caps. Our response had to be instantaneous, and the sound of our caps being slapped against our legs had to be just right or we would be shot on the spot. Even if we hadn't committed some infraction, the Nazis might shoot one of us just for the fun of it.

Our rations consisted of *ersatz* (fake) coffee, a piece of bread that was made with saw-dust instead of flour, and sometimes a mysterious spread that was called "margarine." Sometimes, we would be given a small amount of what might once have been liverwurst. There was also a big pot of something called "soup," but was actually just water

---

*In the women's section, it was a common practice for prisoners to prick their fingers and then rub the drops of blood onto their cheeks in order to look healthier.

16. Auschwitz-Birkenau and Durnhau

with bits of garbage and who knows what else thrown in. Sometimes it could even be a rat or a piece of shoe leather. Can you imagine being grateful for a rat? Whatever was heavier than this filthy "broth," sank to the bottom. If we were on good terms with the prisoner in charge of filling our metal cups he would slide the ladle along the bottom, so that we might get some nutrients along with the dirty water. Our meager portions wouldn't have kept a bird alive—and of course that was exactly the point: we were being starved to death. Starvation is excruciatingly painful: the body breaks down its own organs and tissues in an effort to obtain energy. Skin rashes, diarrhea, heart failure, and indescribable pain at any movement due to muscle atrophy, dehydration . . . the list goes on.

After about two weeks, we were transported to a rock quarry labor camp or *Arbeitslager*, in Durnhau, located close to the Czech border. The Germans ordered workers to put dynamite charges into the mountain. These would then be detonated, causing huge boulders to tumble down. It was our job to use sledge hammers to break them into manageable pieces which we then threw into carts. Next, we would run the mining carts down the hill to the grinding machines, where the pieces would be ground into gravel. Then, of course, we had to push the empty mining carts back up the hill and repeat the whole process. Again and again. Needless to say, it was brutal, dusty, dirty work. I feared that my uncle would not be able to survive much longer. I decided on a plan that might save him—or at least buy him some extra time. It would involve taking a huge risk, and paying a huge price.

Since the kitchen chef lived in our barracks, I had gotten to know him, and I felt that he might be trusted. So, using the diamonds that my uncle had so carefully hidden in

Part I: The Nazi Nightmare

my shoes, I was able to bribe the chef into giving my uncle a job in the kitchen. It was ironic that these diamonds ended up helping my uncle—at least for a little while. He was relatively safe, and even able to eat decent food in the kitchen. He could not sneak out any of this good food because they were searched daily. However, since he'd already eaten, he could share his own regular daily rations with Isaac and me. Naturally, the chef kept coming back for more and more diamonds until they were all gone. Fortunately, even without these payments, he allowed my uncle to remain on his staff. It's amazing how some of the experiences I learned in the camps taught me lessons that have helped me throughout my life. This time I had learned the importance of having good contacts. A support system. And money or valuables put away for, as my father always called it, a "rainy day."

Just when our lives, such as they were, seemed to have taken on a routine, something different happened. And in a camp, "something different" never meant anything good. One evening as usual, when we returned from the labor camp, they made us line up in rows of five for the *Appell*. This evening, however, was different from others. After the count, they refused to dismiss us. They just kept counting and re-counting instead of letting us go get our rations, wash up and go to sleep. Filthy, exhausted and starving, we could barely stand up. After a very long time, the Commandant finally came down and announced to us, "I am going to teach you *Schweinehunds* (pig-dogs) a lesson you'll never forget."

Terrified, we wondered what could have happened—and as a consequence, what would now happen to us. It turns out that three inmates had somehow managed to escape. This escape would certainly have a cost. And we were the ones who would have to pay it. Punishing inmates

16. Auschwitz-Birkenau and Durnhau

for the escapes of others usually provided an effective deterrent for potential escapees. Very few inmates wanted to be the cause of someone else's torture and death. And today's punishment, even by Nazi standards, would be an extreme.

Commandant Wolf suddenly appeared and ordered his underlings to pull out every tenth person in line to receive 25 lashes as punishment for those three escapees. Well, as they were counting and pulling out people from line, I could see that my uncle, who was in front of me, would be a number ten. Once again, knowing that he would never withstand a beating like this at his age, I decided to switch places with him, and become a number ten. They then took me and all the other "number tens" to await our fate in the middle of the yard. They ordered two inmates to bring down bundles of one-by-one inch hardwood stakes, that were about two feet long, with razor sharp edges—and guaranteed to inflict maximum pain. We "number tens" were so special that we were in for a very special beating.

Then the tall, brutally handsome, and infinitely sadistic Commandant came over to us with a drink in one hand and his dainty little *fraulein* (unmarried woman) hanging on his other arm. He proceeded to order the guards to bring a sawhorse, and position it in the center of the yard. Then we were given our own detailed orders. When it was each man's turn to be beaten, he would have to stand very close to the sawhorse, go up on his tiptoes, bend his knees into the opening of the sawhorse, and finally, arch his body up and over the sawhorse without ever touching the cross bar. No part of our bodies could touch the wood; there had to be enough space between our stomachs and the top two-by-four for a hand to pass through. Two other inmates, known as camp *kapos*, were chosen to administer the beatings. One would pull our trousers up, yanking them up by the waist

Part I: The Nazi Nightmare

so that they were tight as a drum. Then we had to count out loud while the other inmate whipped us with the stakes. If we miscounted, we had to start over from one again. If a heel touched the ground, or any part of our body touched the sawhorse, we would have to start counting all over again.

So the first person, who seemed like an older man, but was probably in his early thirties, went up, got into position, and within seconds of the first blow, we could see a line of blood seeping through his trousers. As he shrieked in agony and terror, he lost his count, and they started all over again, yelling at him, "Louder! We can't hear you!" Over and over again . . . until finally, he collapsed. His collapse seemed to be a personal insult to the Commandant,

who quickly stalked over to him, kicked him in the face with those brutal, shining Nazi boots, and screamed, *"Du verfluchte Jude Schweine* (You accursed Jew pig)." The Commandant then pulled out his revolver and shot the crumbled, helpless man in the temple. Following this grisly action, Wolf's smiling, giggling *fraulein* walked seductively over to him and gave him a huge hug and kiss — it was as if he had just performed some heroic act.

The next prisoner was even older, maybe in his early forties, and when he miscounted after ten hits, he started crying and begging for mercy. This of course only made the Nazis more vicious. After a few more hits, with his blood and bits of flesh spraying through the shredded fabric of

16. Auschwitz-Birkenau and Durnhau

his trousers, he collapsed again. The Commandant ordered this broken remnant of a human being to get up and face him. When he just could not stand up fast enough, the Commandant once again took out his revolver and shot the man in the head.

By the time the third prisoner was in the same situation, the *kapo* who was beating him seemed to feel sorry for him — maybe they were friends or relatives — and eased up just a little. This of course infuriated the Commandant, who then made a point of selecting a new, even sharper stake — which he then broke over the head of the *kapo*, commanding him to keep hitting with all his might. When it looked as if he was losing his power, he changed places with the second *kapo* who had been pulling the prisoner's trousers tight. Soon the prisoner also lost consciousness and was shot dead.

So now it was my turn. Three brutally murdered bodies lay on the ground in front of me, their blood soaking in to the dust. I was 15 ½ years old, but despite all I'd been through, I was still determined to live. I must have developed some kind of self-hypnosis in order to let my mind leave my body for a while, because without a thought I walked over to the sawhorse and "assumed the position." I arched my body over the top, shifted my weight to my toes so I could bend my knees underneath, and made sure that no part of my body touched the flesh and blood splattered sawhorse. A fresh new inmate pulled the top of my trousers as tight as the top of a drum, and then his partner began hitting me with all his power. It almost seemed as if I was some carnival attraction and that these "men" wanted to make a special impression on the crowd. With each hit, even though I could feel my flesh being torn from my body, I stayed focused on my task, counting as loud and strong as I could. I almost barked the last three numbers: 23 . . . 24 . . . 25. . .

Part I: The Nazi Nightmare

Much to everyone's surprise—mine most of all—I'd made it. There was a shocked silence, as if everyone had stopped breathing. No one had expected there to be a survivor of this ghoulish game. And this unexpected change in the game was cause for alarm. Was the Commandant offended that someone had lived? Would I be punished for living? Then, to everyone's relief, the quick-thinking *kapo* broke the silence by telling me to go over and thank the Commandant. So I unbent my cramped, tortured body, stood up, and with blood running down my wobbling legs, I walked shakily over to him, saluted smartly, and said, "*Danke Schoen, Herr Kommandant.*"

I just did what I had to do in order to survive. And I chose to do it with as much dignity as possible. Even though it seemed as if I'd become a robot, no longer possessing human thoughts or emotions, I was shocked when the Commandant put his immaculate white-gloved hand on my shoulder. It was almost a caress. I stopped breathing. Was he going to kill me himself for having had the audacity to spoil his fun by living?

But no, now he was going to use me as an example. Since I had somehow managed to survive his little game of death, I would now be his trophy. He twisted me around to face those prisoners who were still waiting to be beaten, and announced to them, "Now you see a perfect example of how it should be done. This *junge* (young man) followed instructions perfectly. I told you it could be done. If the rest of you follow his example, you'll have nothing to worry about." That was probably his idea of a little joke since the only reason I'd survived was that I was so much younger than the others.

In the midst of his lecture to those who still awaited their beatings and probable deaths, there was a sudden frenzied commotion at the gate. Once again, we wondered what had

16. Auschwitz-Birkenau and Durnhau

happened, and how we would end up suffering because of it. We soon learned that the guards had caught the three escapees and were dragging them in—literally beaten into bloody pulps. Their faces looked like lumpy, smashed plums. When the Commandant saw them, an expression of fiendish joy crossed his face. It was as if he now had an exciting new project. We no longer had any interest for him so he turned away from us, just like a spoiled child who would throw away a boring toy. So since the escapees had been found, it turned out that I was the last to be beaten that day. I know that I wasn't the only one who was angry that they had put their own escape above the welfare of the other inmates. And I couldn't help wishing that they'd been found and brought back 30 minutes earlier.

The Commandant then ordered his underlings to bring down a single portable gallows, consisting of a wooden frame, made of a crossbeam on two 10-foot uprights, from which a condemned person could be executed by hanging. Which is what they proceeded to do. They hanged each man, one by one. We were awed when we heard the last one call out the *Shema*, the Hebrew prayer when all hope of living is gone. Throughout his ordeal, he had not forgotten his religion. We all had to stand there and watch the slow, cruel process. Somehow despite my weakened condition, and with a back that looked like hamburger, I once again managed to go on automatic-pilot, forcing myself not to collapse during this hideous demonstration of Nazi discipline. This supposedly superior German "Aryan Master Race" clearly demonstrated once again, their own utter inferiority as human beings.

After this grizzly display, they dismissed us, and, of course, we went for our rations and then back into our barracks. Can you imagine that? After what we had seen and experienced, we just went to get our food as usual.

Part I: The Nazi Nightmare

That night was the first of many where it was necessary for me to lie on my stomach. It was a long time before I could tolerate anything touching my lacerated back. I couldn't even imagine ever sleeping on my back again. What a small but wonderful victory it was for me when I could finally turn over in my sleep, without waking up, shrieking in pain. Looking back, I am amazed by how even the most vicious of injuries—physical as well as mental—can sometimes heal when we are young. The lesson I learned is to never, never let adversity or injuries break my spirit or keep me from accomplishing my goals.

Soon there was something strange in the atmosphere. And one night, we'd gotten very little sleep because of a strange rumbling in the air—almost like cannon fire. There was a sense that something different was about to happen. We got up as usual for the routine line-up to get our *ersatz* coffee and little bit of bread with the so-called margarine, and a spoonful of liverwurst. We were ready as usual to leave to go to work. Unexpectedly, there was an announcement telling us that today we would not be going to work. Of course we were all curious and concerned about this change in routine. Changes usually meant something was about to happen that was even worse than what we had gotten used to. We wondered if it had anything to do with the rumbling cannon fire we had heard throughout the night before.

A harsh voice over the public address system told us that the whole camp was being evacuated. NOW. Everyone who could walk would be marched out of the camp. We could only guess what happened to the others. My uncle was already in the kitchen with his co-workers. The rest of us lined up, and started to march out. I never saw my uncle again. Apparently, the kitchen group was fated to go

16. Auschwitz-Birkenau and Durnhau

somewhere else, somewhere that even diamonds couldn't have helped him. My cousin and I were grateful to still be together, and we managed to hope that our next trip would take us to a better place. *Little did we know that we were embarking upon the notorious Death March...*

17. THE DEATH MARCH

> *"I ask not for a lighter burden,*
> *but for broader shoulders."*
> ~ Old Jewish Proverb

And they called it a Death March for a good reason: Its purpose was to kill us. Anyone who couldn't keep up the pace over the brutally rough terrain was simply shot and left on the road. Sometimes we walked through villages where the people averted their eyes, as they went about their usual daily routines. It was winter time, but we had no warm clothes or shoes to protect us from the endless sleet, snow, or ice, and we were barely fed. Some prisoners just stopped walking, fell down, and died on the spot. Of course, the whole point of this "march" was for us all to die. My cousin got weaker every day, and I kept supporting him, begging him not to give up. He felt guilty that he was such a burden on me, and even ordered me to let him go, but I didn't see him as a burden—in fact, I felt guilty that I couldn't take better care of him. I was so grateful to still have him with me. The truth is that he inspired me to be strong.

Eventually, however, even I could see that he had lost his will to live. With a raspy, barely audible voice, he begged me to let him just lie down and be put out of his misery. I'll never know if it was the right thing to do, but I refused to let him die. I felt that if he had to die, he deserved some respect, some dignity. My determination to protect Isaac and keep him alive gave me the motivation to stay alive. To this day I don't know if I would have survived on my own.

All along this journey of death, the road was littered with the grotesquely contorted and exposed corpses of people who had been shot and left like stray dogs on the

Part I: The Nazi Nightmare

side of the road. The SS guards and even the Wehrmacht, who were marching with us, kept busy with their horrific game of target-practice, never letting up on the roadside executions of the helpless. As we continued our deadly trek, I wasn't sure how much time was passing. It was probably three or four weeks. Time no longer had meaning for us — days, nights — they all flew together. We just stared at the road and took it one agonized step at a time...

It was spring when we finally arrived at a place called Buchenwald. Established in 1937, in the beautiful area of Weimar, Germany, this concentration camp was one of the first and the largest built in Germany. Camp prisoners of all nationalities came from throughout Europe and the Soviet Union to be worked to death in local armament factories. Just like the slogan over the gates of Auschwitz, these gates also had a slogan: "*Jedem das Seine,*" which means that "everyone gets what he deserves." Of course in our case it ironically meant that the Jewish People deserved to die.

At first, this camp seemed different from the ones we'd been to. For one thing, just inside the gates, in stark contrast to the dusty barren grayness of the camp, there stood an ancient, very well-tended oak tree, surrounded by a small, lush, neatly trimmed, emerald green lawn, and safely protected by its own fence. Years later I would learn that this magnificent, healthy example of the beauty of life, was known as *Goethe's Tree** in honor of the famous writer and philosopher Johann Wolfgang von Goethe (1749-1832). It turns out that just over a century before Germany would descend into the depravity of the Holocaust, this world-renowned genius and humanitarian often wrote and visited with his friends under this majestic tree. Another of the

---

*For interesting info on *Goethe's Tree*, see: www.bbc.co.uk/programmes/b00swq96

17. The Death March

many ironies of the Nazis was that they would revere and protect a tree that was at the entrance of one of their most infamous concentration camps. The tree was destroyed during Allied bombing of the camp, but its stump was preserved and is now part of the Buchenwald Memorial.

We were also surprised to receive some bread and soup. This "luxury treatment" continued when they sent us to our barracks, allowed us to shower and gave us clean clothes. We were even able to sleep in bunks instead of on the frozen, blood-crusted ground. But even though it looked as if things might be less brutal here than in previous camps, we had learned not to get our hopes up. And as it turned out, our "comforts" wouldn't even last 24 hours.

Early the next morning we were ordered to assemble in the center yard of the camp. We were going to be evacuated yet again. Immediately. This was the spring of 1945, and we had no idea of what was going on in the world outside our prison. In fact, we didn't even know if the world still existed outside the deadly fences. But apparently, the *Allied Front* (the areas where the Germans were fighting the Allies: the USA, Britain, France and Soviet Union) had surrounded the Germans, and the Allies were rapidly closing in from all sides. And while Hitler's determination to liquidate the Jewish People was stronger than ever, he had two reasons to move us out. One, the Nazis were terrified that thousands of diseased, hungry, angry, walking-dead Jews would somehow manage to rampage through the villages and exact vengeance on the Germans. Two, Hitler didn't want the Allies, and thus the world, to see what had been going on in the camps. *Of course we knew none of this...*

18. *THE DEATH TRAIN TO DACHAU*

> *"It is a brave act to despise death;*
> *but where life is more terrible than death,*
> *it is then the truest valor to dare to live."*
> ~ Sir Thomas Browne (1605-1682)
> English Author

So once again we were led out through the gates to a long line of waiting cattle cars. We were somewhat relieved that at least we wouldn't be going on another Death March. We had learned to appreciate even the most minor lessening of our torment. They divided us into groups of 80 to each car, and I helped my cousin get inside. I told him to go to the back end of it so that we could support ourselves against the wall. I knew from previous experience that this would be better than being in the middle of the car with people on all sides. I followed closely behind him, making sure that he didn't fall. As our eyes got used to the dim light, we noticed two buckets of water in the car. After a little while, the doors slammed closed, sealing us in. When the train didn't move, a petrified silence filled the sealed car. Was this to be our death chamber?

Around a half an hour later, the doors were suddenly thrust open, and loaves of bread were thrown into the car; supposedly one for each person. This really was a test of survival of the fittest because those people who were close to the door took two or more breads, and those of us at the back were left with none. So much for my good idea of leaning against a back wall. Feeling guilty, and knowing that I had to do something, I immediately climbed on top of the other people in order to get to the door to get a hold

Part I: The Nazi Nightmare

of a bread or two. As I struggled to cross this constantly shifting field of angry and terrified humanity, I felt a quick stab under my chin. Ignoring it, I kept going until I was able to find the last remaining bread. Grabbing it quickly and putting it under my jacket, I climbed back to Isaac. Stepping on shoulders, heads, slipping between bodies—it was as if they weren't really people anymore. They were just part of a grotesque obstacle course that I had to complete on the way back to my cousin. It's interesting how my caring for Isaac kept me from worrying about myself.

Suddenly, my face felt wet—I touched it, and I realized that blood was gushing down my chin. Apparently I'd been stabbed as I walked over all those other prisoners. When I got back to my cousin, I put my finger to the spot where I was stabbed. It was quite a shock when my finger went right through my chin and my tongue! There was a gaping hole in my face. Isaac's terrified eyes told me how serious my injury was. I tore a piece of soiled fabric from my trousers and bandaged my chin. It was really a miracle that I didn't get an infection in those filthy conditions. Even though it healed, today I can still find the spot where that knife cut through my chin . . . another miracle for which I've never stopped being grateful.

For approximately four weeks they kept shuttling us back and forth from one railroad siding to another. During that entire period they wouldn't feed us. Periodically they would fill the two buckets with water, but most of the prisoners were dying from starvation and sickness. The only reason that Isaac and I were still alive was because of my disciplined restraint from eating all of the bread at once. It was hard to deprive him, but I knew our survival depended on being careful with the bread. Every day I rationed out a piece the size of half an egg for each of us. That was it. Nothing more. We had to eat it secretly so no one would

18. The Death Train to Dachau

kill us to get it. Those people who quickly devoured two or three loaves of bread at the very beginning of the trip had all died. And they were horrific deaths. Their dehydrated bodies couldn't accommodate so much food. Their digestive systems failed them.

No one had expected this trip to last so long. Not even the Nazis. In fact, even the guards were without knowledge about our destination. This was because no authority had yet decided where our destination should be. The German Army was in total disarray, and the previously so efficient "decision-makers" were busy deciding other things. Trainloads of dying Jews were not a big concern for them. And since no one was making decisions or giving orders, we just kept shuttling back and forth. Eventually, when some prisoners went completely crazy and killed those who were weaker, there was even cannibalism. As inconceivably bad as the conditions inside the cattle cars were, they just continued to worsen until almost everyone was dead. Those few of us who somehow still survived were vastly outnumbered by the stiff and decomposing corpses that enveloped us. We seemed to be floating in a stench-filled sea of death. By some miracle, weak as I was, I either managed to look powerful enough to keep the others away from us, or Isaac and I were just too wasted-away to bother with.

After what seemed like four weeks of this torture, we finally arrived at a place called *Dachau*. Opened in 1933, this was the first regular concentration camp established by the Nazis to imprison political prisoners—anyone who might be seen as a threat to Hitler's newly forming Third Reich—doctors, lawyers, teachers, journalists, clergymen, businessmen and others. It's interesting to note that some people erroneously think that the word "concentration" was used so that the prisoners could "concentrate" on their crimes. In fact, the word means a place where undesirable

Part I: The Nazi Nightmare

people can be "concentrated" in one place in order to be easily watched and controlled.

When the doors to our cattle cars were finally opened up, we were once again brutally ordered to go into the camp. Can you imagine being brutal to the living dead? Only about a handful of skeletons, including my cousin and me, managed to climb through the corpses and out of this hell. But yet another hell awaited us inside the camp. The first thing we saw was a mountain of skeletal corpses, frozen in hideously unnatural poses and stacked up like pieces of ancient driftwood. Our barracks was located right next to this mountain of bodies. There were no bunks, so we were directed to lie down on the floor. We learned later that the only reason we weren't immediately incinerated was that a coal shortage had prevented the Nazis from running their furnaces. Here was a rare occasion when a coal shortage turned out to be a benefit. At that point, there was no question that we were going to die. *The only question was: How long would it take?*

19. *APRIL 29, 1945: LIBERATION!*

> *"Freedom is the oxygen of the soul."*
> ~ Moshe Dayan (1915-1981)
> Israeli Military Leader
> & Statesman

Three days later, not having moved from the floor, Isaac and I thought we were imagining the jubilant noises coming from the yard. It sounded as if the almost dead prisoners were trying to shout, "Liberation! Liberation!" — in many different languages. The one we understood the clearest was Yiddish: *"Bafreiung!"* Confused and curious as to why so many *Musselmans* (almost dead men) were faintly screaming this word so ecstatically, my cousin and I leaned against each other for leverage and somehow forced ourselves to stand up. We held on to each other and hobbled shakily outside. We saw a joyful mob of inmates rushing to hug our saviors. Sadly, we also saw many of them fall and die before they could touch their liberators. As so often had happened in those heinous years under Nazi Oppression, we were once again shocked by the sight before our eyes.

But this time the shocking sight was very different. This time it looked as if something good was actually happening in that hell on earth. How strange that this beautiful sight was even harder to believe than all the atrocities we'd seen and endured. It seemed as if we must be experiencing some kind of pre-death delirium as we watched what appeared to be an *American G.I.* (an abbreviation of "Government Issue") climbing in a crazed frenzy up the Nazi guard tower. When he reached the top, he just picked up the guard, like a bag of garbage, and heaved him down into the yard among the inmates. The guard didn't even bother defending himself.

Part I: The Nazi Nightmare

The faces of our Liberators expressed both horror and satisfaction at justice finally being done. The Americans had been so shocked and disgusted by the sight of emaciated walking skeletons and corpses scattered and piled all over the place, that many of them were on their knees, sobbing and throwing up. Later, they'd said they just felt someone had to be punished immediately — and that guard was their first target.

According to Rabbi Eli A. Bohnen, the Chaplain of the 42nd Rainbow Division that liberated Dachau, he and his men first saw the cattle cars outside the gates. The Rabbi's words accurately describe both the Death Train from which my cousin and I had emerged on April 26, 1945, and the inside of the camp:*

"Nothing you could put in words would adequately describe what I saw there...The human mind refuses to believe what the eyes see."

Those straggling, ghostly inmates who were no longer recognizable as human beings . . . those hollow-eyed, brutalized, barely walking, barely breathing, scarred, vermin-infested and diseased skeletons who had made the traumatized and sobbing GI liberators throw-up . . . those painfully unforgettable examples of the evil that humans can inflict on other humans . . . were us. Isaac and I barely stood there hanging on to each other, too numb to move and too stunned to even think. We watched as two young, clean, and healthy American soldiers approached us. We didn't even know what to think or feel. They tried to mask their horror at the sight of us with friendly smiles. They stretched out their hands and gave us a can of Spam (a precooked, preserved, mashed and molded pork product),

---

*For Rabbi Eli A. Bohnen's impressions of the Dachau Liberation, see: www.jewishvirtuallibrary.org/jsource/Holocaust/GI22.html

19. April 29, 1945: Liberation!

which they had taken out of the German warehouses. Of course these soldiers meant well in giving us this food, but the after-effects of eating it were ghastly. And deadly. We were so malnourished, that even though we knew better, we made a big mistake: we ate some of it.

Unfortunately, as a result, most of us came down with severe, excruciatingly painful *dysentery*.* And although we were both just barely living, Isaac was in even worse shape than I. So in that long-awaited night of the liberation, after surviving so much horror, my frail cousin Isaac, who was already on the brink of death, soon became violently ill. As his poor body heaved in agony, I held him close and spoke softly to him, telling him to hang on because we were finally free—whatever that might mean. It was over. We would have lives again. We would be reunited with our family soon. We would celebrate holidays and eat, laugh and dance. I just kept talking to him, as if my voice could keep him alive. Saying anything that came into my head. I forced my own deteriorating voice to speak stronger as I felt Isaac grow weaker and weaker. Almost as if I could command him to live. It seemed as if every loss, every torture, every humiliation that we'd suffered during the previous six years would have some meaning if only I could keep him alive.

I rocked him softly in my arms all night. Even after he had died. I wouldn't let him go. Just kept on talking to him as tears streamed down my face. In the morning, when they took his body away from me, I tried desperately to hang on to him, to go with him. But to my shame, I lost consciousness and collapsed. Somehow, unlike my cousin Isaac, I didn't die. Why not? Through the following years, I've often wondered if maybe he'd been trying to watch out

---

Dysentery is a serious illness causing such severe and painful diarrhea that death will result if untreated.

Part I: The Nazi Nightmare

for me in some way. *Maybe he had only felt free to die once he knew that I would be free to live.*

PART II

"Survivor"

20. *HOLOCAUST SURVIVOR*

> *"I never dreamed that such cruelty, bestiality, and savagery could really exist in this world."*
>
> ~ **Dwight D. Eisenhower (1890-1969)**
> **American General &**
> **US President (1953-1961),**
> upon entering newly liberated
> Ohrdruf concentration camp, April 1945

Not many people know that the American Liberators were confronted by two distinctly different kinds of prisoners at Dachau. This was because there had been two distinctly different categories of inmates. So if you've seen pictures of fairly healthy-looking inmates smiling and cheering at the Liberators, you weren't seeing us. You were seeing pictures of the non-Jewish prisoners. They had been fed better, and treated more humanely than we were. We were the walking dead. We could barely breathe, let alone smile and wave. We were in such bad condition that we couldn't even make sense of what we were seeing. Was it some kind of Nazi joke? A rush of strange sights and confused emotions flooded our long-numbed minds and bodies.

And as it slowly became clear that we were free, the bitter irony of this freedom also became clear: physically, we were just hours away from death, so what difference did it make if we were liberated? To the degree that we could feel anything, of course there was joy that the killing and torture would stop. But since we weren't capable of coherent thought, much less taking care of ourselves, even if we did somehow manage to live another day, what would

Part II: Survivor

that mean? The non-Jewish inmates who were in much better physical shape, had homes and families to return to. But we had no place to go, and no one waited to embrace us. We "walking skeletons" were suddenly left to fend for ourselves. Many who were too weak to survive this surreal moment of liberation, died as they pitifully crawled through the dirt to welcome the horrified Americans. What kind of future lay ahead for any of us who managed to survive? Even if we somehow regained our physical health, could we ever regain our stolen humanity?

Today, when people ask what Liberation was like, I can only piece together the events of the early days. Before I lost consciousness for three months, I remember thinking that a Polish Jesuit priest was carrying me on his shoulders to a medical area. At that point, and in my condition, this made about as much sense to me as anything else that had happened since September 1, 1939. Much to my surprise, however, I later learned that this priest was not a hallucination—he was real! He had joined a group of French doctors and nurses who had come to set up a field hospital in tents in the yard. He'd carried me as if I were a 65-pound bag of bones—which is exactly what I was. He tried to comfort me by talking softly, and asked me my name. I'd managed to whisper, "Benek."

Then he said something to me that I'll never forget, "Benek, remember to be proud of your religion. From the way your people have suffered, you've paid such a high price for being Jewish. Don't ever abandon your noble religion." Even if it had been a hallucination, hearing these words from a Catholic priest who was saving my life, made such an impression on me that it forever changed how I looked at Gentiles and Poles. I realized that every religious and ethnic group has righteous people. That despite our differences, we share a common humanity. And that it is

20. Holocaust Survivor

better for all of us to honor our shared humanity rather than to despise our differences.

When we reached the medical tent, the attendants gently and respectfully placed me on a cot, covered me with a real sheet and blanket, and gave me nutrients through an *I.V.* (intravenous) feeding tube. After being beaten and starved, this was a reality that I couldn't comprehend. Then I passed out. All I know is that when I regained consciousness, I was in a comfortable hospital bed in a beautiful Bavarian monastery called St. Ottilien. The monks had dedicated one wing for the purpose of medical care and rehabilitation for Holocaust Survivors.

For the newly liberated, our time together at St. Ottilien was very therapeutic — medically and emotionally. For the first time in years, instead of being tortured and murdered, we were being taken care of. There were so many of us in the same situation, that it seemed as if we'd become one

St. Otillien Monastery
Landsberg, Germany (1945)
Lesser Family Collection

147

Part II: Survivor

big happy family instead of despised outcasts, something that we hadn't experienced in a very long time.

We took care of each other and became surrogate relatives. So thanks to the medical care, all the food I could eat, friends and my youth--much to my happy surprise, I began to recover. And as time passed, I grew stronger and began to feel more and more human. So instead of hoping to live for another hour, I began to think about maybe having a tomorrow or a next month. And in experiencing the goodness of human beings, for the first time in many years, I felt a little hope that life might be worth living. And that there might even be a God.

21. *A PURIM IN JULY!*

> *"Praised are You, Adonai our God,*
> *Sovereign of the Universe,*
> *Who brings forth bread from the earth."*
> ~ Hebrew Prayer

Further adding to this hope was the dedication of a Lithuanian Rabbi who had come to help the patients and *Displaced Persons*.* He felt very close to all of us, and rejoiced in our recoveries. At this time, even though it was summer and months past the *Purim* that had taken place in February of 1945, he decided to make a *Purim Seuda*, a *Purim* feast, to celebrate our escape from death. He wanted to make up for all the *Purims* we had missed during The Holocaust, and figured that since we had all just been delivered from horror and annihilation, that God would understand and approve of this *Purim* in July.

This was a very ambitious undertaking because there were a couple hundred of us to feed. And although the St. Ottilien cooks had volunteered to assist with the meal, the rabbi really needed more helpers to bake the traditional challahs and, of course, the hamantashen. So he asked for volunteers to do the baking. First he asked all the young women to help, but for some reason, none of them would volunteer. Maybe they were shy or didn't think that they had the baking skills that were needed. As I sensed his

---

* Jewish refugees who were considered *Displaced Persons* (DPs) had no homes or countries to return to, and most other countries refused to take them. So even though the war was over, once again, Jews were forced to live in specifically designated locations. In fact, many of these Displaced Persons camps had previously been concentration camps. However, sometimes camps were set up in hospitals, churches, military barracks, children's camps, school buildings and even luxury villas and resorts.

149

Part II: Survivor

disappointment, I suddenly had my first conscious flashback of my life before the camps. I remembered baking with my father in Niepolomice—the loving warmth of that memory just enveloped me. I knew that baking challah for this *Purim* was something my father would have wanted me to do. So, despite my fear that I wouldn't be up to the task, I volunteered.

The grateful rabbi took me into the monastery's huge bakery which the monks had generously given up to us for the occasion. They said, "Go ahead. Here are all the ingredients—the flour, the sugar, the cocoa. Take whatever you need." Then they showed me a room with large vats where the dough would be kneaded. When I saw all this massive equipment, I began to wonder if I should have volunteered! It had been years since I had done any baking, and it certainly hadn't been in this kind of set-up! I was used to doing small batches at a time, using a bowl, a *schissel*, for mixing things together.

But at that point everyone was depending upon me, and I couldn't let them down. I knew that if I wanted to accomplish something, I had to find out what needed to be done, and then just go ahead and do it. And now, for some reason, the girls were eager to volunteer. It turns out that despite our circumstances as Survivors, we still possessed the usual teenage interests—like flirting with the opposite sex! So, in order to properly celebrate the many miraculous escapes of the Jewish people, I decided to make one big beautiful challah. Since we had recently heard the horrifying rumors of the Holocaust's Jewish death toll, I decided that this would be a memorial challah. It would be six feet long in order to commemorate the six-million who had been lost.

Just as my father had taught me, except for the much larger proportions, I began by sprinkling the yeast over warm water, and then beat in the oil, eggs and salt. I added

21. A Purim in July!

the flour, one big bowl full at a time, beating after each addition—I began to sense when the dough had reached the right consistency. I then covered it with warm cloths and waited until it doubled in size. Next, I punched the dough down, placed it onto the greased baking sheet, divided it and carefully rolled it into four strands for braids. At that point, we all saw that there was no way for any of us to reach across that baking sheet in order to start the braids. And although I wasn't sure that my father would have approved, I realized that to braid a challah this big, something very unusual would have to be done. So I told the girls my plan—hoping that they would agree to it.

Would you believe that these previously shy, quiet girls took their shoes off and got right up on top of table? I assigned each one her own number, one through four, and each was in charge of her own yeasty strand of the braid. Once they settled down, I said, "#1, move over to number #3!" And then, "#4, cross over to #2!" As I directed them, they carefully changed places with each other until enough of the bread had been braided for me to reach it and finish the loaf. Somehow, in the midst of much giggling and shrieks, as feet missed the table and the girls barely missed falling on the floor, the loaf had been transformed into a beautiful braid. It was like choreography! We weren't just creating bread—we had created a dance of joy! *L'Chaim!* A dance to life.

Next, we let it rise again for about an hour, and finished it up by brushing the top with beaten egg yolk, and sprinkling it generously with poppy seeds. Finally, all together, we carefully carried the heavy baking sheet with its precious cargo to the oven. Suddenly the giggles stopped, and we looked at each other solemnly, each thinking the same thing. Our hearts, minds and souls had suddenly been flooded with images of other, deadly ovens.

Part II: Survivor

As the bread was baked, we set ourselves up like an assembly-line to make other traditional pastries—none more meaningful than the Hamantashen! While we were occupied in the bakery, the monastery's chefs were busy in the kitchen, cooking the food for the banquet. And they even made sure it was all Kosher. When everything was ready, the tables beautifully decorated, and several hundred residents and staff-members were all seated, the girls and I carefully carried the challah into the dining room.

With me at the front and two girls on each side, we looked and felt like pall-bearers. Everyone in the room felt the same way. We also knew, however, that this procession carrying the challah represented life—we were alive! And we would be celebrating an ancient holiday of freedom from oppression—something none of us thought we'd ever do again. As you can imagine, our 1945 *Purim in July*, at the Benedictine St. Ottilien Monastery in Germany, was the most unforgettable *Purim celebration* of our lives. From beginning to end, it was full of miracles.

22. THE CHALUTZIM

> *"To be a free people in our land,*
> *The land of Zion and Jerusalem."*
> *"Hatikva"*
> Israel's National Anthem

The next few months in the hospital were uneventful as I concentrated on recovering my health and growing stronger. Early one morning, as I lay in my second-floor bedroom, I heard something very interesting outside. It sounded like a group of young people singing Hebrew songs! Curious, I looked out my window and was surprised to see a group of robust teenagers, wearing crisp blue and white uniforms, marching past my dormitory. And they were singing Hebrew songs like "Arza Alina," which is about ascending into our Promised Land; and "Hevenu Shalom Aleichem," we bring you peace. A third inspiring song, "Lehitraot B'arzenu," says we will meet again in our land.

These sights and sounds were extraordinary to me! It was like an instant flashback to my childhood when my family and friends sang these same joyous songs. Even now, today, I still get very emotional when I think about these songs. Even the Nazis weren't able to burn away the power and beauty of our Jewish music. In a rush, I dressed, ran downstairs, walked up to the *Madrich*, the leader, and asked him who they were. He said that they were all orphans whose families had been murdered by the Nazis. It was inspiring to learn that these orphans, who had suffered so much, were already part of a very important new undertaking. They were *Chalutzim*, or pioneers, who were dedicated to establishing a Jewish homeland in Palestine.

Part II: Survivor

They would reclaim the land of our ancestors—Israel—where they would build *kibbutzim*, collective farms where everyone worked and everyone benefitted from the work. They would learn specialized trades and the technical skills necessary to become self-sufficient individuals, in a self-sufficient country. They would also be trained to protect themselves and their own land. There would be a strong, well-trained military. Never again would Jews be powerless minorities in the all too often unfriendly countries belonging to other people. Never again would our existence depend upon the naïve and futile hope that the voices of "good people" would speak out against evil.

These spirited, industrious and highly competent young *Chalutzim* had already established a *kibbutz* in Feldafing,* near Frankfurt, Germany. It was named *Ma'apilim*, a Hebrew term describing Jews who attempted to reach Palestine despite obstacles. And there were plenty of obstacles. Following World War I, the League of Nations had appointed Britain to administer the area now called the *British Mandate of Palestine.* In the 1930s, European Jews, escaping the alarming growth of Nazi oppression, began to immigrate to Palestine. Oil-rich Arabs fearing an influx of Jews, put extreme anti-Jewish pressure on the British. Oil-hungry Britain then severely restricted the immigration of Jewish refugees. Having survived the Nazis, the Jews now needed to survive the British. What had happened to the civilized world?

Eager to learn more about these young pioneers, I asked what their plans were. I was stunned when they told me

---

*It is a testimony to the resilience of the Jewish People that refugees in in the Displaced Persons Camps quickly created as normal an environment as possible by establishing libraries, social clubs, choirs, theater groups, orchestras, newspapers, schools, synagogues and small businesses. A council of rabbis functioned as a government.

22. The *Chalutzim*

that their goal was to reclaim part of British-occupied Palestine. Their plan was to form a Jewish state in the land from which we were exiled by the Romans neary 2,000 years ago. Since then, the Jewish people have been forced to live as minorities all over the world in what has since been known as the *Diaspora*. Then they told me something that I hadn't known — something that was almost as hard to believe as had been my experiences in the concentration camps. Something that has haunted me to this day. This unbelievable information was that the whole world had stood idly by while six million of our people were being slaughtered. No one cared. No one came to our aid. No one bombed the railroad tracks to the concentration camps. No one issued a meaningful warning to the Nazis to stop their crime against the Jewish People, their crimes against humanity.

Then the *Chalutzim* explained that the Holocaust would not have been possible if the Jewish People had had their own country — their own military — and alliances with other countries. It was only because we were so scattered and fragmented around the world that we weren't able to protect ourselves. And since we were in the minority wherever we lived, we just weren't very important to anyone and were always available to use as scapegoats for anything that went wrong wherever we resided. This was a radically new point of view for me, but it made a lot of sense.

So I enthusiastically offered to join the group, and was honored and grateful to be accepted. I was more than ready to become part of a movement that would build a Jewish homeland, thereby ensuring the safety of our people. Happily, a few days later, I was considered well enough to be discharged from St. Ottilien. A delegation from the group came to pick me up and took me to their

Part II: Survivor

compound in Feldafing. Once again, I was introduced to a whole new world—a world that was filled with learning, ideas and brand new possibilities! The best thing about it was being part of a Jewish group that absolutely refused to be victims. I'd never seen Jews strategizing and taking collective, organized physical action to protect themselves. They had an attitude of pride that I had never experienced.

Ben as a *Chalutz*
Feldafing, Germany (1945)
Lesser Family Collection

These *Chalutzim* would never cower and become victims, waiting in vain to be rescued from monsters. They were proud, competent Jewish people. And they had much to be proud of.

While I was with the *Chalutzim*, I studied Hebrew and how to live the cooperative life of a *Chalutzim kibbutznik*. This community was based on the ideals and practices of Zionism, emphasizing mental and physical fitness as well as maintaining constant vigilance and unity. We were also shown how to fight so we could defend ourselves. It was clear that we were being trained mentally, emotionally and physically for combat. Never again would we be passive victims. Since our group had no money, and only the most primitive equipment, however, we had to use sticks instead of rifles while marching. We were able to learn how to load and use the one and only gun the Kibbutz possessed: a German Luger.

22. The *Chalutzim*

Ben (back row, fourth from right) with *Chalutzim*
Feldafing, Germany (1946)
Lesser Family Collection

I lived at *Ma'apilim* for almost four months. Our days were very regimented, much like a military boot-camp. And near the end of 1945, I was honored to be chosen to participate in the first *Aliyah Bet*.* This extremely dangerous, illegal mission, code named *Ha'apala*, enabled Jewish refugees to immigrate by ship to Palestine. We would be aboard the very first ship carrying Holocaust orphans to arrive there. The reason it was illegal was that the British had decided that a large influx of Holocaust Survivors into Palestine would not be in the best interest of Great Britain. This was because the British felt their best interest was to stay on friendly

---

*For more information about *Aliyah Bet*, see: http://www.zionism-israel.com/dic/Aliya_Bet.htm. Also of interest is the 1996 video documentary, *Exodus 1947*, which tells the story of the SS *Exodus*—the *Aliyah Bet* ship made famous by Leon Uris' 1958 novel, *Exodus*, and the 1960 movie of the same name.

Part II: Survivor

terms with the oil-controlling, anti-Jewish, Arab countries. So instead of trying to help us by granting us visas, the British declared that we were now "illegal immigrants." They vigilantly patrolled, blockaded, intercepted, and searched any ships in the Mediterranean Sea that might be carrying Jewish refugees. They arrested any Jews, including children, and then sent them to Detention Camps. In fact, over 50,000 were imprisoned on Cyprus. While many were released at the end of the 1948 Arab-Israeli War, many others remained in captivity until the early 1950s.

To be chosen for the first crossing to what would become Israel was a great honor. I studied and trained with great dedication and even became a teacher for the younger ones. Of the 200 members of our organization, there were only ten leaders. I was honored to be one of them. It seemed that my life suddenly had meaning and that I was of value to a very important cause. Soon I was promoted to a position of greater responsibility. Apparently they thought I had something to contribute to the future of Palestine. I had gone from being near-death as a concentration camp inmate, to being a healthy, highly trained, effective leader, helping to create what would become the new, independent Jewish State of Israel.

We now had false papers and identities, and were excitedly preparing to join hundreds of other *Chalutzim* from all over Europe. There would be enough of us to fill an entire ship! We were to meet at an as yet undisclosed location near Frankfurt, and then journey to a port on the Mediterranean Sea. From there we would be on our way to *Arzeinu*, our Promised Land. We were never told anything in advance because any information that was leaked out could sabotage the entire plan, and possibly cost lives. Our joy and excitement about the upcoming mission were tinged

22. The *Chalutzim*

with sadness, however, because one of our 10-member group, a lovely, determined young woman named Rachel, suddenly took ill just two days before we were scheduled to embark on our adventurous illegal journey. Despite her protests, Rachel was rushed to St. Ottilien, which by now was a hospital strictly for Holocaust Survivors. We were devastated that she would not be able to make the journey to Israel with us. We were such a closely-knit group, each person possessing unique and valuable skills, that the loss of one was a real hardship on us all.

The next day, my closest *Chalutz* friend, Avrum, decided that we must go to see Rachel and say goodbye. So we took a bus from Feldafing to St. Ottilien to visit her. We would have only two hours for the visit because we had to catch the bus returning to Feldafing in time for our last group meeting before departing for Palestine. We found Rachel in a hospital ward that she shared with five other women. She looked so pale and helpless compared to the strong, fearless fighter who had trained with us. And she was angry that her own body had betrayed her, forcing her to let us all down. Avrum sat close by on a chair, and I sat on her bed facing her. We talked for almost two hours, letting her know that we understood that she had no choice; and that we wanted her to get healthy so she could join us later. We all tried not to let our emotions show. All the while, in the bed next to Rachel, was a very pregnant lady, who was totally immobilized because her leg was in a cast and elevated by a traction-sling. At that moment, however, since the only thing that mattered to me was that we were saying a sad farewell to Rachel, I didn't pay any attention to this woman.

I would later learn that after we left, the "pregnant lady" asked Rachel, "Who were those two nice boys? The one who sat on your bed with the beautiful black wavy hair reminded me so much of my younger brother."

Part II: Survivor

"Oh, that's *Benyameen*," Rachel responded, pronouncing my name in Hebrew.

With rising excitement, the woman then said, "I had a younger brother by the name of Baynish! Do you by any chance have a photograph of this young man?"

And Rachel, who just happened to have a photo of the 10 of us, showed it to her. When the lady took a look at the photograph, she almost passed out. She screamed, "*Oy*! This is my brother Baynish!" She'd had no idea that I'd survived. And since she'd only seen my hair and my profile as I sat on Rachel's bed, of course she hadn't recognized me—especially since in the last two years, I had matured, grown taller and my voice had changed. I bore little if any resemblance to the young brother she remembered. We'd never thought we'd see each other again. And here I had been in the same room with her—only a couple of feet apart—for two hours! It appeared as if another miracle was happening.

Even though our group was involved in a highly secret underground mission, Rachel finally understood that she must give Lola some information about my location. From this information, Lola realized that the particular group that I joined, the *Hashomer Hatzair*, was a left-wing, Zionist, secular (non-religious) organization.* In the midst of her joy at having found me, she knew that I should not belong to a group that was contrary to our background as Orthodox Jews. Lola felt that my youth, loneliness and Holocaust trauma had made me vulnerable to ideas that were contrary to our family's beliefs. Even in extreme discomfort and pain, she felt that she had to take drastic action to prevent

---

*"Left-wing" political organizations can range from Progressives to Social Liberals, from Socialist to Communists and Anarchists. The "right-wing" can span from Conservatives to Reactionaries, Capitalists, Monarchists and Fascists.

22. The *Chalutzim*

me from being brainwashed away from my religious upbringing. She knew full well that it would not be easy to make me leave this organization, especially now that I was on the way to the Promised Land. Lola immediately screamed for Mechel, who came running from down the hall to her room. Frightened, he rushed to Lola's bedside both greatly relieved to hear the wonderful news of my survival and somewhat confused by her anguished wailing.

She explained the problem, making him promise to retrieve me from the group and bring me back to her, no matter what he had to do. Of course if Lola's broken ankle hadn't been in traction, she would probably have tried to come after me herself. Being incapacitated, however, wasn't the only reason that Lola couldn't come after me herself. At nine months pregnant, she wasn't in any condition to go anywhere! And as an expectant mother, she was even more formidable than usual! Understandably, Mechel was reluctant to leave Lola in her condition, so they decided to ask a recently found cousin, Baynish Horowitz, from my father's side of the family, to help.

At that time, finding lost relatives comprised the major part of our daily lives. In the midst of the post-war chaos, there were some primitive centers where important lists of information could be collected and distributed. These lists were then posted in hospitals, synagogues, newly organized Jewish Community Centers and the Red Cross. Whenever survivors came to a new town, they would immediately go to these centers to get their names and information put on a list. They would also search for the name of a loved one or a *Landsman*, a person from their hometown. Lola and Mechel had checked these lists daily and they had been overjoyed to find that my cousin was living in another Displaced Person's Camp in Feldafing. Just like Lola, he'd been so close to me and we'd never known it!

Part II: Survivor

Mechel got word to cousin Baynish that he must come to see Lola immediately. When he arrived, breathless and worried, she instructed him to do whatever he had to do to find me—even if he had to tell me that she was in the hospital critically ill and on the brink of death. Being Lola, she made him swear not to return without me. Of course my cousin agreed to do it. Since none of them had a clue about where to look, Lola turned to Rachel and using all her considerable skills eventually persuaded Rachel to tell them that I was somewhere in Frankfurt. Even though she had been sworn to secrecy, Rachel cared deeply about me and felt that I deserved to know I had a living relative. Besides, no one could deny Lola something when she was determined to get it!

So without any specific information, my cousin went to Frankfurt, where he just aimlessly wandered the streets. He struck up conversations with people, hoping to run into someone who might reveal to him my whereabouts. After hours of searching the neighborhood, he noticed some young adults who were conversing in Yiddish. He approached them and asked whether they knew me. At first they denied knowing anything, because we were "underground" and sworn to secrecy. But when he pleaded with them, telling them about my "dying" sister, he must have been persuasive because they agreed to take him to me.

Later, when my cousin Baynish told me the story, all I could think was that it was a good thing that he wasn't an enemy spy because if he had been, our Zionist mission would have been discovered and we could have all been imprisoned—or worse.

23. *A JOYOUS REUNION!*

> *What greater thing is there for human souls than to feel that they are joined for life - to be with each other in silent unspeakable memories?*
> ~ George Eliot (Mary Anne Evans)
> (1819-1880)
> English Writer

Well, while my sister was busy making plans for our reunion, I was quietly studying our Zionist group's plan for the next day's early departure for Marseilles, where we would board the *Aliyah Bet* ship bound for Palestine. You can imagine how shocked I was to look up and see my cousin come strolling through the door! He had survived! I was stunned to learn that I wasn't the only family member left alive! I was even more stunned when he told me that he'd found Lola! Needless to say, I was ecstatic — until he lowered the boom on me with the agonizing news that she was in the hospital, ill and dying. He also told me that he could not go back to her without me. I knew my sister, so I knew that he was telling the truth. This put me in a difficult situation since our Zionist group was scheduled to leave early the next morning.

In order to better evaluate the situation, I took my cousin to meet our leader, a young man who was part of the *Haganah*, a section of the British *Palestinian Jewish Brigade*.*

---

*Founded in 1920 in order to protect Jews in Palestine, this independent, underground militia actively worked against British anti-Zionist policies to facilitate "illegal" immigration of Jewish Holocaust refugees to Palestine. For info see: http://jewishvirtuallibrary.org/jsource/History/haganah.html.

Part II: Survivor

His highly dangerous mission was to enable Jewish refugees to immigrate to Palestine in spite of the British Blockade.

At first he sympathized with my predicament, but then he told us that any idea of me leaving was absolutely unacceptable. Replacing me at such late date would be impossible. He pointed out that a great deal of money, time and trust had been invested in my training. A lot of people depended on me. I had been chosen from many other candidates who were willing to pay any amount of money just to have the chance to join them on this historic journey — the first *Aliyah Bet*. I had sworn to be part of the mission. I was overwhelmed with guilt and grief, and joy and hope.

I had been so honored to have been chosen, I was well-trained for the mission ahead, and I knew that if I were to leave them it would be considered an unforgivable act of treason. I stayed up all night long agonizing over this decision. Helping to establish and protect the new State of Israel had become the center of my existence. In some ways, I had become just as focused on this goal as I had been in surviving the concentration camps. It gave some meaning to the hideous suffering of the Jewish People. Not going to Israel the next day was unthinkable. Little did I know that I was about to make a choice that would affect the rest of my life.

By early morning, after a sleepless night struggling with my mixed feelings, I managed to gain some perspective and see the big picture. I came to the conclusion that this is what was meant to be; that it was destiny that had caused this turn of events. Of course my sister was more important than my dream. I would have to postpone going to Palestine. Needless to say, the *Chalutzim* group was shocked and angered by my decision. In fact, when I told my group leader about my decision, he angrily tore off the lapel pin

23. A Joyous Reunion!

that had signified my respected status in the group. It was his way of showing his utter contempt for my disloyalty. Even my so-called best friend, Avrum, turned his back in disgust and walked away from me. We never spoke again.

Once my agonizing decision had been made, however, I focused all my attention on my impending bittersweet reunion with my long-lost, and now "dying," sister.

With my departure from the *Chalutzim* the next morning, I was once again homeless — a condition that by then seemed almost normal. I had no clue about where I would spend the next night. So having packed my few possessions in my back-pack, I met my cousin and we took the bus to the very same hospital ward where our *chaverah* (dear friend) Rachel was still in the very same bed. I could barely contain my emotions when I saw that the hugely pregnant, woman in the next bed really was my beloved, "terminally ill" sister. How could I find and lose her at the same time?

After an emotional reunion, she told me the good news about her health, and why they'd had to use such extreme measures in order to retrieve me. As I heard this news, I was stunned. Wild emotions raged through my heart and soul. On the one hand, I was very upset that I'd had to go against my own integrity and Zionist beliefs by letting down the people whom I respected, and who respected me and depended on me. I was devastated by my decision to forgo my commitment to help build and protect Israel. At the same time, of course, I was indescribably ecstatic that Lola was not only healthy, but that she was about to bring a new member into our family. A precious new life who would be one of the first born to a Holocaust Survivor. A living, breathing, laughing, crying, jubilant answer to Hitler's monstrous "Jewish Question." We are still here! And we will continue to survive and thrive!

Part II: Survivor

My homeless situation was resolved when Mechel arranged for me to move into the little room that the staff at St. Ottilien had provided for him so that he could be close to Lola. Over the next few days, he and I visited her room as often as possible. Together, the three of us talked with great joy about the future. During the evening of January 18, 1946, the "future" seemed to be approaching fast! Lola began having terrible pains and eventually realized that she was going into labor. Since St. Ottilien wasn't a maternity hospital, it was necessary for Mechel to find a cab to take us to the hospital in Landsberg,* about an hour away. Needless to say, it was an amazing night for all of us!

And after some unexpected challenges, baby Hershel Lieber was born bright and early the next morning. So less than a year after I thought I was the only one left in my family, there were now four of us! Although we hated to leave Lola and Heshi, Mechel and I eventually had to return to our little room that St. Ottilien. Of course we visited Landsberg daily until Lola and Heshi were able to come "home" to their own little room at St. Ottilien. Since he was the first newborn at St. Ottilien after the war, you can imagine what a big fuss everyone made over him! And us! I was getting attention just for being an uncle! I was such a proud uncle! Happy to feed him, bathe him, change his diapers, make him laugh—and just gaze into his already wise eyes, knowing that through these eyes, the future would be bright!

And in fact, newborn Herschel Lieber brought a bright future to those of us who had thought that our own was lost. Sixty-five years later, along with countless others, I am still awed by my nephew Heshi. Because even though I'd

---

*Years later we found it ironic to learn that Hitler wrote, *Mein Kampf* (published in 1925) while he was in the nearby Landsberg Prison.

23. A Joyous Reunion!

known that his very existence would be a blessing to the Jewish People, his actual achievements continue to exceed anything I could have imagined. His entire life has been devoted to finding Jews who as children had been hidden in Poland and brought up as gentiles. Many of these people who never knew who or what they really were, had been haunted throughout their lives by torturous nightmares. Because of Heshi's dedication, hundreds of families have been reunited. In a way we couldn't have imagined on that sparkling morning in January, 1946, Heshi Lieber is still bringing a future to people who literally had lost their pasts.

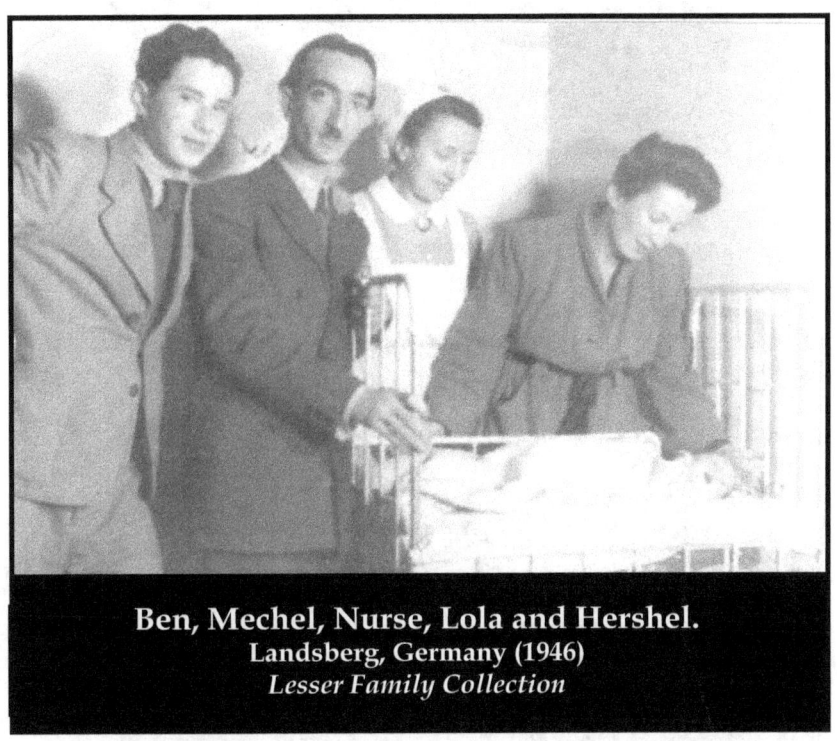

Ben, Mechel, Nurse, Lola and Hershel.
Landsberg, Germany (1946)
Lesser Family Collection

Part II: Survivor

Heshi, Lola and Ben
Munich, Germany (1946)
Lesser Family Collection

Heshi, Lola and Ben
Brooklyn, NY (2011)
Lesser Family Collection

24. LIFE IN POST-WAR GERMANY

> *"Rejoice with your family
> in the beautiful land of life!"*
> ~ Albert Einstein (1879-1955)
> German-born Jewish American
> Nobel Prize-winning Physicist

When World War II ended, the Allies (Great Britain, France, the USSR and the US) divided Germany into four sectors. This was called West Germany's post-war Allied Occupation Government. Many Jewish refugees settled temporarily into apartments in the British and American sectors until they could get the documents that would allow them to immigrate to England or the US. A few weeks after Heshi was born, we received the wonderful news that *HIAS** had arranged for us to move out of St. Ottilien and into a big apartment on Munich's beautiful Prinz Regent Strasse, in the American sector. The Allies had confiscated German homes in order to provide housing for Jewish refugees. So here we were about to live in a German's apartment, that might even originally have been a Jewish family's home.

In some cases, including ours, the Jewish refugees agreed to let the German residents stay in their homes, so the two former enemies now lived together. A Mrs. Bremer, the German woman who had been living in our newly

---

*For more than a century, *HIAS*, the Hebrew Immigrant Society, has provided essential life-saving services to needy Jewish people throughout the world. They were particularly effective after World War II, arranging reunions and resettlement. According to Jewish tradition and values, HIAS also helps non-Jews who are threatened and oppressed. For more information see: http://www.hias.org/

Part II: Survivor

assigned apartment, agreed to move to a small bedroom and do our laundry and cooking in exchange for being allowed to stay. She was as poor as we were since her Nazi soldier husband had committed suicide. So there we were: Three religious Jewish Holocaust Survivors, an infant, and the widow of a Nazi. Today this would have been the basis for a TV show! Mrs. Bremer was very kind to us and Lola stayed in touch with her and her son after moving to the USA.

In addition to providing me with a family and a home, Lola and Mechel also introduced me to a professor who taught me math and German. While the opportunity to study hard might not seem like a gift to many young people today, to me it was, and continues to be something to treasure. I was eager to spend hours studying. And

Sharing a bench with my math tutor.
Munich, Germany (1946)
Lesser Family Collection

24. Life in Post-War Germany!

will never forget the professor's kindness to me — I don't know how Mechel paid him, because at that time we had no income. I'm sure, however, that there was a mutually agreeable arrangement. In spite of our poverty, our days in Munich were quite happy. *HIAS* gave us rations and they kept records for each of us in order to help anyone who was trying to find us. They even gave us cigarettes — which we smoked like crazy — and could also sell for other necessities. We waited for our visas to America, and inquired at *HIAS* about other survivors on a daily basis. We met with friends. We shared meals and information. We walked the baby, went to the park, enjoyed each other's company and planned for a future we'd started to believe would now actually happen.

Since I was only 17, I still qualified for *Kinderjugend*

I proudly take my nephew Heshi for a walk.
Munich, Germany (1946)
Lesser Family Collection

Part II: Survivor

(Children-Youth) Transport, an organization that arranged housing and travel for Jewish refugee children under the age of 18, to go to America. Once I was accepted into this program, I moved out of Lola and Mechel's apartment and into a lovely room the organization provided for us at a beautiful former lakeside resort in the nearby village of Prien am Chiemsee. I was lucky to be assigned a remarkable roommate named Martin, with whom I shared the horror of being an orphaned Holocaust Survivor. We also shared our dreams for the future. We spent a lot of time together while waiting our turns to be transported to America. We never could have predicted that over sixty years later, Martin and I would still be close friends, who enjoy remembering some of our adventures during those months we lived together.

One such adventure in particular, involved a little cigarette manufacturing enterprise. Back in those days, cigarette smoking was very popular. If you didn't smoke, you were considered to be unsophisticated. Cigarettes were also very valuable. Many people used them almost like currency to trade for other goods and services. I don't need to tell you how badly Martin and I both enjoyed smoking and needed money! Well, coincidentally, right across the street from our dormitory, there was a large tobacco farm. Don't ask me how tobacco grew in that climate.

Every morning we'd look out our window at the tobacco fields and try to figure out how to get some tobacco to start a little cigarette manufacturing business. First we bought a device that filled cigarette papers with tobacco. And then, just as if we knew what we were doing, we went across the street and bought some leaves from the farmer. Each wet green leaf was about 18 inches wide by 24 inches long. Unfortunately we had no clue what now needed to be done with them. Since they were wet, we thought we probably should dry them, so we decided to

24. Life in Post-War Germany!

hang them outside on the clotheslines* with clothespins to dry for a couple of hours.

Once they were dry, we crumbled enough bits to roll our own test cigarettes. The first few batches were so strong that we thought we'd cough our lungs out. Then Martin said he remembered from back home that boiling the leaves would take some of the nicotine and harshness out. So we went out and got some pots, filled them with water and leaves, and put them on the small stove that was in our room. When the pots started to boil, an odor fouler than a human could imagine began to fill the room. And then it filled the yard. And then it proceeded to fill the neighborhood. Terrified, screaming people came running out of their homes trying to find out what new catastrophe had befallen our community. There was no way for our little venture to go undiscovered, and the noxious odor lingered for days. Needless to say, Martin and I weren't very popular.

Undaunted, we once again dried the leaves. Then, with great anticipation, we crumbled them up and then filled the papers. At last we were ready to sample our product. Well, the instant that I put a match to mine, it ignited into A BALL OF FLAME! It singed my hair and eyelashes! I thought that this was it. I was about to be burnt alive.

Martin Kohn and Ben
Las Vegas, Nevada (2009)
Lesser Family Collection

After Martin helped me put the sparks out, we took a

---

*Since very few people had automatic, in-door clothes-dryers until after WWII, they hung their laundry outside on clotheslines.

Part II: Survivor

couple of deep breaths and had a good laugh. Martin might have laughed harder than I did. Needless to say, that was the end of the whole enterprise. All these years later, Martin still talks about what I looked like when that cigarette exploded! And he still thinks it was pretty funny.

In February, 1947, Lola, Mechel and baby Heshi finally received their visas. They packed their meager belongings, and left the horrors of Germany for the dreams of New York City aboard the steam ship SS *Ernie Pyle*.* As was so often the case, mixed emotions surged through me. While I shared their joy at this exciting opportunity to begin new lives in America, I was filled with sadness that the only family I had was leaving me. I would be on my own in Germany — the place where Nazism began.

Well, I turned eighteen in October before my *Kinderjugend* Transport paperwork could be completed, so I no longer qualified for the program. As a consequence, I no longer qualified for housing. Fortunately, I didn't have

**S.S. *Ernie Pyle*
(1946)
*Lesser Family Collection***

---

*The SS *Ernie Pyle*, was a transport ship used as a carrier for displaced persons (DPs) and World War II refugees emigrating from Europe to the United States.

24. Life in Post-War Germany!

to face being homeless because the kind German woman welcomed me back into her home for as long as I needed to stay. And this turned out to be much longer than I expected. It wasn't until the following September that my father's brother, David Leser, who had immigrated and settled in America years before the war, finally succeeded in getting a visa for me.

Those months were like being in limbo—especially without Mechel, Lola and Heshi. It was a stressful and lonely time. And all these years later, I still appreciate that despite the awkwardness of the situation, Mrs. Bremer welcomed me back into her home as if I were her own son. She did my laundry and made special meals for me to enjoy. When it was especially cold that winter, she would even fill a hot-water bottle and put it in my bed to keep me warm. Of course I helped her whenever she needed me to do something.

Strange as it might seem, our situation wasn't at all unusual. There were many Jewish refugee families living in German homes, with German families. Somehow they managed to get along under extremely difficult circumstances. In some cases, unique and even caring bonds were created between these former enemies. I often wonder why it took a Holocaust to make these bonds possible.

During this time, something very unexpected occurred. Through the Jewish refugee grapevine, my brother Moishe's widow, who we all thought had perished, was able to find me. I was overjoyed at the thought of seeing her again. This joy was quickly extinguished, however, when she explained that as a Jewish widow she had only two choices if she hoped to ever marry again. One, she could marry her deceased husband's brother—me—or two, be symbolically "kicked out" of her in-laws' family (*Chalitzah*). Clearly I wasn't in a position to marry her. So in order for her to be

Part II: Survivor

free to marry again, I had to comply with her request to participate in the ritual of casting her out of our family. Treating this lovely woman with even symbolic cruelty was extremely painful for me. It went against everything I believed in.

It wasn't until September of 1947 that I received a visa and enough money from my Uncle David to book passage on a ship. I am forever grateful to him for making it possible for me to begin a new life. He'd been determined to succeed in his efforts to bring me to this free country despite the determination of the American immigration bureaucracy to keep Jewish refugees out.*

None of the challenges that I'd experienced in the previous seven years, had prepared me for getting on a ship along with hundreds of strangers, crossing the Atlantic Ocean, and beginning a brand new life in the golden land of America. And that's how we thought of it. The Golden Land. Everyone would be free to do whatever they chose. We could eat whenever and as much as we wanted; money could be earned and used as we saw fit. We could have goals, make plans—and be free to work to achieve them. Families would not be torn apart and murdered. There would be no formerly good neighbors to turn us in and then move into our homes. No monstrous Nazis to beat and kill us at their whim. No horrific concentration camps, Death Marches or Death Trains. No fear. *Strange how something so normal could be unimaginable. . .*

---

*The US State Department's man in charge of helping Europe's Jews during the Holocaust was Breckinridge Long. Tragically, he deliberately created bureaucratic obstacles for refugees seeking visas, and found ways to block many humanitarian efforts. In fact, most of the immigration quotas in the US and European countries were never filled. Had they been, it's estimated that the lives of 200,000 people could have been saved. For more info on anti-Semitism in the US during the first half of the 1900s, see: http://www.pbs.org/wgbh/amex/holocaust/peopleevents/pandeAMEX90.html

25. *LEAVING THE OLD WORLD*

> *"Home is where the heart is."*
> ~ Pliny the Elder (23 CE-79 CE)
> Roman Author

I had faced the terrifying unknown so many times, that the idea of sailing off across an ocean to a foreign continent really didn't seem daunting. Home would be where my family was. Just like Lola and Mechel, and so many other refugees bound for America, I would be sailing from Bremerhaven, Germany, on the SS *Ernie Pyle*. In fact, I looked forward to the adventure. The displaced refugee community was close-knit, and most of us were in the 17-40 age range, because older and younger people had not survived. So it turned out that I knew a couple of the people on the ship. And since we were all in the same situation, it felt like one big extended family going on a trip together. If you've ever taken a cruise, however, you might be surprised by our living conditions. We definitely weren't aboard a vacation cruise line!

Originally a military transport ship, the SS *Ernie Pyle* had never been intended or equipped for passengers. We refugees didn't have staterooms or private lavatory facilities. The men slept in hammocks in a big windowless ship's "Hold," that had been designed to carry cargo below the water line. With 200 hammocks arranged in three tiers, it looked like an underground hammock warehouse! And since the weather was stormy for most of the trip, at night, we all swung around like crazy. Almost every man was continuously seasick! You can imagine what this looked, sounded and smelled like. The men on the bottom tiers

Part II: Survivor

really suffered — in more ways than one! I was lucky in two ways: first, I didn't get sick, and second, I'd been able to get a hammock on the top tier.

Despite the terrible weather, we spent as much time outside as possible to escape the terrible situation inside. On the decks above the "Hold," the women and children shared small four-bunk rooms. They were also horribly seasick and couldn't eat for most of the trip. This disappointed the chefs, who took pride in their food. Fortunately, since I could eat anytime and anywhere, the chefs happily welcomed me and my insatiable appetite. They always gave me whatever I wanted — including steak, which they made to order. Try to imagine for a minute what it would be like for a teenager who had experienced over six years of brutality and starvation, to be presented with a 24-hour a-day banquet of luscious food and beverages by people who kept encouraging him to eat.

The dark, stormy voyage across the Atlantic Ocean seemed like something out of a science-fiction movie. Here we were, the impoverished and traumatized remnants of Europe's devastated Jewish community, battered and seasick. We lacked language skills and had little hope for jobs or adequate housing. We carried our pitifully few belongings in small tattered sacks and wore ill-fitting, cast-off clothes — some of which had actually been confiscated from the German military. What a strange sight to see Jewish Holocaust Survivors walking around the drenched and wildly rolling decks wearing German military coats! Ahead of us lay even more strangeness: the uncertainty of a new world. But just like the ship, we forged ahead to this strange new world where we would make new lives

After two turbulent weeks, having lost hope that we'd ever see sunshine again, suddenly, just as we approached New York City, the weather magically calmed down.

25. Leaving the Old World

The sun shone brightly in a clear blue sky like a good omen — almost as if even the weather in the New World would be beautiful! We all crowded the decks — laughing and cheering — excitedly catching our first glimpses of the wondrous New World that would become our home. Just as with so many immigrants before us, when we passed the Statue of Liberty, we each felt as if we were being welcomed personally to this land of milk and honey. And it was at that moment that I actually felt my life begin. September 21, 1947, was the first day of my life.

I was astonished by the sight of the massive, proud, skyscrapers. It was overwhelming, and I suddenly was filled with anxiety about this fairy-tale land that was far beyond my imagination. So temporarily, my exhilaration and bold dreams were tinged with anxiety. It was so vast — how would I avoid getting lost? How on earth would I fit in? I couldn't even understand the language. I was so shabby and ignorant of modern American ways. What if the people hated me? Worse, what if they laughed at me? What if I had to be a beggar on the street? What if my American Dreams turned into American Nightmares?

Instead of going to Ellis Island, a customary destination for immigrants, the SS *Ernie Pyle* pulled right into a dock in the New York Harbor, where a cheering crowd awaited us. Somewhere in that crowd were Lola, Mechel and Heshi, who would be taking me to their apartment in Brooklyn. What if we couldn't find each other in the crowd? But first all the refugees had to go through Customs — a big open room where all foreigners must check in with immigration officials to make sure that their papers are in order and that they are not bringing any *contraband* (illegal items) into the country. Fortunately, the clerks spoke many different languages, including Yiddish, so we were able to understand what was going on and follow directions. Many

Part II: Survivor

of the refugees were terrified that they would be sent back to Europe where they were unwelcome. With a big sigh of relief, I cleared Customs and was directed to another huge hall that was packed with people awaiting the arrival of their loved ones. Amidst the frantic waving, whistling, shouting of names, screams of joy and sobs of agony and relief, my anxiety about finding my family increased.

This anxiety evaporated instantly, however, when I finally spotted Lola and Mechel waiting for me right outside the exit door! They were smiling and waving like crazy. And when we fell into each other's arms, laughing and crying, I knew that everything would be okay. Because I knew that one day, I'd be an American. And I would earn the right to live the American Dream.

PART III
"The American Dream"

Part III: The American Dream

25. 1947: AMERICA!

> "Give me your tired, your poor,
> Your huddled masses yearning to breathe free,
> The wretched refuse of your teeming shore,
> Send these, the homeless, tempest-tost to me..."
> ~Emma Lazarus (1849-1887)
> Jewish-American Poet
> whose poem, "The New Colossus,"
> is inscribed on the Statue of Liberty

So, here I was in America. I was a Holocaust Survivor, a refugee—an inexperienced greenhorn. I had no education, no trade, no profession, no money, and did not speak or read a word of English. In other words, I was in perfect condition to go after the American Dream! And I couldn't wait to go after it! After all I'd been through, and despite my many challenges, how could I not be optimistic? I was in the USA! I had my youth, my health, my freedom, and my whole future ahead of me.

What more did I need?

Well, what I needed was money to live on. And I'd hoped to go to school, learn English, and finish my education. But our little family of four had very little money and needed me to bring in some income as quickly as possible. So instead of going to school, I went to work. I was determined to do whatever was necessary to achieve my goal: a happy, safe, secure life for me and my family here in America. Fortunately a friend in the refugee community got me a job working for a furrier as a shipping clerk. Since furs were very popular in New York at that time—especially during

Part III: The American Dream

the cold winters — it was a busy enterprise. So I worked and attended night-school to learn English. In addition, hoping to renew my Hebrew education, Mechel had enrolled me in the Mesivta Torah Vodaas Hebrew School in Brooklyn.

Busy as I was, however, I felt the need to contribute even more to the household. So Mechel and Lola, who both worked out of the apartment as sales representatives for hosiery (ladies' stockings) dealers, helped me get extra work peddling hosiery on *Delancey Street*.* Finally, I was earning a little spending money! To learn the business, I went along with Mechel as he met store owners who carried his hosiery. In the 1950s, ladies' stockings were an essential part of well-dressed women's wardrobes, so there was plenty of business. Before World War II, stockings had been made of silk and therefore were very expensive. During the War, however, it had been necessary to use whatever silk was available to make parachutes, so for years, no silk stockings had been available. As a consequence of this shortage, women would actually put dark makeup on their legs so it would look as if they were wearing silk stockings. And since real silk stockings had a single dark seam running down the back of each leg, these women would also use an eyebrow pencil to draw a fake center seam down the back of their legs! Of course as soon as the women went out of their homes, the fake stockings would smear and become very messy! The solution to this problem, was the result of newly developed technology, and would end up providing us with our first little business.

One of the many chemical/technical advances that developed in the mid-1930s and became popularized during

---

*The *Delancey Street* neighborhood on New York's lower East Side, was well-known for its dense population of refugees. For info see: www.tenement.org/

26. America!

the war, was the invention of *nylon*. This miracle substance could be turned into fabric and used as a substitute for silk in parachutes, textiles, and many other products, including ladies nylon stockings. Since all stockings are pretty similar, we decided to make ours unique—and therefore popular.

Lola's creativity and artistic talent provided just what we needed. She carefully hand-painted a beautiful flower, bird or butterfly on the top of each stocking. Our customers couldn't get enough of them! Although it seemed like a small, maybe even frivolous detail, this taught me an important lesson in salesmanship: Even if your product is commonplace and ordinary, you can be successful selling it if you do something to make it uniquely appealing. Always make your product or service different from the others.

Bright and early every morning I would take my carefully packed display suitcase and go down to Delancey Street where I peddled our products right out on the street. I was taking a bit of a risk, because I didn't have a license. In order to avoid getting arrested, I kept all my wares in the suitcase so I could close it up quickly and walk away whenever a policeman came into sight. Of course, some of the policemen, whose families were also recent immigrants, knew what I was doing and were kind enough to walk very slowly as they approached my corner!

So for six months, right along with Lola and Mechel, I worked hard, sometimes 12-15 hour as day, six days a week. At night I went to school and, of course, I helped take care of my quickly-growing, very active nephew, Heshi. We also visited with Uncle David's family. It was wonderful being part of a family again, with everyone so strongly committed to each other's welfare. Each of us choosing to work together for a better future; working hard to better our lives. My family was like a safety net for me, allowing me

Part III: The American Dream

to grow and explore my new world while staying securely connected to the love and familiarity of the Old World.

At the same time, we were also very much aware of another new and beautiful country that was being born right in the middle of the Old World — and that country would be Israel. A Jewish homeland. Its birth became possible when, under world-wide pressure, the United Nations finally ended the British Mandate over Palestine in 1948. Unfortunately, this was done without the establishment of any transitional governing body. So it was no surprise that the immediate result was utter chaos and violence between the Jews and Arabs who lived there. When Israel announced its independence in May of 1948, its new status was quickly recognized by many countries, including the US. To the surrounding Arab countries, however, the establishment of the Jewish State of Israel was justification for war. In fact, their stated goal was to push Israel into the sea. And with their combined military power and huge military, this did not seem to be an unrealistic goal.

But despite being vastly outnumbered and out-gunned, little Israel won this David and Goliath war. Jews all over the world rejoiced that the Jewish People finally had a homeland. Never again would we be subject to the whims of the countries where we lived. And in Brooklyn, USA, amidst the joyous celebrations for Israel, we couldn't help but wonder to what degree the loss of six million men, women and children had influenced the United Nations to allow the birth of this new nation. To this day, I have remained an ardent supporter of Israel, making sure that our children and grandchildren know about and visit our precious homeland.

Our little family had developed a comfortable routine, and the months passed quickly. As wonderful as it was to be living with my loving family, however, I was a healthy

26. America!

young man who had missed all the fun and excitement of growing up. It didn't take long for me to realize that I needed a place of my own. It seems strange now, but one of the reasons I needed to move was that like most Europeans, I was an avid smoker. So were Mechel and Lola, but since they were ultra-Orthodox, smoking was forbidden in their house on the Sabbath. Well, for me, not being able to smoke on Saturday was very frustrating and inconvenient. It's interesting how such a minor circumstance can change the course of a person's life.

It was also interesting that I was easily able to reunite with my dear friend, Martin, from the *Kinderjugend* Transport dormitory in beautiful Prien am Chiemsee, Germany. The New York City Jewish refugee community was small, and word spread quickly through the refugee "grapevine," providing information about lost relatives and friends. Ironically, it turned out that Martin lived in a nearby apartment with his cousin, Jack. When the three of us got together and discussed my living situation, it was quickly decided that I should move in with them. This would be beneficial for all of us — I could smoke whenever I wanted, and they now had a third person to share expenses.

Although I wouldn't have believed it then, this would be the next step of my American entrepreneurial (business) career! Martin and Jack were already trained upholsterers by profession, and since Martin had a well-paying job, Jack and I decided to go into the upholstery business for ourselves. What did we know about business? Nothing! But since, back then, people reupholstered instead of buying new furniture, we figured that we couldn't lose. We were so excited about this venture, that we went ahead and rented two small side-by-side stores that were connected by a door. One store was for our upholstery shop and the other would be a fruit and vegetable store. We were partners in both. Our

Part III: The American Dream

reasoning was that the *hausfraus* (housewives) who would buy their family's fruits and vegetables every day, would, perhaps one day, also need their furniture reupholstered. Since they would already know and trust us, it would be natural for them to bring us their business.

Wonderful as this idea was, however, we just didn't have the financial know-how to make it work. So we struggled along for a few months. One of the major problems that we should have foreseen, was that neither one of us drove a car. And it was quite a *schlep* (a big hassle) to go to the wholesale produce market and back to the store on the bus at three o'clock every morning. So Jack and I decided to liquidate our stores and salvage whatever little money we could—and I emphasize "little."

That summer, young, free and eager for adventure, we decided to use our little bit of money to go West, to golden California, and start a new chapter in our lives. Even though we didn't know anyone in—or anything about—California, we were convinced that moving there would change our luck. Helping to convince us was this old Jewish proverb:

> *"M'shana Mokaum, M'shana Mazel"*

Meaning, as you change your place, you change your luck—which is exactly what we wanted to do. Our friends and family, however, had all tried to dissuade us from going to Los Angeles. They told us that there were no Jewish people there, and that we would be completely isolated and removed from Jewish life.*

---

*I later found out that there had, indeed, been a Jewish community in Los Angeles at least as far back as the 1840s—before California had become a state! For more info see: http://www.jgsla2010.com/hotel-los-angeles/timeline-of-jewish-history-in-los-angeles/

26. America!

At that time, although neither one of us wanted to abandon Jewish life, we strongly felt that we could no longer stay under the strict yoke of Orthodoxy. The constraints it imposed seemed to have a stranglehold on our lives and spirits. We didn't want to leave our families, but we had to escape their restrictive life style. So we packed our still very meager belongings, said tearful goodbyes to our friends and family, purchased our Greyhound Bus tickets and we were off! During our four-day trip across the country, we tried to absorb as much as we could of the amazing landscape, and practice our primitive English. We were filled with gratitude to be able to live in this beautiful country...

Speaking of places where we lived, any illusions we might have had about comfortable accommodations in LA quickly evaporated when we arrived at the bus station in Los Angeles. We got off the bus and walked around the corner to Main Street, and sadly realized that we were actually on Skid Row, a very squalid, dangerous section of town inhabited by drunks and derelicts. However, it did have a shabby hotel, and since we had so little money, the one dollar cost per night for a room was the right price. And bad as it was, I'd survived in far worse conditions, so I wasn't worried. We decided to stay there for just a few days until we found employment. To the degree that we could understand the English, Jack and I immediately started checking out the help-wanted ads in the newspapers. We were willing to take anything that came our way. But even though we changed our location from the east to west coast, our luck didn't seem to be changing. We ended up staying in that dingy hotel for a month, each day more hungry and less hopeful than the day before.

Despite all of our efforts, neither one of us could find any work. And as we ran out of money, we had no choice but to start hocking (trading possessions for money at a

Part III: The American Dream

pawn shop) our few personal belongings. Considering the financial circumstances of the neighborhood's inhabitants, we weren't surprised to find that pawnshops were the most successful businesses on Main Street! All too soon we had pawned all of our personal possessions, including wristwatches and coats. We ran out of money to even pay the one dollar a night for the hotel room. However, for some reason, the manager was nice enough to extend us credit, telling us that he had faith that we would eventually repay him. We were most appreciative of his kindness, especially since by this time we had also run out of food money. So Jack and I rotated scavenging for food. One day, he would go to Clifton's, which was a cafeteria, and the next day I would go. We would take our trays down the serving counter, make sure to fill our pockets with food for each other, and then buy only a cup of coffee at the end. Clearly, we had hit rock bottom.

One Friday afternoon when I was feeling particularly melancholy I turned to Jack and said that it would soon be *Shabbat*, or *Shabbos*,* and there we were, completely detached from Jewish life. Despite my family's assurances, I had a hard time believing there were no Jewish people living in this city and that there were no synagogues. I certainly felt like praying tonight, especially now that we were in this desperate financial predicament. Jack felt the same way, so we both started to inquire about the whereabouts of a Jewish community. And that's when we found out about the Jewish community on the east side of Los Angeles. Known as Boyle Heights, this neighborhood was densely populated with Jews from Eastern Europe. In

---

*Shabbat, the twenty-four hours celebrating the Jewish Sabbath, starts at sundown on the sixth day of the Jewish week (Friday), and is followed by a day of rest (Saturday).

26. America!

fact, by the 1930s, there were almost 70,000 living there, making it the largest Jewish community in the western part of the United States. This was just what we were looking for!

So we hopped on a streetcar that we hoped was going in the right direction—especially since once we paid the fare, we would be completely out of money. We watched all the amazing sights of Los Angeles from our window, but felt our optimism fade when we didn't see what we were looking for: some evidence of a Jewish community. Just when we were about to lose all hope, however, we saw a bearded man and two small boys walking up the street. And they were wearing the traditional black coats and hats of Orthodox Jews. The man even carried a familiar-looking velvet pouch that we knew would contain a *tallith*!

We rushed to the conductor and demanded in our broken English and vigorous hand gestures that he let us out immediately! Fortunately, he somehow understood us—or else just wanted to get rid of us fast—and he stopped the streetcar, letting us out on Wabash Avenue. We scrambled down the steps, excitedly dashed up to the very surprised man on the sidewalk and asked him in Yiddish if he was going to a synagogue. Then, in our beloved Yiddish, he told us that he was going to Rabbi Tarshes' Temple (Congregation Talmud Torah of Los Angeles) down the street. In spite of our ragged appearance, he kindly invited us to accompany him. When we saw the Temple, we breathed sighs of relief.

How indescribably comforting it was to find ourselves in a familiar environment. We tried to straighten our hair and clothes so we'd look more respectable before solemnly entering the Temple. To our great relief, the rabbi greeted us warmly—as if we two shabby strangers were just what the congregation needed! And it turns out that we were. With

Part III: The American Dream

so many young people leaving the community for more affluent neighborhoods, most of the remaining parishioners were senior citizens. So young and eager faces were rare — and very welcome.

Now it so happened that Jack had been trained in Hungary to become a rabbi. In fact, he actually had received *Semichut* (ordination as a rabbi). Even though Jack and I were the same age, he'd actually had five years more education than I did. This is because he was from Hungary, and the Germans did not occupy Hungary until March of 1944. Poland, where I came from, was occupied in 1939 — and that's when my education stopped, the first week of 6th grade. Jack was so exhilarated to find himself in a Jewish Temple in the middle of an American-Jewish community that he dared to ask the rabbi if he could lead the congregation in the holy prayer songs. For some reason, the rabbi had been instantly impressed by Jack, and without knowing whether he had any talent at all, motioned him enthusiastically to the podium.

And then, right before our eyes, as he walked to the podium, it seemed as if Jack was entering another spiritual dimension — he seemed to change physically, gaining more assurance in his posture. Holding his head higher. Looking older and dignified. This was something I had never seen, so I was as transfixed as everyone else. When he reached the podium, he paused, breathed deeply, and then slowly and deliberately looked around the sanctuary, seeming to gaze into each pair of expectant eyes, making a personal connection with each of us. It was as if instead of Jack being a newcomer, a greenhorn, he really belonged right there at the podium, as if the congregants were all his guests. And then he began to sing.

26. America!

It was as though the music was coming through him from some otherworldly source, and the mesmerized congregation went right along with him. In Hebrew the word *Kavanah* means that it's not enough to merely read, listen or repeat the sacred prayers and songs by rote, we must be totally absorbed by the meaning of the sacred words because they are meant to convey our hearts, souls and spirits into the presence of God. We try to make ourselves worthy of this honor by entering a state of such profound concentration that all other thoughts are blocked out. Some people find it helpful to rock back and forth while praying in order to focus more fully. The more effective the cantor is in establishing this mood, the more powerfully the congregation is filled with *Kavanah*.

It would not be an exaggeration to say that the beauty and power of Jack's singing induced the essence of *Kavanah*. When he'd sung his last note, the sanctuary was filled with a totally stunned silence. And then, as if on cue, the crowd suddenly rushed to hug him, and lifted him up from the podium. They just couldn't believe that such power and beauty had come from this 20-year-old refugee. And they knew they might never again have such an experience. The overjoyed rabbi asked us to stay for *Oneg Shabbat*, the special after-services celebration meal.

Needless to say, we took grateful advantage of the delicious and plentiful food, and then we both sang many joyous songs welcoming the Sabbath. Later, the Temple's board members congratulated us again, and asked if it would be possible for us to come back in the morning to lead them in the Saturday services. When they heard about our miserable living arrangements, they were appalled. They immediately went over to a Mrs. Greenberg, who just happened to have a spare room with two beds and close

Part III: The American Dream

access to a real bathroom! Then and there arrangements were made for us to stay overnight at the house she shared with her husband. We were delighted to accept this offer.

Later that night, before we could go to sleep, Jack and I went over some prayers and hymns together for the morning's service since I would also be participating. And then, on very full stomachs, in comfortable, clean beds, in a warm and safe Jewish home, we had our first good night's sleep in a very long time. Maybe our luck was changing after all.

The next morning, Mrs. Greenberg served a wonderful breakfast. And once again, we ate as if we were bottomless pits! The lively mealtime conversation included Yiddish, English, and smatterings of Polish, German and Hungarian—with many sentences containing more than one language! After this body-and-soul-nourishing meal, we walked to the Temple for services, anticipating another joyous event. As we rounded the corner, however, we almost choked when we saw a crowd of waving, people rushing in our direction. Unlike our recent experiences in Europe, where a crowd rushing toward us usually meant we were about to be beaten—or worse—this time it was a smiling crowd, coming to wrap us in warm hugs. Apparently word had spread throughout the Jewish community that an extraordinary young man would be conducting Saturday services, so the synagogue was packed. And they would not be disappointed. Once again, when Jack began to sing, the congregants were mesmerized by his extraordinary talent and charisma. Again, it was indeed *Kavanah*.

Later that night, after *Havdala*, the ceremony marking the end of *Shabbat*, the board of directors called us in to their

26. America!

office, and offered Jack a *cantorial** position for the upcoming High Holidays** — which were only a month away. They offered him $350 dollars for three days! This was an unimaginable sum of money! And that was when I became his business manager and gave them a counter-offer of $500 dollars. I also told them that we needed $250 in advance because we had to pay off all of our debts. Miraculously, they met our conditions, and we shook hands in agreement. That same night we also made an agreement to become boarders at Mrs. Greenberg's home on a more permanent basis. And as soon as the bank opened on Monday morning, we were there to cash the check. We immediately paid up our hotel bill in full and thanked the manager for his trust in us. We then redeemed all of our pawned personal belongings and moved into Mrs. Greenberg's comfortable home. It was September of 1949, and things were finally beginning to look up for us.

Always on the alert for ways to improve our circumstances, Jack and I immediately got busy applying for all kinds of jobs. Any job. He got lucky first, although it was a job he hadn't even thought of or applied for. It seems that one of the members of the Temple owned a sheet-metal factory and had offered Jack a job. This was cause for a great celebration! It meant that he would never go back to upholstery. He had, however, already contacted every upholstery business in town, trying to find a job. And

---

*A cantor, or *chazzan* in Hebrew, is a highly trained singer who leads the congregation, along with the rabbi, in sacred songs and prayers.
**The Jewish High Holidays consist of *Rosh Hashanah*, which marks the beginning of the New Year, and *Yom Kippur*, the "Day of Atonement," the holiest day of the Jewish calendar. On *Yom Kippur* observant Jews attend a day of prayer services and fast for 24 hours in the hopes of being forgiven for their sins. A festive meal marks the end of *Yom Kippur*.

Part III: The American Dream

unlike today, when everyone has their own cell phones, in those days, no one had a personal phone. In fact, most homes only had one phone, and it was usually on the wall or a little table in the hall on the first floor. Well, one day, I happened to be near the phone when it rang, so I answered it. When the caller asked for Jack and said that there was an opening for an upholstery job starting the next day, I didn't even stop to think. I had to make a fast choice, so I told him that I was Jack and that I would be there the very first thing in the morning, ready to work. Of course, since I had absolutely no experience as an upholsterer, once again, I was in a position where I had to figure out what needed to be done, and then just go ahead and do it.

Well, needless to say, Jack and I never got to sleep that night. He had to teach me how to be an experienced upholsterer in just a few hours. He started at the beginning by showing me how to spit nails into a box in a straight line. This was the mark of an experienced upholsterer. This also was a complicated and often painful process if you didn't know how to do it, which I clearly didn't. So over and over again he showed me how to take a mouthful of these little sharp tacks with my tongue, and line them up along my lips so that the sharp points were inside my mouth. Next, I had to learn how to retrieve them from my lips, one-at-a-time, with a magnetic hammer. And then, without a break in the action, I had to pound them into a box or a piece of upholstered furniture in a perfectly straight line. A real pro could do this very quickly. I, on the other hand, took a while to catch on—all too often hitting myself in the mouth with the hammer, sometimes pricking my tongue with the nails. So that's what we did. All night long. Eventually, despite my raw, bloody lips and tongue, I became pretty good at it—so I have to admit that sometimes pain is an effective motivator!

26. America!

Bright and early the next morning, I did my best to look alert, confident and unscathed when I arrived at the Acme Chrome Modern Furniture Factory on Temple Street. I walked through the door and introduced myself to the owner as Jack. You can imagine my huge sigh of relief when he just shook my hand and nodded absently. He then sent me over to the secretary who helped me to fill out all of the documents — as Ben Leser. Apparently she didn't know I had used an alias on the phone with the boss. And apparently he really didn't care what my name was as long as he had an upholsterer! Anyway, it worked, and I worked there for three years. And, yes, I got pretty good at upholstering!

My responsibility was to put the plastic upholstery on those 1950s dinette chairs. I knew my future depended upon becoming indispensible to the boss. And despite my lack of experience, I was determined to excel at this new job. So I figured out what to do, and did it. And then, I figured out how to do it better and faster! I figured out an assembly-line process that allowed me to work even faster than my supervisor! So I asked the owner to pay me by the piece instead of by the hour. Soon I was making more money than my supervisor who'd been there for 35 years. Of course this information we never told him! I did so many chairs in the three years that I worked there that sixty years later, I still could probably do it blindfolded!

Since I was determined not just to work, but to achieve the American Dream, I also went to night-school and took on whatever odd-jobs I could find! Plumbing, plastering, painting, electrical — whatever needed to be done, either I did it or found a partner who could. I was never satisfied just going to work and doing the job. I always wanted to achieve excellence, to be the best at whatever I did. And this required knowing how to deal with the bosses, figuring

Part III: The American Dream

about what would be good for the whole business, going way beyond the call of duty at my work, and being alert to additional opportunities. So while many other workers stayed at the same job for their entire careers, I was able to get promotions, and move ahead.

And I wasn't the only one who was working hard toward achieving the American Dream. In addition to his own full-time job at the sheet-metal company, Jack also began taking lessons in order to pursue his dream of becoming a certified cantor. So between all of our jobs and religious services, we were very busy young men, each of us fully confident, as only young men can be, that the future would be very bright. We even let ourselves dream of the beautiful young women we would meet when we'd finally made our fortunes!

Now, between the war, the concentration camps, coming to a new country, my need to learn English, make a living, and pursue the American Dream, I hadn't had much time for girls. In fact, I was really looking forward to eventually spending some time making up for all I'd missed! So as you can imagine, the last thing I was expecting to do was to fall in love. I'd assumed that my more experienced friend would be way ahead of me in that department. And he probably assumed the same thing! Well, I always find it interesting that there's an old Yiddish proverb for every situation. And in this case, it couldn't have been more perfect:

> ***"Mensch tracht, und Gott Lacht"***

which means, "Man plans and God laughs. " And God must have been having a good chuckle at my expense, because for me, the future came much quicker than I expected!

27. TRUE LOVE

> *"BASHERT!"*
> Hebrew word for fate.

One Friday evening, when Jack and I left the temple, we couldn't stop chattering excitedly about all that had happened to us. And we were all wound-up from the congregation's enthusiastic reaction to us. When we entered the Greenbergs' home, were surprised to see that they had company: a middle-aged couple and their very attractive daughter. Jack and I glanced at each other, trying to take stock of this new development. What could it mean to have this beautiful young woman at our table? And why were her parents and the Greenbergs looking at us with such cheery, expectant expressions?

Why? I'll tell you why. Because it turned out that our own Mrs. Greenberg was a bit of a *Shadchan* (matchmaker)! Mrs. Greenberg had invited their good friends, Mr. and Mrs. Julius Singer and their very lovely daughter, Jean, to join us for that night's *Shabbat* dinner! Mrs. Greenberg knew that Jean would make some lucky man the perfect wife! So, of course, it was perfectly natural for the four of them to cook up that evening's little get-together. What loving Jewish parents could pass up the opportunity to surround their daughter with two such eligible, hard-working, and religious bachelors?

With all of their eyes upon us, we felt as if we were supposed to do or say something, but to our humiliation, we had no clue what that might be! We didn't even know what to do with our own eyes. We certainly couldn't look

Part III: The American Dream

at the young lady — and while she was visibly blushing, she was clearly not looking at any of us!*

So we just sat down at the elaborately spread table and tried to act as if there wasn't anything unusual about these additional guests. Jack, who was never at a loss for words, began and maintained a lively conversation, while I sat there like a lump. Little did I know that this *Shabbat* would change my life! Because despite my deficient social skills, I had somehow managed to sit at the end of the table, right next to the very appealing Miss Jean Singer: the incredible woman who would soon become my wife, my partner, the mother of my children, and the love of my life!

Somehow, in the midst of everyone else talking and laughing, and despite my halting English, she and I managed to strike up a quiet conversation just between the two of us. Given her lively personality, I suspect that she had more to do with this conversation than I did. Soon we quietly moved from the table and into the living room. Well, it turns out that despite our different backgrounds, Jean and I had a great deal in common. Our values, our dreams, and our determination to reach our goals were the same. At age 19, having graduated from Roosevelt High School, Jean could drive her family's Pontiac and had already started what would become a successful career! I didn't know all this yet, however, because it took me a whole week to work up the courage to call this amazing young woman. It felt like a tremendous risk. On some level, I must have realized that I wouldn't just be asking for a date. This might be the most important phone-call of my life. Brave as I was, this

---

*Sixty years later, as I write this memoir, Jean now tells me that she had most definitely not wanted to accompany her parents to the Greenbergs that evening, and had tried to get out of it. Furthermore, she would have flatly refused to go if she'd known that she was the center of a matchmaking plot!

27. True Love

was frightening! But I'd learned the hard way that the best course of action when confronted with a risk, was to just get it over with. So brave Ben Lesser called lovely Jean Singer and asked for a date! And to my everlasting gratitude and delight, she most graciously accepted!

On our first date, we took the bus to the RKO (the Radio-Keith-Orpheum) movie theater on Hill Street, and saw *Golden Earrings*, with Marlene Dietrich and Ray Milland. I could really relate to many events in this movie. It told the story of a daring English military officer on an espionage mission in 1939 Nazi Germany. He is helped by a beautiful Hungarian Gypsy woman, and of course they fall in love. She disguises him as a Gypsy so that he can elude the Nazis. To make the disguise more authentic, she pierces his ears for golden earrings. This movie's beautifully haunting title song, written by Ray Evans and Jay Livingston, became a big hit for the famous vocalist, Peggy Lee. And of course, it became "our song." And it still is. At our recent 60th wedding anniversary celebration, the song was played, and Jean and I felt the same way as we did the first time we heard it!

Well, after this glorious first date, I unexpectedly had to return to New York to help a friend from our post-war days in the hospital at St. Ottilien. There were so many complicated arrangements to take care of that I ended up staying for two months! During that time, I lived with Lola, Mechel, my quickly growing nephew, Heshi, and his new baby brother, Yossel (Joseph). It was wonderful to be back with my family. And in order to help out, as well as earn my own money, I worked for Mechel in his hosiery business.

I missed Jean terribly, but for some reason, I didn't contact her. Maybe subconsciously, I felt insecure about how she might really feel about me after our one date. Maybe I'd felt she could do better with someone else. She

Part III: The American Dream

deserved an educated, American Jewish man instead of a refugee. Maybe I'd thought I was doing her a favor by not contacting her. I figured that Mrs. Greenberg had told the Singers that I had gone back to New York, so as far as I knew, Jean probably thought that I'd left her. Little did I know, however, that she was waiting for me to return. And when I did return, the first thing I did was call her, hoping that she remembered me, and wasn't too angry to speak with me.

Well, much to my relief, she did remember me and, lucky for me, she decided to forgive my neglect and even agreed to a second date. This time she picked me up in her car, a big Pontiac. We went to the world-famous Ambassador Hotel* on Wilshire Boulevard for dinner, and the show at its legendary Coconut Grove Nightclub. This level of luxury was a whole new world for me, and I began to worry that the $20.00 I'd brought might not be enough! I doubted that Jean would appreciate washing dishes to pay for our second date! Fortunately, after looking at the menu, she mysteriously decided that she wasn't very hungry. But since there was a cover-charge and a two-drink minimum, she went ahead and ordered the minimum two drinks. Martinis. Which Jean had never had before. She just nursed one of them all evening long. We talked, we laughed, and we danced to the wonderful big band, and dared to dream of the future. But long before the future could arrive, we had to deal with a more immediate need. We were both starving! So we left the very expensive Coconut Grove Nightclub and headed for the very inexpensive Steinberg's Cafeteria and ate our fill!

---

*Between 1921, when it opened, and 2006, when it was demolished, the Ambassador Hotel was the premier "hotspot" for celebrities and politicians. It was the site of many historic events including the tragic assassination of Robert F. Kennedy on June 5, 1968.

27. True Love

Then we went back to Jean's house. It was hard for us to say goodnight. Especially for Jean, because the last time I'd said goodnight I'd disappeared for two months! Well, we talked very quietly together on the front porch so we wouldn't wake her parents up. We shared a prolonged goodnight kiss, and then I had to leave. My legs may have walked slowly back to the Greenbergs' house, but my heart was racing, and my thoughts were dancing. I was in love. And I had no intentions of ever neglecting Jean again—not even for two hours, let alone two months. There would be no more wasted time! In fact, our second date had gone so well, that we quickly planned our third. And this third date would be very special. Jean put together a picnic and we went to MacArthur Park, a lush urban oasis surrounding a beautiful lake right in the middle of Los Angeles. After a wonderful meal, we rented a little boat and paddled it out on the lake. It was one of the most beautiful days of my life. I knew I had reached a point in my life where a very serious decision had to be made.

And it was a decision that carried a huge risk. But as in the past, I knew what had to be done, so I just went ahead and did it! As we floated along, I told Jean how I felt about her, and asked her to be my wife. And then I held my breath. Fortunately, I didn't have to hold it too long because Jean quickly said, "Yes!" I still wonder how we

Jean and Ben Engagement
Los Angeles, CA (1950)
Lesser Family Collection

Part III: The American Dream

could have known after just three dates that we were meant to be together for the rest of our lives. But we did. Truly, it was *Bashert*. Destiny.

As far as I was concerned, at that moment, I had indeed attained the American Dream. I had my life. I had liberty. And I looked forward to pursuing happiness whenever I had a minute between working and attending classes. I still marvel that within a short span of four years, I had gone from being an orphan on the brink of death in a Nazi concentration camp, to being an employed, healthy young man in America, with a loving family and the future waiting for me, as I floated on the cool blue water of a lake in Los Angeles, California, USA with my beautiful bride-to-be.

28. ACHIEVING THE AMERICAN DREAM

> "... *Life, Liberty, and the Pursuit of Happiness.*"
> ~ Thomas Jefferson (1743-1826)
> Author, Statesman,
> American President (1801-1809)

Much, much later that evening when we went back to Jean's house, we were so excited, that this time we deliberately woke her parents up to tell them the good news. When it finally sank in that we were bringing happiness instead of an emergency, Mr. Singer brought out a 15-gallon barrel of his very special home-made wine. This wine was to be used only for the most important occasions! Then Jean phoned her brother, Mitchell, who lived nearby, and woke him up! When she told him we were going to get married, he mumbled, "That's nice." And hung up. Less than a minute later, he called back, asking excitedly, "To who?" A few weeks later, on Jean's 20th birthday, April 25, the Singers made a beautiful combination birthday and engagement party for us at their home.

And on June 17, 1950, just two quick months after our engagement, Jean and I were married in a lovely Orthodox Jewish wedding at the Park Manor Banquet Hall. Put on by Jean's parents, this celebration overflowed with love, joy and hope. It was so open and free, that of course it brought back painful and poignant memories of my sister's small and terribly dangerous wedding in the bleak little backyard of our house in Niepolomice. Since it had been illegal for Jewish people to gather together for any purpose, Lola and Mechel could only invite a few close friends and immediate family. Making do with scraps of food and borrowed and

Part III: The American Dream

tattered clothes, we had all tried to make the best of it for the newly-weds' sake. How could we have known that except for Lola, Mechel and I, all of the wedding guests would soon perish in the Holocaust?

At our wedding reception in a festive ballroom in Los Angeles, 125 beautifully dressed wedding guests were able to dance to a live band—and none of us had to fear for our lives. Sadly, due to my brother-in-law Mechel's illness, no one from my own family was able to attend. My best man was Jack and my ushers were my dear friends Martin, Dave and Jean's brother, Mitchell. The rabbi conducted our Orthodox ceremony under a *Chuppah*, the traditional

Jean's parents escort her to the *Chuppah*, where I wait for her to become my wife.
Los Angeles, CA (1950)
Lesser Family Collection

28. Achieving the American Dream

canopy that symbolizes the new home of the bride and groom. According to tradition, Jean's mother led her around me seven times. This circling is a bride's way of demonstrating how central the groom is to her thoughts and to her very existence. And then of course, I crushed the glass under my shoe. At the end of the wedding ceremony, the groom steps on a wine glass and crushes it in memory of the destruction of the Temple during Roman times. For some people, it is also a reminder that even in the amidst of a joyous occasion, we must remember where we came from, and what we've survived. Every time there is a *Simcha* (happy occasion) we must always remember that there will always be bad times as well.

Once the glass was crushed, Jean and I kissed and then with huge smiles and holding each other's hand tightly, we turned toward our friends and family. Everyone joyously shouted, "*Mazel Tov*! (Wonderful! Good luck! Congratulations!)"

After the ceremony we had a wonderful *Kosher* dinner. Then the tables were arranged in a big circle so that dancing could take place in the center. Jean and I have always loved to dance and that night, in addition to dancing the *hora* (a traditional circle dance) to "*Hava Nagila*" ("Let Us Rejoice!"), we waltzed to the "Anniversary Waltz" and of course to our special song, "Golden Earrings." Everything was perfect.

Well, not entirely perfect. I found out much later that there actually had been a few glitches. First of all, there was a big International Shriners* convention in town, and their downtown parade had caused such a huge traffic jam that the rabbi was late. Also, because of Daylight Savings Time, the sun had set later than we'd anticipated. This was

---

* Established in 1870, the *Shriners* provide free hospital care for children in Shriners' Hospitals.

Part III: The American Dream

a problem because Jewish tradition requires that we begin the wedding ceremony after sundown. So we had to wait an hour to begin. And then, right before the ceremony, when Jean and I were signing the *Ketubah* (wedding contract), Jean got so nervous that she signed her name on the groom's side! We both let out deep sighs of relief when the rabbi said it was okay — our marriage was still valid.

Additionally, the beautiful, sparkling shoes that my bride was so gracefully dancing in hadn't always been so perfect. In fact they'd caused a state of emergency in the Singer household the previous night! Apparently in the hustle-bustle of preparing for our wedding, Jean had somehow forgotten to buy white shoes to go with her gown, and was quite distraught to say the least. As usual, her father came up with a unique solution. He told her not to worry, and asked her to give him her most comfortable shoes. Much to her surprise, he then painted them silver! And Jean wore them with pride.

And 60 unbelievably quick and happy years later, I'm still in touch with Martin and Dave. In fact, Dave, who is a rabbi, conducted a very special wedding-vow renewal ceremony for Jean and I at our recent 60th Anniversary Party.

After the wedding, we spent our first night together in a hotel. What a luxury! But it was also bit of a challenge. This was because when we went to our wedding, we had only $20.00 between us to start our beautiful life together. Needless to say, we stayed up late counting our wedding gift money until we confirmed that we had enough to pay both the hotel bill and the honeymoon expenses! The next day we went downtown to Union Station and began our long honeymoon train-trip to New York City.

We didn't have enough money for a Pullman (sleeper) compartment, so we sat in the Coach section on nice soft seats — for three days! There we were, giddy newly-weds,

28. Achieving the American Dream

With joyful smiles, Jean and I begin our honeymoon.
Los Angeles, CA (1950)
Lesser Family Collection

With joyful smiles, we celebrate our 60th wedding anniversary.
Las Vegas, NV (2010)
Lesser Family Collection

Part III: The American Dream

trapped and embarrassed in front of everyone. Every so often, we would get up and walk through the train to get some exercise and steal some privacy. This trip to New York was to be more than a typical honeymoon because it would be the first time that Jean would be meeting my very loving and very Orthodox family. After sight-seeing in New York, we would all get together at a cousin's chicken and egg farm in Flemington, New Jersey. While I was eager to see my sister and her family, I was grateful that they had already left the city for the farm so that Jean and I would have their apartment to ourselves for three whole days!

Since it was Jean's first time in New York City, I was happy to be the expert! Ellis Island, the Empire State Building, Broadway, a midnight horse-and-buggy ride in Central Park—it was all so different from Los Angeles! We were particularly excited when Jean's employers, a distributor for *Manischevitz**, provided us with an especially lovely wedding gift. We were invited to visit the Manischevitz factory and have lunch in the Executive Dining Room! They also provided us with tickets to a Broadway play!

Early on our fourth day in New York, my cousin, Usher, picked us up so we could join our extended family of almost fifty people in celebrating *Shabbat* at his farm. It would be at this dinner that my family would hold a *Shevah Berachot* in our honor. This is the reciting of seven traditional blessings for the bride and groom. This was all pretty new to Jean, who wasn't Orthodox, but of course, she learned fast!

---

*Going back to its founding in 1888, by Rabbi Dov Behr Manischevitz, the national success of the *Manischevitz Company* is a perfect example of achieving the American Dream. For info see: www. manischewitz. com/aboutus.html.

28. Achieving the American Dream

In fact, the very first thing she learned occurred the first night when she excused herself during dinner to use the restroom. Naturally, she turned on the light. When Usher immediately called out, "It's *Shabbos!*"* Jean realized that she wasn't supposed to turn on the light! So she instantly turned it off—but that's not allowed either! This was a real awakening for her, but true to her resilient nature, she overcame her embarrassment. Afterwards we were able to spend a private night by ourselves in a room that Lola had generously rented for us at a nearby farm.

Saturday night all of us went out to the chicken coops and gathered eggs. Then we sorted and *candled* them, which means we passed them through a machine with bright lights—like an x-ray machine—in order to look for blood clots. According to Jewish tradition, we can't consume any blood. Any eggs containing blood-clots would be destroyed. The others we carefully packed in crates for the market. It was enjoyable work, filled with fun and the singing of Hebrew songs. Gathered together in this beautiful location with loved ones, Jean and I could barely conceal our joy at what life had brought us—and what the future held in store for us.

Well, apparently, the Leser honeymoon wasn't the only exciting event that was taking place that week. Two days before we were to take the train back to Los Angeles, two major events occurred, and one was of international significance. The Korean War* broke out on June 25, 1950. The other important event was a massive train strike, which meant that the only way we could get back to Los Angeles would be by flying—in a propeller-plane. Neither one

---

*During the 25 hours of the *Sabbath* or *Shabbos*, Orthodox Jews refrain from any kind of "work." This prohibits doing anything that is creative or changes the environment.

Part III: The American Dream

Jean and I relax on our honeymoon!
Flemington, NJ (1950)
Lesser Family Collection

of us had ever flown so, naturally, we were very apprehensive, but, having no other choice, we did it. Flying was very different then than it is today. Since at that time plane cabins weren't pressurized, the flight was particularly difficult for me because I'd had childhood ear problems, and the pressure made it seem as if my head was about to explode. It was excruciatingly painful. Flying was also much slower then. This trip from New York to Los Angeles made three stops and took all day.

Much to our relief, we arrived home safely. And Mr. Singer was there to meet us and take us home. Jean had let him know when we would be landing at tiny Burbank Airport, so he could pick us up. He would take us straight home to our own little "love-nest," which as they used to say, "was about as big as a minute!" It had one bedroom, a living room, sun-room, small breakfast room and a tiny kitchen. In fact, in order to open the refrigerator you had to go into the bathroom! We paid $31.00 per month. But it was all ours!

---

*The Korean War was a military conflict between the Republic of Korea, (supported by the United Nations) against the Democratic People's Republic of Korea (supported by the People's Republic of China and the Soviet Union).

28. Achieving the American Dream

Always considerate of other people's feelings, Jean's father had not told Mrs. Singer that we were flying in because she was terrified of planes. It would be an understatement to say that Mr. Singer holds a special place in my heart, and I would like to tell you a little about this man. Having lost all my older male relatives during the war, I was truly blessed by my relationship with Jean's father, Mr. Julius Singer. This was a man who had experienced severe chronic pain and survived innumerable tragedies. And he didn't just survive, he succeeded in creating a beautiful life for himself and his family. Having overcome so many obstacles himself, he was a wonderful role model for me. He showed me the importance of taking responsibility for solving problems instead of using them as an excuse for not succeeding.

When I met the Singers, they owned and operated their own small trucking business. Mr. Singer, being a Jack-of-all-trades and master of everything he did, took care of everything in that business but the books. These were taken care of by Jean. He could build and repair just about anything, and could drive any kind of truck, including the huge semis in which he hauled loads of scrap metal and bales of paper to the docks. And he had a real head for business. When he realized that the gas rationing of World War II would have a negative effect on the trucking industry, he converted his whole fleet of trucks from gas to butane.

Mr. Singer had an old Packard automobile, and every week when he was finished with work he purchased lumber and tied it to the top of the car. He then drove it 35 miles, all the way up to his property in San Bernardino County's beautiful Carbon Canyon. About an hour and a half away, and right next to a magnificent Regional Park, this rural oasis seemed very remote at the time! And all by himself,

Part III: The American Dream

he built a beautiful home. A real work of art. It was almost like a villa. He set up a generator for electricity and even figured out how to get his own water supply. Through the years, as I watched his projects develop, I marveled at his strength, resourcefulness and talent. And I learned about his amazing past.

Back in Russia, where he grew up, he had been a very prosperous jeweler who'd owned a gold and silver smelting factory. As a successful entrepreneur, he was very unpopular during and after the Russian Revolution*, because the new Communist government did not allow free enterprise or individual wealth. In fact, there was a price on his head, which meant he and his family could be murdered at any time. So he knew it was time to give up everything and try to get to America. Having used walking canes all of his life as a result of a childhood injury, he decided that everyone in his family should also have walking canes. Not because they were all afflicted by the same "handicap," but because canes would provide them with the financial wherewithal that they would need to escape.

He'd decided to melt down as much of his gold as possible and pour it into the hollowed out canes. So from little 5-year-old son Marcus, to Mr. Singer's sister, wife and himself, each member of the family walked with not just one, but two canes! There were many additional complicated and very daring arrangements needed to take the whole family out of the country. In fact, in order

---

*The Russian Revolution was really a series of revolutions that ultimately destroyed the centuries-old rule of the Russian Czars (Kings) in 1917, and resulted in the creation of the communist Soviet Union (USSR) government. Communists theoretically believe in a form of government where there are no economic classes, and everything is owned communally — by everyone. Unfortunately, the old saying, "Power corrupts and absolute power corrupts absolutely" applied just as much after the Revolution as it did before.

28. Achieving the American Dream

to do this, he had to buy an entire train. And hire a staff, including engineers. Can you imagine buying an entire train in order to save your family from death? Then they had to cross Siberia. Whenever they needed money, he'd break a piece of gold from a cane. This dangerous journey took a year, during which time they'd lived in exotic places such as Shanghai, Manchuria, and Japan! In 1923, when they finally got to the US immigration station at *Angel Island** in San Francisco Bay, their plan had been to call Mrs. Singer's brother, Dave, in Los Angeles. Well, at that point, they had nothing left, not even a dime to call him.

Fortunately, HIAS, the Jewish relief agency—helped them contact his brother-in-law. After not hearing from them in such a long time, of course he was ecstatic and immediately wired money to them. Otherwise, they would have been sent back to Russia, where they most certainly would have been killed.

A man of great character, profound love, infinite talent and awesome strength, Mr. Singer never stopped working for the benefit of his family. I saw a lot of my own father in him, and was honored that he treated me as if I were his son. I never wanted to let him down. Jean felt the same way about her parents and we were determined to work hard and be successful. We wanted to bring them *nachas*—the blessings of good children.

Jean, who'd had a head-start on bringing blessings to her parents, had begun working as a young teenager. Starting as a file clerk for a kosher food distributor, she had diligently worked her way up to bookkeeper, and then to buyer of food products. And she had made a point of

---

*Angel Island, located on the West Coast in San Francisco Bay, is similar to Ellis Island, the island immigration station located off of the East Coast in New York City. Both were entry points for refugees coming to America.

Part III: The American Dream

learning every function of the business, so she was able to deal with any issues that developed. I was so proud to have such an accomplished wife!

Eventually, the Singers retired from their trucking business and moved to the beautiful summer home that Mr. Singer had built. That was when Jean and I decided to take over their two-bedroom apartment on Wabash Avenue. It was bigger than our little house, and since Jean was "expecting," we needed a larger place. As if these weren't enough challenges, this was also an exciting time because, thanks to Jean, I was offered an extraordinary business opportunity. Through her job, Jean had been introduced to a very successful gentleman, who owned a large hotel with furnished apartments at Hollywood and Vine Street. He had been impressed by Jean, and when she told him that I was an upholsterer, he told her that he would like to meet with me.

When we met, he showed me around his 150-unit furnished hotel, pointing out that each unit had a couch and some chairs. And all of the furniture in the entire building had to be reupholstered! He then made me an amazing proposition. He asked me if I wanted to re-cover each piece. He told me that this would be a chance for me to open my own upholstery shop, and that he would not rush me, I could take my time, feel free to accept more lucrative jobs, and only do his as fill-ins between better paying orders.

Trying not to look stunned by this offer, I told him that I had very little money and no credit, so I couldn't possibly open a shop. He responded that he would advance me whatever I needed, and that I could use his credit to open accounts at fabric and supply houses. Of course, knowing that I would somehow figure out how to do all this, I took him up on his offer. And as soon as I got home, I contacted

28. Achieving the American Dream

Robert, my supervisor at Acme Chrome Modern Furniture, who had 35 years of experience in upholstery. We discussed this new opportunity, and decided to become partners.

After doing much research, we opened up our business on the busy corner of Wabash and Fickette. We carefully created an inviting, comfortable showroom and a well-equipped workshop. Business started to trickle in, and we still had the big hotel job to fall back on. Always looking out for my best interests, my father-in-law decided that I needed a truck. So he took my old car, and with his own two hands, converted it into a flat-bed-truck that could carry eight to ten sofas at one time. Once we could transport more furniture at a time, business really started to pick up. We now employed four upholsterers, including my dear friend Martin.

So there I was: seven short years after the end of World War II, an orphaned survivor of the Nazi concentrations camps, an uneducated, unsophisticated refugee who, thanks to God and my own determination and hard work, now had my own business — with employees! And a truck! A great apartment! And best of all, a beautiful, smart wife who was expecting our first child! What more could any man want?

My American Dream was coming true.

This was 1952, however, and since the major powers in the world still hadn't learned how to live in peace after the horrors of World War II, the Korean War was dragging on. Most of us didn't know exactly where Korea was, or why there even was a war. I had, of course, registered, as legally required, for the Draft, the US Selective Service agency that has the authority for conscripting, or drafting, men into the military. And I had noticed that many other young men, including Jack, were already in the military. We, however, were too busy building our new lives to even think about

Part III: The American Dream

war again. So when I got a letter from the Draft Board to appear for my physical, I was stunned.

I was immediately overwhelmed by conflicting emotions. I was thrilled to be finally achieving the American Dream — which I felt was the best way of all to counteract the devastation of Hitler's Third Reich. I was also frustrated because all my recent achievements were about to be taken away. At the same time, however, I was flooded with gratitude to this great country for taking me in, and making it all possible. Clearly, I needed to participate in keeping the American Dream safe from its enemies. So, in spite of my mixed emotions, I never doubted what I should do. I went in for my physical. And of course, I passed it, thereby earning the classification of "1-A," meaning I was eligible to serve in the US Military. They only gave me four weeks' time to close up my business and report for active duty.

So Robert and I sadly settled up with the hotel owner and started to liquidate our business. Just like that, I went from being an up-and-coming business man to being a man who was out of business. Upsetting as this was, however, it was not in my nature to wallow in disappointment, anger or frustration. I'd refused countless times in the past to let much more difficult obstacles get me down. Since we needed an income, I immediately began delivering laundry for a local dry-cleaning business. And, as always, I was determined to become a valuable employee. So I made a point of taking on additional responsibilities in order to impress our customers. My boss knew that I'd always take on extra work, like making deliveries after hours and on Sundays. By providing extra services, I was able to develop a positive reputation throughout my delivery area. As word spread, my actions and reliability began to attract additional customers, so my boss was happy, and my route expanded

28. Achieving the American Dream

so I earned more money. As always, going beyond the basic job description paid off for me.

Jean was getting closer to her delivery date, and as if we didn't already have enough on our minds, she was involved in a car accident. She was at a stop sign and someone plowed into her from behind. They didn't have seat belts then, so she really got smacked around. Self-disciplined as always, however, she just took the other driver's contact information and went on in to work. Jean didn't even call me because she didn't want to bother me while I was working. So she completed her work as quickly as possible, took the rest of the day off, and went to see her doctor—who ordered her to stay in bed until the baby was born.

This frightening time brought up memories of when I found my sister Lola in that St. Ottilien hospital bed, nine-months pregnant. It was almost like history repeating itself—and the thought of leaving Jean in this condition to go into the Army was unbearable. Unexpectedly, however, some good luck came our way. Jean's doctor, who knew about these things, was kind enough to give us a very special letter for my Draft Board. This letter permitted the Draft Board to give me a *deferment*, which would postpone my military service until after the birth of our baby. And so we were able to breathe a little bit better knowing that I would be around for the arrival of our first child.

As it turned out, Jean had had a couple of false alarms and was now two weeks late. Since my in-laws had come to stay with us to help, we had a full house, with everyone anxious about when the baby would arrive. Around four in the morning, it became clear that it was time to take Jean to the hospital. After some discussion about what to do if this was another false alarm, my father-in-law decided that he

Part III: The American Dream

would take Jean to the hospital. I could follow them so that I could go straight to work if it was another false alarm. This time, however, it was for real. I spent seven very nervous hours in the waiting room with my in-laws. And typical of my considerate wife, she gave birth to our first daughter at 11:55 am, just in time for lunch. As if any of us could eat! I did, however, manage to buy and distribute the traditional cigars in celebration of becoming a father.

When I was finally allowed into Jean's room, I carefully hugged and kissed my wife, and then, with some butterflies in my stomach, looked into the incubator to see our perfect little girl. I couldn't really believe what I was seeing. A brand new human being created by the love Jean and I shared. Such a miracle! I touched her softly, almost afraid that she would bruise or break. Then I counted her tiny, perfectly formed fingers and toes. So it was official. I was a father. I thought about my feelings for my own father, and finally understood how he must have felt about his children. Now there was someone who was going to feel the same way about me. I couldn't let her down. Lots of emotions seemed to dance through me: responsibility, joy and sorrow — fear. How I longed to be able to show my parents their granddaughter. How proud they would have been. We named her Sherry, after my beloved mother, Shaindel. Her middle name, Michelle, was in honor of Jean's brother, Marcus, who had been killed while serving in the highly dangerous US Glider Infantry.*

For five days, I visited Jean and Sherry in the hospital, always bringing flowers and little gifts. Jean and I held

---

*Many Jewish families observe the custom of naming newborns in memory of a beloved relative who has passed away. It is thought that this keeps the name and memory of the deceased alive, and creates a bond between the generations.

28. Achieving the American Dream

each other's hands, and talked excitedly about our little girl's future. What a beauty she would be. What talents she would have. What dreams and accomplishments!

Well, my lessons on fatherhood weren't the only lessons that I learned once our precious daughter was born. Had I done some research when I first received my draft notice, I would have known that my temporary draft deferment for being an expectant father would change on the very day that the baby was born. The good news was that they did not draft fathers. The bad news was that I was already and unnecessarily, out of business. It was a hard lesson to learn, and one that I never forgot. To this day, I always do research on any project that I plan to take on.

29. *A NEW CAREER*

> *"No labor, however humble, is dishonoring."*
> ~ The Talmud

Well now that I wasn't going into the military, I needed to get a better job. I'd heard from another delivery-truck driver about the great pay and working conditions at UPS (United Parcel Service). So I went there and applied for a job. Luckily for us, they hired me, and I remained a devoted employee for 25 years. Throughout my time at UPS, I understood, as always, that my success depended upon doing my best and becoming indispensible to my bosses. So, as usual, I found out what had to be done and then went ahead and did it well. I was surprised that the trucking industry has so many functions, and I made a point of quickly learning everything that I could — from loading the trucks, to hauling huge, long-distance loads through the middle of the night.

As routine as this kind of job might seem to some people, there were occasions when our shipments had historic international significance. For example, during the early 1950s, there had been a worldwide polio epidemic. This horrific and often deadly disease targeted children, often leaving survivors deprived of muscle control and paralyzed for life. Of these, the "lucky" ones were only unable to walk. Many others were unable to even breathe on their own, and had to live inside metal ventilators called "iron lungs."

Since the former American president, Franklin Roosevelt was a polio survivor, he had spearheaded our government's interest in curing this hideous disease. Fortunately, a brilliant young medical researcher, Jonas Salk, who was the son of Russian Jewish immigrants, would soon develop

Part III: The American Dream

the miracle vaccine to cure this devastating plague. The entire world celebrated this medical achievement, and Salk became a national hero. And in 1955, when this vaccine finally became available across the United States, much of it was distributed through UPS!

Needless to say, I was thrilled and honored to be connected, even in a small way, to this important moment in history. Little did I know that this "small way" was about to become quite big! One afternoon, my supervisor called me into his office. His supervisor and some other members of UPS management were also there. You can imagine how anxious this situation made me. Had I made a terrible mistake that would result in my being fired? However, upon seeing everyone's warm smiles, I quickly realized that all those important people wouldn't be needed just to fire me, so I relaxed a bit.

My supervisor then explained to me that they were all very impressed by my service, and that something very special had come up. It seems that the *Los Angeles Times* wanted to spotlight the first shipment of the polio vaccine. They would be writing an article and needed a photo for the front page. They'd asked the management to select a worthy employee to be included in the photo. Well, among all their hundreds of employees, they chose me. When I got over the shock, I was deeply honored. This photo was a very big deal, and ended up on the front page! In fact, it was picked up by other newspapers and seen all over the country. Talk about achieving the American Dream! Here I was less than 10 years out of a Nazi concentration camp, and I was now on the front page of a major American newspaper as part of a celebration of one of the most important advances in medical history—a life-saving vaccine that was developed by a Russian Jewish man!

29. A New Career

Since I never turned any assignment down, sometimes I unexpectedly ended up doing UPS work that was not delivery related. Our station had a monthly newsletter, "The Big Idea," that suddenly was in need of a reporter. I was already very busy and since I knew that I'd be the last person to write a column in English, I figured that someone more competent—more American—would do it. When no one else would volunteer, however, I figured, why not? I knew that behind every door there were opportunities that I wouldn't have dreamed of, so I decided to go through this new door. And for some reason, they agreed! My responsibilities included reporting on employee achievements, promotions, and special personal events. I even had my own column with my photo at the top! Jean corrected my English, but I did my own titles. It was like being a gossip columnist! I really enjoyed meeting and interviewing so many people, and I became well-known for my human-interest stories and contests.

One time in particular, I stirred up quite a bit of interest when I wrote that my dear wife and I would be spending the weekend engaged in one of our favorite pastimes: "ghoating." Whenever any of my co-workers brought the subject up, instead of explaining what this meant, I just told them to read next month's column and find out! As an immigrant who was fascinated by the spelling of English words, I'd wanted my readers to understand how it felt to be mystified by the meanings and pronunciations of what looked like familiar words. So in the next month's column, I explained that "goating" was really "fishing." In other words, I used phonetics! So the "f" of "fishing" was represented by the "gh" sound as in "enough." The "o" stood for the "ih" sound in "women," the "a" is silent, and the "ti" expressed the "sh" sound in "nation." Everyone loved it, and I never tired of being asked how the "ghoating" went!

Part III: The American Dream

Adding to the pleasure of this job was the annual huge banquet honoring each station's writers, and I always won a prize. Who could have ever imagined that I would win a trophy for writing in English? Who could have imagined that yet another kind of writing would become important to me in the future?

Among its many other benefits, UPS provided a very nice financial incentive system to encourage drivers to complete their routes more quickly. I was always up for this kind of challenge, and made it a point to finish my route as rapidly as possible. Whenever I returned early to the station, my supervisor would ask me to take on other routes for people who were running late. This was hard work, but it meant that I was able to earn overtime pay. My bosses knew that at a moment's notice, day or night, that I would fill-in and meet their highest standards. I never turned down any work, whether it was on my day-off or even on a holiday. Although I may have started at the bottom of the job-ladder, and faced many personal challenges, I was determined to make it to the top. And as a result, I became one of the highest paid drivers in all of Southern California.

Another highlight of my years with UPS was the very impressive Annual Awards Dinner. In addition to the wonderful food and entertainment, there was the presentation of the prestigious "Safe Driver Award," given to those drivers who had not had a single accident during the preceding year. And for each and every one of my 25 years driving for UPS, I was honored to always be one of the recipients. This was considered quite an accomplishment. As I look back now, it's astonishing to think about the number of hours I put in behind the wheel, and the miles I covered in 25 years, without ever having an accident.

Well, achieving the American Dream was definitely keeping me busy. Being a new Dad and having a busy

29. A New Career

career as a professional truck driver didn't lessen my determination to make a success of myself. So I also had a side-line business with a friend doing odd jobs. Between us, we could build or repair just about anything, and if we couldn't, we brought in someone who could. On top of all that, I attended Roosevelt High night-school to prepare for my citizenship test!

Unlike my various jobs and classes that were for the most part routine and predictable, my life as a new father was a combination of the routine and the completely unpredictable. It was amazing how such a tiny creature could impose her own fluctuating routine on two adults! And depending upon her eating and sleeping and diaper-changing habits, Sherry didn't hesitate to let us know whenever the routine changed! Everything we thought and everything we did, revolved around her and her needs. So whenever I wasn't at work or school, I did all the same things with the baby that Jean did. From feeding to bathing to changing diapers, I was a real participatory father! If she cried in the middle of the night, I let Jean sleep while I rushed to make sure Sherry's needs were met. Every activity was a joy and a delight! Fortunately, Jean was able to stay home with Sherry during the day, so I was able to go to my various jobs and attend night-school. My lack of sleep however, sometimes made my daytime activities challenging! What was indescribable was the range of intense emotions that flooded through me on a continuous basis. I was in a constant state of awe of this little creature, and each time I made her smile, I felt as if I had won a victory. Every new accomplishment was cause for celebration. And when she first said, "Daddy," I was totally captivated. It's almost 58 years later, and I still am. With the birth of my daughter, I finally understood why I had been allowed to survive. I could see how my parents

Part III: The American Dream

would live on through her. And hopefully, in some way, through me, she has been able to know them.

30. AN AMERICAN CITIZEN

> *"Go confidently in the direction of your dreams.
> Live the life you've imagined."*
> ~ Henry David Thoreau (1817-1862)
> American Author

My life seemed to be progressing well. I was working hard and achieving my goal of living the American Dream. Following Liberation, marrying Jean, and becoming a father, the next major milestone of my life occurred in 1953, when I became US citizen. This was a very big deal for me and I was indescribably proud and honored to be a citizen of the country that had allowed me to have a life. So along with other immigrants, I had to know English, history, and all about American federal, state and city governments. I studied very hard in preparation for achieving this goal.

Taking the test was a strange experience, because we each had to take it individually, one-on-one with a judge. And of course, it would be all oral—and in English! I was especially worried because my formal education had ended when I was 11, and I felt that this could be a handicap. I studied hard and with high hopes went in to take the test. Despite my determination and effort, however, passing the test was not easy. In fact, I failed the first time because I missed one question about California! One question! Instead of letting this disappointment overwhelm me, however, it motivated me to try again. I'd certainly faced tougher challenges in the past. So I returned to the books, made sure I knew everything about California, retook the test, and passed it! Needless to say, when I received my official citizenship papers, there was a big celebration!

In case you were wondering, it was during the process of becoming a citizen, that I added the second "s" to my

Part III: The American Dream

My Certificate of U.S. Citizenship.
Los Angeles, CA (1953)
Lesser Family Collection

30. An American Citizen

last name, making it Lesser. This spelling corresponded to how my name was pronounced by Americans. Having finally become a real American, I wanted my name to be easier for Americans to pronounce and spell.

Having now achieved what I had set out to do, I eagerly looked forward to what life would bring next! Well, what life brought next, in 1957, was a beautiful new house, complete with a backyard for barbeques, in the San Fernando Valley. And we moved in just in time for the arrival of our second precious daughter, Gail. Even though I thought I had become a "pro" at fatherhood, I was just as nervous this time as I'd been with Sherry! And Jean's labor was so short that I didn't even have time to run out and buy cigars! As with Sherry, our joy at Gail's arrival was indescribable. It was yet another miracle for our little family.

In 1962, in order to start building towards the next stage of the American Dream, we sold our house and purchased a four-plex back in Los Angeles, right around the corner from the Singers' duplex. We moved into one apartment and rented out the other three, an arrangement which would allow us to earn money on our investment. Little did I know then that this would be the beginning of my career as a real-estate investor. Throughout the following years, we worked hard to purchase, renovate, manage and sell rental properties.

One particular property would present an unexpected and unpleasant challenge. We went to look at it to see if might be good for a rental property investment. And then we surprised ourselves when we fell in love with it on the spot. Even though it needed some modernizing, we just knew that this was our dream home. And in a move that was out of character for us, without doing any research, we went ahead and purchased it that same night from the owner. So we sold our four-plex, and moved into the

Part III: The American Dream

upper unit of new 2-family duplex. We all were so excited to have such a big apartment—with three bedrooms plus a den, there would be plenty of room for everyone. Things were looking up for the Lessers!

Soon after moving in, we started remodeling the apartment to better suit our needs. After checking out the work and references of a local contractor and liking what we saw, we enthusiastically hired him to completely redo the place. Much to our shock and frustration, however, the whole remodeling experience soon turned out to be a nightmare. It became very clear that I had been too trusting. I had believed everything that the smooth-talking contractor had verbally promised us—specifically that he was a *licensed* and *bonded* contractor. Later, in reading the fine print, I saw that he was *bondable*, not bonded. I would soon find out that there is a huge difference between the two.*

The contract I signed was on bright pink paper, with pink ink, and many of the terms were on the reverse side and were in very fine print. We had given the contractor a deposit, and the next day his crew started dismantling the kitchen and bathroom. And then they abruptly stopped, saying that they wanted more money. When we contacted the contractor, he pointed out that according to the contract, after a certain amount of work had been completed, he was entitled to more money. By the time he had demolished the kitchen and the bathroom, he had received more than 60% of his money, and then he stopped again. It seems that he had conveniently left out the completion date in writing, even though there were many verbal promises made. After

---

*The phrase, Licensed and Bonded, means (1) that the contractor has fulfilled government competency requirements and is permitted to conduct business in a specific city, county or state; and (2) that money has been set aside by the contractor, and controlled by the state, to be available for claims that might be filed against him.

30. An American Citizen

numerous telephone calls and pleadings, he finally sent a couple of the guys over to start some of the frame work. But this didn't last long. Once again, the contract indicated that he had some more money coming to them. By this time, even though the job was less than 50% completed, he already had received 75% of his money.

Every so often, he would send someone over who would stay for an hour, pound in a few nails here and there, and then disappear. This dragged on for months. We had no kitchen, no master bathroom. Our dream home was filled with dust and chaos. Fortunately, Jean and the girls were good sports so we acted as if we were camping and just made the best of it. Finally, I couldn't stand it anymore and decided to go to see the contractor. Jean, of course, wouldn't let me go alone. Since neither one us is particularly intimidating, we figured that going together would be a show of force.

When we arrived, it was clear that the contractor was not pleased to see us. In fact, instead of inviting us into his office, he led us out to a balcony at the end of the building's second floor hallway. We thought this was strange, but the whole situation was so strange that it didn't occur to us that it could also be dangerously strange. He was a big man — almost bigger than both of us put together. At first we tried speaking reasonably with him, but he used his threatening manner to intimidate me. I just couldn't believe that this kind of thing could happen in 1964 in America. So I stood up to him by making what I thought were very logical and justifiable requests. His immediate response was a hate-filled glare, and then he silently reached out, picked me up several feet from the floor, walked me over to the edge of the balcony, and as Jean screamed, threatened to throw me over the railing. He shook me violently, bellowing that he

Part III: The American Dream

would finish the job whenever he was good and ready, and not a minute earlier. And he added with a laugh, that if I didn't like it, I could sue him. And then, to top it all off, he said that the next time I came to his office, he would kill me.

At that point I don't think that I was even breathing. I don't know what was more terrifying, the fear that he would drop me, or that Jean would try to rescue me and end up getting hurt. Fortunately, he put me down and we were able to make a hurried escape. Shaken, we rushed home and immediately contacted an attorney who promised to look into the situation. The next thing we heard was that the "contractor" had declared bankruptcy and disappeared. This experience was a shocking reminder of the evil of the human spirit. And it reminded me to always read the fine print.

After this rude awakening, we still had to finish the remodel, so we decided to hire individual subcontractors for each individual part of the job. After we had ended up paying twice to remodel our home, I realized that even if I always went over the fine print on contracts, it was often written in such a confusing way that ordinary people really needed help from an expert. So I decided that I needed to become an expert and enrolled at City College to study contractual law. This meant that I would be working full-time at UPS, working part-time buying and managing properties, in addition to being a good husband, father, and citizen, plus also going to school!

30. *AMERICAN ADVENTURES*

> *"Without ambition one starts nothing.*
> *Without work one finishes nothing.*
> *The prize will not be sent to you.*
> *You have to win it."*
> ~ Ralph Waldo Emerson (1803-1882)
> American Essayist, Poet

To me, attaining the American Dream meant owning property, actually owning a piece of America. So in addition to the various full and part-time jobs I worked, I was always on the lookout for suitable properties that I could buy. I would then fix them up and either keep them for income, or resell them in order to buy something bigger. If I kept a property, it was necessary to maintain and manage it. Today it's hard to imagine how Jean and I packed so much work into each and every day, but we were young and strong and somehow able to keep it all under control.

While attending City College, I found that the more I learned, the more interested I became in the business of real estate. It became clear that I would enjoy working full-time in this field. So I decided to prepare myself to eventually leave UPS and make real estate my career. This would have to be a gradual transition because, as a family man, it would be very risky to give up a good paying job. Additionally, I feared that my lack of both an education or a life-long circle of friends would put me at a real disadvantage when competing with other American-born realtors. Furthermore, since I was not going to give up my job for quite a while, it would mean that any time I wasn't working would have to be spent studying and in school. I would be separated from my family a great deal. And it

Part III: The American Dream

would put more responsibility on Jean's shoulders. So this was a time of intense pressure and soul-searching. How could I succeed despite my shortcomings? How could I risk putting an uncertain career goal ahead of my family's current security?

Well, although I was questioning my own ability to take on this challenge, my family had no doubts about my competence. With their encouragement, I realized that the many obstacles that I had overcome in the past were far more demanding than the one I now faced in becoming a realtor. They also assured me that I wouldn't be doing it alone — they would support me in every way. So I decided to go for it. And just as in the past, I knew that in order to compete, I would have to be much better than just good. I would have to be the best in this profession.

So in addition to my courses at City College, I enrolled in Real Estate School. I hit the books pretty hard until I passed my real estate salesman's test in 1966 and received my salesman's license. My confidence grew once I had proven to myself that I could achieve my goals despite the obstacles. I soon became a part-time salesman with a well-known local realtor. I started out by "sitting in open houses." This means that I greeted potential buyers at open houses, and provided them with the information they needed to make a good decision. I went beyond this responsibility, however, and also did research to find them the right house for their likes and needs. This was very time-consuming, but it demonstrated my commitment to providing excellent service. You can imagine how busy I was. And when, on top of everything else she was doing, Jean volunteered to get a real estate license to help me out, we became as great a team in real estate as we were in our marriage.

I soon realized that my goal was to open my own real-estate office. According to the requirements, however, I

31. American Adventures

needed to work for four years as a part-time salesman before I could apply for a broker's license. So while I worked both jobs, went to school, and managed our properties, I also studied for the broker's test. And as frugally as we always lived, we needed to live even more frugally in order to save money to invest in the new real estate business. I also needed to have a financial cushion in place after I left UPS because, realistically, we had to be prepared for the possibility that we wouldn't make a single sale that first year.

After two years of this, I decided it was time to speed things up. Since I would eventually have to compete with full-time agents at large well-established companies, I thought it would be a good idea to get my name circulating in the area as soon as possible. I wanted to find a better approach than distributing the typical fliers and cold-calling. But what could it be? Well, one sleepless night after much brainstorming, an unusual idea came to me: Why not write a column in a local paper about real estate? I'd learned how to write a column at UPS, so I knew I could do it! And by this time I felt fairly knowledgeable and pretty well-versed in most aspects of real estate. I knew that I could always research the answers when necessary, and Jean would make sure that my English was correct.

Having made this decision, I didn't want to waste time, so the very next day I went over to the office of *The Reporter*, which was a small weekly, throw-away paper delivered to each home in our area. I met with the editor, told him my idea, and waited hopefully for his positive response. Which he soon gave me. He particularly liked the idea because no other small papers had a real estate column, so this would make his paper unique. Of course since the column was considered to be advertising for my business, I had to pay him for the use of the space. The cost was not cheap, but

Part III: The American Dream

as long as he promised me exclusivity — meaning that no one else could write a real estate column — I figured that in the long run it should pay off. He was generous with the space, giving me two full-length columns, and even put my photograph at the top. The headline was, "All You Need to Know about Real Estate, Questions and Answers." Of course I included a "disclaimer clause" stating that I was not an attorney, and therefore readers should be sure to consult an attorney before acting on any advice from my column.

Well, much to my surprise, after my first few articles appeared, questions from readers really started to roll in! In fact, the mail-man soon was trudging up our sidewalk with heavy bags of mail on a daily basis. We began to feel sorry for him! Jean and I spent hours sitting on the floor and sorting the mail. We categorized each pile according to topic, and prioritized topics by how many questions each received. Then, in order of popularity, I would research and then discuss each topic in my column, making sure to incorporate the answers to each question. For months we were unable to use our living room for anything other than sorting the mail!

Exciting as this was, however, I still felt somewhat handicapped by my lack of a formal American education. I worried about competing with educated American agents who I figured spoke and wrote excellent English. Another challenge I faced as a newcomer, was my lack of local contacts. Between their families, friends, neighbors, schoolmates and colleagues, it seemed as if American realtors already had a large base of potential customers. Despite these drawbacks, however, once I had made my choice to become a realtor, I just plowed ahead, worked hard, and did the best job possible. So along with my job at UPS, my college and real-estate classes, studying for my broker's license, managing our properties, holding open-houses

31. American Adventures

on Sundays, being a husband and father, and researching and writing my column, I was slowly but surely becoming known in the community as a real estate expert!

I soon realized that despite my lack of a basic education, I had managed to develop many important skills and behaviors that other realtors might not possess. When contrasted with the many real estate courses I had taken, my work ethic, integrity, authentic desire to help people, and determination to succeed, my lack of a formal education and English fluency really had very little importance. I was further encouraged and delighted that my little newspaper column had turned into an effective way to become well-known and respected. And although it didn't come quickly or easily, its success helped to compensate for what I had initially lacked in contacts. I realized that just as in the past, hard work and determination would help me overcome what had seemed like overwhelming obstacles.

Little by little, I started to become successful in the prestigious West Los Angeles/Beverly Hills real estate market. And in 1970, after much study, I passed the test to earn a broker's license, officially making me a realtor! I joined the Greater West Side Real Estate Broker's Association, and Jean and I looked forward to a bright future. Adding to the joy of our accomplishments was the birth in 1973 of our granddaughter, Robyn. And while this unimaginable joy was accompanied by the sadness of my own parents' absence, Jean and I were particularly fortunate and grateful to have been able to share our joy with her wonderful parents. Sadly, this pleasure would only last another few years. In 1975, my beloved father-in-law, Julius Singer, passed away. This was a great tragedy in our lives. Both Mr. and Mrs. Singer were like parents to me, and I loved and respected them very much. Mr. Singer was always very supportive of all my endeavors, even if it

Part III: The American Dream

was something so ridiculous, as me deciding to go uranium prospecting!

What did I know about uranium? Or prospecting? Nothing. But I was determined to find out. And what I found out was that uranium is a radioactive chemical element that is necessary for nuclear power. In 1945, the United States used the newly invented atom bomb to end World War II by bombing the Japanese cities of Hiroshima and Nagasaki. It is used in science, space exploration, medicine and nuclear power plants that provide electricity for homes, businesses and industry. And since the nuclear industry was just beginning to emerge in the 1950s, it was all very exciting. Everyone thought that nuclear energy would be bigger than electricity, and since uranium was essential to nuclear power, the international race to find uranium was on — there were fortunes to be made!

And so there began a mad frenzy all over the western United States. People seemed to go crazy just like during the California Gold Rush in the mid-1800s. Imagine, going prospecting in the 1950s! Today, no one who hadn't seen it would believe it. And one of the places that this race was particularly popular was around a little town called Rosemont near Lancaster, California, only two hours' drive from Los Angeles.

Well, at that time I had two buddies who loved hunting for just about anything, and they often invited me to go along. I'd always declined because I couldn't stand the violence, but this time, they weren't hunting with guns, so I accepted their invitation. This would be a real American adventure!

Since prospecting, just like driving a truck, was an unusual activity for a young, religious Jewish man, I decided to discuss it first with my father-in-law. Much

31. American Adventures

to my surprise, he said, "Okay, so maybe it's foolish, but if you really want to do it, go ahead. Maybe you'll learn something; just be careful." I realized that this adventure was totally out of his world, but since he didn't try to talk me out of it, I knew he wouldn't be disappointed in me if I went ahead with it—even if I failed. And of course, I'd be very careful. So my adventure in uranium mining began.

The first thing we needed to do was to get outfitted with the right clothes and equipment. My buddies already had the clothes and guns, but I had to go shopping! I didn't want or need a shotgun, and certainly didn't plan to use it, but I wanted to fit in with my friends, so I bought one. Since I didn't plan to shoot anything, I didn't bother doing any target practice. Looking back, it's interesting to me now to realize that this would be the first time since my training with the Zionist group after the war that I'd be handling any kind of weapon. And this one was much different than the old German Luger that we had all practiced on.

One of the guys had a pick-up truck, which was all we needed at first. Later we rented a trailer that included a power source for the big drills we would be using once we started mining. We chipped in and bought a large, very fancy tent at Sears, along with all the other essentials we thought we'd need. I even bought something called a *Scintillator*, which was an extremely expensive and highly sensitive version of a *Geiger Counter*,* the device typically used by miners to detect the presence of uranium in the ground. The Scintillator, which unlike the Geiger Counter

---

* The *Geiger Counter* was invented in 1908 and named for one of its inventors, Hans Geiger. It's interesting to note that during the 1950s, the Las Vegas area was famous for its nuclear testing, and today, 60 years later, the use of nearby Yucca Mountain to store nuclear waste is still a source of national controversy.

Part III: The American Dream

didn't make any noise, had a gauge that could indicate the presence of uranium from inside a car or even in an airplane! And it had a compass that pointed out the direction of the uranium's location.

Once we were equipped and at least looking as if we knew what we were doing, we headed out. We didn't have a particular location in mind; we just drove inland until the Scintillator started registering uranium. And we ended up in Rosemont, California. When the Scintillator indicated that we were in the midst of a lot of uranium, we looked at each other excitedly, turned off the road, got out of the truck and started using the smaller Geiger Counter. Its loud, rhythmic clicking noises strongly indicated that we were in the middle of a deposit that stretched at least a three-quarter-square-mile area surrounding where we stood. We started walking around in further concentric circles, following the Geiger Counter to try to figure out just how big the deposit was. We couldn't believe what was happening—the Geiger Counter seemed to be going crazy—indicating that there was uranium everywhere! You can imagine the dreams of riches that filled our heads!

We ended up circling all around the mountain. Three grown men following this crazy Geiger Counter and already planning the gifts we would buy for our wives—who had laughed at our plan to get rich! Turns out that the whole huge mountain was "hot"! Meaning that it was filled with uranium—and that we definitely were going to be rich! We had to circle the entire area and "stake it out" to make a claim, which would legally entitle us to mine uranium within the perimeter of our claim. To do this, we created what we called monuments—big piles of boulders and rocks, around a quarter of a mile apart, on the top of which we placed a can that contained a description of our claim. Then we had to race to the County Registrar's Office to

31. American Adventures

register the claim. While we were staking our claim at one end, however, someone else was doing the same thing at the other end! You can imagine the frustration we felt when we found out about each other! Fortunately, when we met to discuss the situation, we were able to prove that we had gotten there first, so the claim was ours.

The next weekend we rented a trailer that included a power source. Now we needed to get serious and find a place to create a base camp. After doing a careful search, we found just the place between two protective mountains. This was where we pitched the big tent. Now the real work would begin: We had to start digging. Our plan was to come back every weekend, pitch the tent and continue digging until we struck it rich! And that's just what we did. Every weekend for five weeks we went through the same process of packing our equipment and supplies, waving goodbye to our laughing wives, driving out to the site, pitching our tent, finding a likely spot, and finally, digging. This mountain was so solid, however, that even with our powerful sledge hammers, it took two hours of strenuous digging to fill one little bucket! Such pitiful results from such difficult work! We soon started using power-drills to create holes for the dynamite sticks with which we could blast tunnels into the mountainside. I never could have dreamed as a slave laborer back in Durnhau's horrific rock quarry that one day I'd be doing similar physical labor. This time, however, it was voluntary—it was an adventure. And my friends, family and I would be the ones to benefit from the results!

Despite the back-breaking labor, we refused to give up because we could just feel that the uranium was there—all we had to do was find the vein! So we kept trying—digging over and over again. Well, several weeks after we'd begun, we pitched the tent as usual and laid out our sleeping bags.

Part III: The American Dream

That night, totally exhausted after our hard day's digging, we immediately fell asleep. In the middle of the night, there came a sudden terrible howling and a brutal wind seemed to attack us. It felt like a train was coming right through our tent, destroying everything in its path. Within minutes, our beautiful Sears tent was ripped to shreds around us. The two-by-four that supported the ceiling became a pile of splinters. And there I was, hopping around like a crazed bunny trying to hold up another support beam—and in my sleeping bag because in my rush to get out of it, I'd jammed the zipper. Well, when it was finally over, we looked at each other in shock that we'd survived and also with humor because we were each completely covered in black dust. Desperately needing to shower and get some sleep, we quickly cleaned up some of the damage, loaded our stuff in the truck and trailer, and took off toward the nearest town to find a hotel for the night.

On the way to the hotel, we stopped at a drive-in for hamburgers and Cokes. In talking to some of the other customers there, we learned that our safe, calm camping spot between the two mountains was actually a well-known and very dangerous wind-tunnel! It had never occurred to us to research the location in advance. Our problems continued when we got into town and found out that there was only one motel. And it was a real dump. And it only had one room available. And in that room there was only one lumpy bed. But we were so beaten up and tired that we didn't care—we just wanted to shower and sleep. That didn't seem to be too much to ask.

When we'd unloaded our equipment and dragged it all up to our room, one of the guys suddenly turned to me and asked, "What did you do with the detonator caps?" I told him that I hadn't done anything with the caps; I'd never

31. American Adventures

touched them. Once again we all looked at each other in shock—detonator caps could be very dangerous! We raced back to the truck and searched every inch. The detonators were not there. We tried to mentally retrace our steps and realized with frustration that when we'd gathered up and thrown all the food wrappings in the garbage, we must have also thrown away the detonators. We were so terrified that they would somehow detonate and hurt someone that we postponed the shower and sleep and headed back to the drive-in. And just in case the detonators had somehow dropped out of the truck and were laying somewhere along the road, one of us drove slowly while the other two walked, carefully looking for the caps. Can you imagine what we must have looked like? We were lucky not to have been arrested. And we were really lucky because much to our surprise, we did find the detonators! So exhausted, filthy, and by this time, somewhat dazed, but excited by the prospect of a shower and sleep, we once again headed for the motel.

Having just barely dragged ourselves up the stairs, I was grateful when my kind friends told me to go ahead and be first to use the communal bathroom and shower, which was located down the hall from our room. I quickly scraped off my destroyed clothes and reached for the faucet. Would you be surprised to learn that when I turned it on, there was no water? Nothing. I banged and twisted and probably used some colorful language, but nothing worked. So I gave up and returned to our room where there was a little sink. Unfortunately, the only thing that came out was black, oily mud. Just disgusting. You should have seen us. Three grown, sleep-deprived men who had been battered and bruised and now couldn't even clean themselves up. So we dusted ourselves off as much as possible and then

Part III: The American Dream

just dropped on the bed. And passed out. But we would not be having pleasant dreams that night.

In the middle of what was left of the night, one of the guys started grabbing us like a madman and screaming, "What's going on?" Bright lights flashed through the window and the bed was actually moving—rolling across the wooden floor. Nothing made any sense. Was it an earthquake? Martians? We tried to grab our belongings and get out of the building before it collapsed on us, but with everything moving, it was hard to stand up. Then, just as suddenly as it had begun, the noise and vibrating stopped. We looked out of the window and were stunned to see train tracks not ten feet away from us!

Once again we went to bed, almost afraid to sleep. But we must have lost consciousness because we almost leaped up to the ceiling when deafening pounding noises roared through the room. This time, however, it wasn't the wind hurtling through our tent or a train right outside our window. This time it was the motel's old steam radiators. Apparently when the manager turned the heat on in the early morning, the rush of steam hitting air pockets in the pipes caused the ear-drum blasting racket. At this point it felt as if we were in some really bad movie. Since by then it was morning, we gave up on sleep and drove home. Needless to say, this adventure provided Jean and the girls with lots of opportunities to have fun at Daddy's expense!

Despite our challenges, however, we three stalwart prospectors were not daunted! Once we'd recuperated, we decided to take the shredded tent back to Sears to see if they would make good on its guarantee. Much to our surprise and delight, Sears replaced the tent! Over the next couple weekends, we excavated an enormous hole. Upon our arrival one early morning, when we looked into the hole, we were horrified to see that it had become the residence

31. American Adventures

of hundreds and hundreds of slithering rattlesnakes. Fortunately, the other guys, who were life-long hunters, had rifles and shotguns which they didn't hesitate to use on the snakes. Not wanting any part of this mayhem, I took a little walk until it was over.

Well, our work finally paid off when we found some rocks that registered high uranium content. We rushed one to the government Assayer's office to test samples to see what percent of it was uranium. We weren't afraid to handle it because we'd been told uranium wasn't dangerous until it was processed. And of course we wore heavy-duty gloves.

We left our precious rock with the Assayer and eagerly went back a week later for the report. We were so excited about how our lives would change once we'd become millionaires! Much to our disappointment, however, it turned out that we hadn't hit a vein. In fact, even though the mountain was filled with uranium, it wasn't in veins. In fact, it permeated the whole area. And much to our disappointment, we learned that it would require a ton of this kind of rock to be processed down to one ounce of uranium. We'd have to harvest tons of it and then pay to have it transported all the way to Washington State where it would be processed down into small amounts of usable uranium.

So our adventure in mining was over. Disappointing and exhausting as it was, however, I did not regret the attempt. I have found throughout my life that it's necessary to take risks in order to achieve anything. And although sometimes the risk isn't immediately worth it, the lessons learned always come in handy later in life. The main lesson that I learned from this American adventure was to stick with real estate!

32. BEN LESSER AND ASSOCIATES

> *"Nothing can stop the man with the right mental attitude from achieving his goal; nothing on earth can help the man with the wrong mental attitude."*
> ~ Thomas Jefferson (1743-1826)
> Author, Statesman,
> American President (1801-1809)

And sticking with real estate is exactly what I did. Throughout the 1970s, Jean and I continued to work hard toward achieving the American Dream by living frugally and investing in properties. There was one special occasion, however, that I decided warranted a luxurious commemoration. It was April 25, 1978, Jean's 48th birthday. I took her out to a Cadillac dealer because it was the first year that the brand new Seville appeared in the showrooms. This wasn't unusual, because in those days people used to like going to car dealerships just to see what was new. I casually mentioned that I thought that a good-looking new car would make us look successful to potential clients.

At first Jean objected, questioning why we should go and look at cars which were entirely out of our reach. I assured her that I'd heard a lot about this beautiful Seville; that it would be fun to see what all the fuss was about and perhaps, even take it out for a test drive. What I didn't tell her was that years before, on the very day that I'd quit smoking cold-turkey after hearing about the connection between smoking and cancer, I opened up a savings account into which I deposited my daily cigarette money, plus any tip money which I'd collected. This secret account had finally grown large enough to pay for a new car.

Part III: The American Dream

A few days before I took Jean out to the dealership, I'd picked out a car that I knew she would love. I made all the arrangements and paid for it all in cash prior to our arrival. At first she objected to test driving the car because it was entirely out of our reach. After the test drive, I wished her a happy birthday and handed her the keys, complete with a "pink slip" (certificate of ownership), as a birthday present. Well, needless to say, she was stunned and elated. And surprised that I could keep such a secret from her for so long!

We now had the beautiful new car, but it wasn't until later in the year that we felt ready to open up our own real-estate company. Before I could leave my job at UPS, there were two important things that I needed to do. One was to find a suitable location for our first office. Eventually, we found and leased a building on 3rd Street near Fairfax, furnished it, and ordered the outdoor sign saying Ben Lesser & Associates. The second task was something that I wasn't looking forward to, called "farming" for clients. This meant that in addition to working full-time at UPS, I would have to walk up and down neighborhood streets, go door to door, introduce myself and let people know that we were open and ready to service any and all of their real-estate needs. I knew how negatively people can react to uninvited guests at their door, so I feared that this activity would turn out to be awkward and embarrassing. But, since I had always faced unpleasant tasks with the determination to do whatever needed to be done, I just went ahead and did it. And unexpectedly, with the very first house, I found out that even "farming" could have an "up" side.

I walked up the first front sidewalk as if I had been sent to the principal's office in school. I was nervous and just wanted to get it over with. Worrying about the reception I might receive, I rang the doorbell, held my breath, and then

32. Ben Lesser and Associates

was indescribably relieved when no one came to the door. I could scratch that one off the list! Just as I was stepping down off the porch, however, the door suddenly opened. And before I had a chance to utter a word, the lady said to me, "Aren't you Mr. Lesser?" When I said, "yes," she replied, "Oh, Mr. Lesser, I read your wonderful column in *The Reporter* all the time, please come in!

So much to my surprise, what had started out as a long-dreaded assignment, ended up as a wonderful conversation—and a new friend. As I was leaving, I gave her our latest marketing tool, a pot-holder with our new business address on it. Soon it seemed that almost everywhere I went people recognized me from the newspaper. Hard as it was to believe, I actually found "farming" to be pleasant—just like visiting friends. Some people were lonely and appreciated the company. Most liked to ask real estate related questions, and discuss property values with me. It was as if they had their own real estate consultant who made house calls. They considered me an expert in the field of real estate, and I almost felt like a celebrity. And along with refreshments and conversations, I developed many positive relationships. So it turned out that my little idea about writing a weekly real estate column to advertise my business ended up being one of the smartest moves of my career. As a result, people felt they already knew and trusted me. It seemed as if doors simply opened up for me and I started getting listings in the area.

Now that I had gained the evidence and confidence that clients would come our way, I finally gave my notice at UPS. Leaving such a good job was not only a huge financial risk, but also meant the loss of my annual five-weeks of vacation when I worked on side-jobs and enjoyed family camping trips. In fact, working on my own would mean no vacations for a very long time. Despite our fears, however,

Part III: The American Dream

Jean and I looked forward to a future where our hard work, self-discipline and skills would result in success and happiness—in other words, the American Dream. Owning our own agency would be frightening, exhilarating, and a lot of work, but the results would be well worth it.

Much to our delight, the "farming" had really paid off. We received many listings and wherever you looked, you could see "Ben Lesser FOR SALE" signs on front lawns and bus-stop benches. The agency was becoming successful. And we'd reached another step on the way to achieving the American Dream. Soon, other agents started to join our office, and we had to expand. Part of the reason for our success was my decision to associate only with the highest caliber sales agents. We also provided weekly in-house education meetings so that everyone in the office was always up-to-date on the latest developments in real estate. Our focus was on customer service first, and sales commissions last. As a result, we earned a reputation for honesty and excellent service. And I always made a point of letting our agents know how important and appreciated they were. Their effort, dedication and integrity resulted in success for all of us. But along with the rewards of our success, was the painful shadow of my past. No matter how successful I became, I had left the camps, but to this day, they have never left me. Instead of overwhelming me, however, they are a constant reminder that my survival was a gift. And in honor of this gift, I have chosen to live a meaningful life instead of letting Hitler's fires continue to consume me. In a way, living a meaningful life, creating a loving family and a successful business would be my personal solution to the Nazis' problem.

Well, it soon became apparent that continued success would require expansion of our little business. Since we finally had an advertising budget, we began to run large

32. Ben Lesser and Associates

ads in the newspaper. Jean did a great job of managing the office as well as the bookkeeping. We quickly needed more help so we hired Sherry, and then, later on, Gail also came on board. We soon had to double-up on some desks because we were simply running out of space! The community was flooded with "Ben Lesser SOLD!" signs, wherever you looked, and I actually had to turn away new agents until we figured out what our next move would be. Such a problem!

Meanwhile, a romance was brewing between Gail and an impressive young man named Michael Gerber, who had joined our sales staff. I had gotten to know Michael through previous real estate transactions, and was very fond of him, so I was happy that Gail grew to share my opinion! This was a very busy time for us because part of our expansion plan was to open a second office. After much research, we concluded that our next location should be in the prestigious Los Feliz area of Los Angeles because it had huge hillside mansions and sales there would bring in much more money per house than the ones we were listing at the other office. So we were taking a risk and venturing out into new territory.

We found a great location for the new office on Hillhurst Avenue. We gutted and remodeled a six-unit building (and yes, I read and understood the fine print on all the contracts!) into the most beautiful offices in the entire area. This involved a lot of work in addition to keeping up with the agency on Third and Fairfax.

And that wasn't all we were doing. During this time we were also occupied with the joyful preparations for Michael and Gail's August 1980 wedding. The ceremony took place on the spectacular grounds of the Ambassador Hotel — the very place where Jean and I had had our second date. It was such a beautiful wedding that even now, all these years later, people still talk about it. Amidst the joyous

Part III: The American Dream

Our beautiful new offices.
Los Angeles, CA (1980)
Lesser Family Collection

celebration, however, once again my thoughts traveled back to my sister Lola's wedding in Poland.

Then, just two weeks later, we celebrated the gala, red-carpet, grand-opening of our new office. As guests pulled up to the curb, the valets would escort them over the red carpet to the door, where each was handed a glass of champagne. Huge urns filled with flowers and fruit were displayed throughout the building. Several buffet stations offered just about any kind of food anyone could want! A large tent, erected in the backyard, offered desserts, a fully-tended bar, a band and a dance floor. The party went on until the early hours of the morning, and as the guests left each lady was given a single red rose. This grand opening was written up in the area's newspaper as a great success.

32. Ben Lesser and Associates

Always a bright spot in our lives, my son-in-law Michael proved himself to be a great motivational speaker and everyone liked him, so I gave him the job of managing the Hillhurst office. He and Gail worked well together interviewing new agents. We were particularly blessed by Michael's talent in training new personnel. With his support and expertise, the office quickly started making a profit, and for a while we had over 70 agents between the two offices. My name became very prominent in Los Angeles, and I actively participated in The West Side Real Estate Brokers Association. In fact, at the beginning of 1983, I was honored to be elected its president. My installation was held in the Grand Ballroom of the Beverly Hilton Hotel. It was quite an affair! Further adding to our joy, a few weeks later was the beautiful wedding of our daughter Sherry to her wonderful husband, Larry Kramer.

Well, just as we were rejoicing in our good fortune, we learned once again that joyous celebrations can be followed by serious troubles. The booming housing market suddenly began to change, and interest rates climbed sky-high, making it too expensive for many people to purchase homes. The whole real estate market turned sour. Now, since we had an oversupply of listings, very few sales and

My installation as president of the Westside Real Estate Brokers Association
Beverly Hills, CA (1983)
Lesser Family Collection

Part III: The American Dream

two offices, we had very high expenses. Additionally, our listings had to be advertised and serviced, meaning that we still needed to hold open-houses. And our large newspaper ads put us deeper and deeper in the red. During this difficult time, many real estate offices closed, but I continued putting my own money into the business, hoping that the market might turn around. Unfortunately, it didn't.

Then, near the end of 1983, I was approached by the real estate division of Merrill, Lynch & Company,* which at that time was one of the most powerful investment firms in the world. They were seeking to acquire reputable real estate offices that were now having trouble in the down-market. They conducted extensive investigations — almost like the FBI — and came to the conclusion that the unimpeachable reputation and high sales record of Ben Lesser & Associates would make us the perfect agency to acquire. So in a very unexpected way, my efforts to maintain the highest of standards had paid off. Ben Lesser & Associates, a family business built with the hard work and determination of a Holocaust Survivor, an uneducated refugee, had impressed giant Merrill, Lynch — and they made us an offer. Since we were going deeper and deeper into the hole with each passing day, I learned another important lesson: I learned that sometimes the determination to succeed against all odds needs to be tempered by flexibility and directed toward realistic goals.

Apparently, Merrill, Lynch also learned this lesson, because at the end of that year, it sold its real-estate division to the hugely powerful Prudential Corporation. I went right

---

*Founded in 1914, this hugely successful investment and banking firm lost most of its assets as well as its reputation in the 2007 subprime mortgage crisis. Merrill, Lynch & Company was eventually acquired by Bank of America.

32. Ben Lesser and Associates

along with it. To my surprise and relief, it turned out that I couldn't have asked for a better place to work. Prudential had given me the choice of either managing an office as a salaried employee or selling real estate on commission. Once I analyzed these options, I realized that since I had such a large following, that I would do better financially by selling property.

So I left management and fortunately, for the next ten years, I did very well in sales. Consistently one of Prudential's top salesmen, I was annually awarded fully-paid vacations and cruises to exciting destinations all over the world, including Acapulco, Spain, Hawaii and London. The trip to London was made even more exciting because just before our departure, my manager asked if Jean and I could stop by his office. When we arrived, he presented Jean with a full-length mink coat! Who could believe such a thing? Here I was, Ben Lesser, refugee, Holocaust Survivor, and now going on a luxury trip with a wife in a mink coat! Clearly these trips were much different from my first trans-Atlantic crossing.

Even though the years with Prudential were good, Jean and I never lost sight of our goal to achieve and maintain the American Dream. We knew all too well that without any notice, life could bring disaster. It was essential to "save for a rainy day," especially since that "rainy day" could end up being several stormy years. In order to ensure that our family would always be protected against unexpected hardships and despite our success, we worked hard and continued to invest in real estate. And it looked as if our efforts were paying off. We could feel ourselves almost starting to relax.

Then, on January 17, 1994, at 4:31 in the morning, we were shaken out of our sleep by the infamous Northridge

Part III: The American Dream

earthquake. Registering 6.7 on the *Richter Scale*,* it had the highest ground acceleration, which measures how hard the ground shakes, ever recorded in a North American city.

It would be an understatement to say this was absolutely terrifying. And just as if 55 years hadn't passed and I was still that 10-year-old boy who was shaken from a happy sleep by the rumbling Nazi tanks, I practically leapt from my bed to the window. Luckily, I didn't hurt myself—leaping out of bed at age of 65 can be quite a challenge. And while things didn't look unusual outside my window, inside the house was a different story. It was a total mess; it looked as if everything had crashed to the floor. There was broken glass all over everything, and of course my mind traveled back to the aftermath of the Nazis ransacking our home.

The unexpected ringing of the phone shocked me back to the present. It was our now all grown-up, usually very calm, confident granddaughter Robyn, crying that she was scared. So, without first determining if it was even remotely possible, I told her I'd be right there.

My confidence wavered somewhat when I went outside. It looked like a war-zone. Buildings had crumbled, none of the street-lights worked, and the streets seemed to be impassable. But my granddaughter needed me so of course I just did what needed to be done and started driving. Fortunately, there was no traffic—which was very eerie for usually traffic-jammed LA. Unlike me, everyone else must have known that they wouldn't get far. The still-dark ghostly morning was filled with the sounds of sirens and the flashes of fires. It seemed as if all the glass in Los Angeles must have broken, and of course I couldn't help but think about what we'd all heard it had been like on *Kristallnacht*.

---

* The *Richter Scale*, which measures the magnitude of earthquakes, was developed in 1935 by Charles Richter.

32. Ben Lesser and Associates

With grandfatherly determination, however, I somehow managed to navigate the chaos of the streets and get to Robyn. Fearing the worst, I breathed a sigh of relief when I saw that her apartment building seemed to be undamaged. Robin was waiting at her door and when we hugged, I could feel her begin to calm down a bit. Since there could be aftershocks at any moment, I wanted to get us back home as soon as possible. I told her to grab some clothes and whatever else she might need for a couple of days. That's when she told me that she wouldn't leave until we found her cat. Apparently it had found a place to hide when all the commotion started. To me, the idea of searching for a cat instead of getting my granddaughter to safety didn't make much sense. But the look on Robyn's face told me that she wasn't going to budge. So there we were—in the midst of total pandemonium, with the potential at any moment of more pandemonium, not to mention serious danger—grandfather and granddaughter searching for an uncooperative cat. It finally became obvious even to Robyn that the cat was not going to come out until it was good and ready. So we gave up on the cat and left. The streets had begun to fill with traffic, so the ride home took much longer than usual. I tried to keep Robyn distracted from the rubble by telling her stories. When we reached home, her anxious grandmother quickly scooped her into a big hug. And then Jean called me a hero, and gave me a hug of my own.

Since the immediate task of cleaning up kept us focused, we really didn't have time to feel sorry for ourselves. Fortunately there was enough food and water to hold us for a few days. So we figured we'd just settle in for the duration. Of course Robyn wanted to go back to her apartment as soon as possible to check on the cat. It wasn't until three days later, however, that the streets were passable and I was able to take her home. We were all relieved when Robyn

Part III: The American Dream

finally called to tell us that her cat had been waiting for her safe and sound, licking its paws, acting as if nothing at all had happened—and impatient for some food and water!

This terrifying earthquake had a tremendous impact on the comfortable lives we'd created for ourselves. We suffered over $500,000 in damage to our investment properties. While of course we had insurance, it really didn't help. This is because the deductible, meaning the amount of our loss we had to pay out of pocket before the insurance kicked in, was so high that we didn't qualify for benefits. Even so, we considered ourselves lucky because it could have been much worse. And certainly I had lived through much, much worse. But with 72 deaths, over 9,000 people injured and $20 billion in damages, this shocking event made us lose our taste for residing in Los Angeles. Combined with the fact that I was thinking about retiring, we felt that it was time to live somewhere that was safer. It was time to make another important choice.

PART IV

"Zachor!"

33. RETIREMENT AND A NEW CHALLENGE

> *"A man can't retire his experience. He must use it."*
> ~Bernard Baruch (1870-1965)
> Jewish-American Financier,
> Philanthropist, Statesman

After much discussion, Jean and I decided to retire to Las Vegas, where we already owned some investment properties. We had friends there, and knew the town well. We figured that by living in Las Vegas, we would still be close enough to spend time with our family and manage our properties in Los Angeles. Before making this big decision, we carefully researched construction companies and locatons. For the first time in our lives, we would be building a new home to our own specifications. Just like expectant parents, we visited the lot and eagerly watched the progress of the construction. When it was ready, we rented out our duplex in Los Angeles, but kept a small apartment there in one of our other buildings to use whenever we came to town.

Jean and I embarked upon this new stage of our lives with excitement. We looked forward to taking it easy and enjoying our well-earned, semi-retirement. I say "semi" because we would still manage our properties in Las Vegas and in Los Angeles. We thought that after retiring from an extremely busy and eventful life, and having earned and maintained the American Dream, that our lives would soon settle down in to a comfortable routine. But this was not to be the case.

A few months before we moved to Las Vegas, I received an unexpected invitation from my grandson, Adam, who at that time was in the fifth-grade. This invitation brought a

Part IV: "Zachor!"

rush of pain that I thought had been buried along with the dead. It seems that during a class discussion about WWII, he had mentioned to his teacher that his Grampa, "Papa Ben," had been in a concentration camp. This was of great interest to the teacher, but she didn't want to impose on me she so asked Adam to ask me if I would speak to his class about my experiences. I never dreamed that I would hear this in a phone call from my grandson, so his request really threw me for a loop. Over the previous 50+ years, except for occasional conversations with my sister Lola, my wife Jean, who has spent years calming me during nightmares, and a video-taped interview with the Shoah Foundation,* I hadn't talked about the Holocaust. I had been determined not to let its horror contaminate my new American life and family.

It's important to understand something about the younger Holocaust Survivors who were fortunate enough to marry and become parents in the United States during the 1950s. They had to make an agonizing decision about whether or not to tell their children about the horrors of the Holocaust. On the one hand, some parents felt that the best way to honor their murdered loved ones was to make sure that their children grew up immersed in stories of their loss. Hopefully, this would encourage them to remain vigilant against the danger that it could happen again. Many of their homes were filled with ghosts, fear, and never-ending

---

*The *Survivors of the Shoah Visual History Foundation* (Shoah Foundation) was established in 1994 by film director, Steven Spielberg, following his experience making "Schindler's List." Its purpose is to gather video testimonies from survivors and other witnesses of the Holocaust. Its mission is to overcome prejudice, intolerance, and bigotry—and the suffering they cause—through the educational use of the video-oral-history testimonies. Today the Foundation reaches educators, students, researchers, and scholars on every continent, and supports efforts to collect testimony from the survivors and witnesses of other genocides.

33. Retirement and a New Challenge

pain. Every knock at the door could be bringing disaster. They were never free from the terror that they might not be able to protect their precious children from the horrors of another maniacal anti-Semite.

Many of these Children of Holocaust Survivors* grew up feeling that their own existence was a miracle. Many felt that they had to make up for their parents' unspeakable losses. Although they didn't experience the Holocaust directly, growing up with it as a constant part of their lives could cause children to become second generation psychological and emotional victims. They never could fully experience the innocent childhood happiness that life in America could bring.

On the other hand, some Survivors vowed to keep silent about the past—hoping it would never contaminate their new American lives. Hitler would never take over the minds and souls of their American children. For me, achieving the American Dream meant much more than just acquiring property and achieving financial success. It meant that my children would be real Americans—free and healthy, with dreams they would be free to achieve instead of nightmares that would imprison them. So while the girls were young, I never discussed the heinous details of the Holocaust with them. And they didn't ask. Maybe they understood that it was too painful for me. And it was. I didn't want it to intrude on our lives. Why contaminate our children's innocence? Why give the Nazis even more than they have already taken?

By the time Sherry and Gail were teenagers, they'd learned about the Holocaust in school and knew that I'd lost

---

For info see: *Generations of the Shoah International (GSI)* (http://www.genshoah.org)

Part IV: "Zachor!"

my family and been in the camps. But to them this was just history—a subject in school; it was all in the far-away past. While we kept a Jewish household, we deliberately lived in a mixed community, where the girls would have both Jewish and non-Jewish friends, and could participate in all the typical American childhood activities. As teenagers, they had traveled to Israel, and shared my belief that Israel's existence was essential to the well-being of the Jewish people. So even though we hadn't specifically discussed my own experiences during the Holocaust, somehow the girls knew. And understood.

I'd had no idea, however, that Gail had shared this knowledge with Adam. That's why I was so shocked when he brought the subject up. And while my first impulse is to always say "yes" to Adam, this time I really had to take a while to mull it over. This would be a profoundly difficult choice for me to make. Would the information be too shocking to his classmates? Would it be horrifying for him? Would I embarrass him? Would it open up those terrible doors that had been locked closed for so many years? Would it cause me trauma that would affect my current blessed life?

Well, after much soul searching and discussion with Jean and Adam's parents, I decided that of course I couldn't deny my grandson. For him, I would break my silence. Once I had made this choice, my upcoming "assignment" seemed to engulf me. I had to deal with my past. With old memories and emotions—as well as my added anxiety about doing a good job for Adam. This was even more of a challenge because I would only have an hour to tell this story. How could that be done? And of course I had no experience as a public speaker. So I researched, and studied and did my best to create a presentation that would be appropriate and interesting for fifth-graders in sunny, carefree 1990s California.

33. Retirement and a New Challenge

The night before my presentation was very difficult for me. I was nervous for so many reasons, and couldn't sleep at all. Walking into the school the next morning was a strange experience. I flashed-back to the last days of my own education—I was stunned to realize that I had been Adam's age when it ended. I saw his sweet face superimposed over memories of myself as a 10-year-old. It was overwhelming. When I felt my eyes tearing up I got even more concerned that I would become emotional during my presentation. And when I got to the classroom door, I had no idea if the Ben Lesser who was about to walk through it would be the same man who came out.

Well, as in difficult situations throughout the years, I just went ahead and did what I had to do. And I did it the best that I could—by starting off tentatively, in order to judge how my words were affecting the kids. It was encouraging to see that within a few short minutes, the entire class had become spellbound. Their eyes were glued to me. It almost seemed as if they didn't breathe until I took a breath. My presentation was scheduled to take place from 10 a.m. to 11 a.m., but once I got started, the words seemed to carry their own momentum and I talked straight through until noon, when the lunch bell rang. The students were mesmerized; no one budged. They just sat there listening. Finally, the teacher told them they had to go to lunch, so they quietly and reluctantly left the classroom. When they saw me in the hall outside the classroom, they surrounded me, thanking me, touching my arm, asking me to stay. Over their heads, I caught Adam's eye. He smiled softly at me, letting me know that I had pleased my most important audience: my grandson, Adam.

And the students weren't alone in being overwhelmed by my talk. It also had an overwhelming impact on me. Once again, going through a door into the unknown had

Part IV: "Zachor!"

changed my life. In a way, those innocent, respectful and curious 10-11-year-olds in that two-hour class showed me what I had to do in the next stage of my life. They taught me that we Survivors must speak out. So after 50 years of silence, and with great surprise that the students and teachers were eager to hear my story, I began to speak about the Holocaust.

34. 2006: TRANSPORTED TO THE PAST

> *Learn from yesterday, live for today,*
> *hope for tomorrow.*
> ***The important thing is not to stop questioning.***
>
> ~ Albert Einstein (1879-1955)
> German-born Jewish-American
> Nobel Prize-winning Physicist

The years flew by, and as the result of Adam's initial invitation, I spoke to hundreds of classes, as well as religious and community groups. And unbeknownst to Adam, he would be the cause of my going through yet another challenging door to my past. In the spring of 2006, our family gathered in Davis, California to celebrate Adam's graduation from University of California at Davis. We sat together at the ceremony, eagerly searching for his face among the hundreds of smiling graduates who would soon receive their diplomas, and then go on to follow their dreams. Ever since he'd been in fifth grade, and had asked me to speak to his class in school, I have known that Adam understood his place in the history and future of the Jewish people. He knew that his college graduation was a victory not only for him, but also for so many others. This was especially true for his "Papa Ben," whose formal education had been so brutally cut short in the sixth grade. And as is so often the case, my mind flashed to the past. I couldn't help but think of other long lines of loved ones who never got the chance to "graduate" to the next phase of their lives.

Adam's commitment to his family and the Jewish People is evident in the way he lives his life. In fact, his first job

Part IV: "Zachor!"

as a college graduate would be with *Hillel** at U-C San Diego. But before settling down to his new job in the fall, Adam had made arrangements to tour Europe for a month. Coincidentally, his cousin Robyn had decided to tour Italy during that same summer. Always eager to spend time with each other, they made plans to meet in Kraków to explore their family's roots.

After discussing many details, they decided to rendezvous for dinner in Kraków on July 11th. They would meet at the famous *Pod Aniolami* (Under the Angels) restaurant, located in a 13th century building near Wawel Castle. A few days after they had made their plans, Robyn called me to ask about where I was born and the places I'd lived in Kraków. During this conversation, she just happened to mention how nice it would be if I could also be there with them to show them around, and fill in important details. As you might imagine, I wasn't able to give her an immediate answer. Following our traumatic visit to Kraków 10 years earlier, Jean and I had decided never to return to that accursed land, where the soil is soaked with innocent Jewish blood. We had only undertaken that trip in an effort for me to reach some kind of "closure." In other words, we'd hoped that by confronting the past, I would be able to diminish the painful memories that still haunted me.

Instead of "closure," however, the trip had awakened long-dormant memories, causing even more pain. And now, my granddaughter wanted me to return to Kraków to help her and Adam explore their roots. I didn't want to burden her with the anxieties that her innocent request had created. Of even further concern was the fact that I would

---

*Hillel: The Foundation for Jewish Campus Life, with centers on more than 500 college and university campuses, is the largest Jewish campus organization in the world.

34. 2006: Transported to the Past

be traveling on my own because Jean was unable to go with us. But, just as I couldn't refuse 10-year-old Adam's request to speak to his class 10 years previously, of course I couldn't refuse Robyn now.

So, after giving it much thought, I decided not only to go, but to invite the whole family to join us on this pilgrimage. Those who could take the time away from work instantly agreed. Now that it had become a family project, I would have the pleasure of my loved ones around me to soften the pain of my memories. And adding to the enjoyment was our decision to keep it all a secret from Adam, so that instead of just meeting his cousin Robyn, he'd be surprised to also see his parents, Gail and Michael, his Aunt Sherry and most surprising of all, his Papa Ben! We couldn't wait to see his face!

Since we would all be staying in the same hotel in Kraków, one of our biggest challenges that first day would be to remain quiet and inconspicuous! Here we were, three generations of exuberant, somewhat giddy relatives, arriving from a long, exhausting trip, excited about the upcoming reunion with Adam—and we had to sneak around! When we finally arrived at the restaurant for dinner, we sat at the table Robyn had arranged for our group, right next to her reserved table for two. We waited impatiently for Adam to come through the door. He saw us as soon as he walked in, and his face quickly flashed emotions from shock to confusion to disbelief to joy! He was completely taken by surprise! Needless to say, we had a wonderful dinner, and while no one really remembers the food, none of us will ever forget Adam's reaction!

Bright and early the next day, inside the chauffeured car that Robyn had hired, we started our tour of remembrance in Kraków's Jewish section: Kazimierz. As we passed

Part IV: "Zachor!"

Wawel Castle, I told the "kids" about King Kazimierz and his lovely Esterka. Next we visited the old *Szeroka Synagogue*, which dates back to the 15th century, and is known as *The Old Synagogue*.* The Nazis destroyed the inside and its sacred contents when they turned it into storerooms during World War II. Thankfully, it has been restored and is now a branch of the *Muzeum Historyczne Miasta Krakówa* (Historical Museum of the City of Kraków). Our next stop was the *Remuh Shul*, which was built in 1556 and is the smallest in Kraków. Except for during the Occupation, when its interior was destroyed, and the next few years during its restoration, the *Remuh Shul* remains the only synagogue in Kraków that has functioned continuously every week as an actual place of Jewish worship.

We then went around the corner to see my grandfather's apartment at #6 Pobrzezie Street. When we told the man who answered our knock on the door who we were, he quickly closed the door in our faces. Actually, this is a common reaction because the Polish inhabitants are afraid that Jewish visitors will try to reclaim the property that was stolen from them and taken over by the Poles. It's interesting to note that much of the stolen Jewish property had been insured by insurance companies that have still not provided compensation for post-war claims. Further complicating the ownership problem was the Communist nationalization of most businesses in Poland following World War II.**

I imagined that the Polish family now living in my grandfather's apartment would still be using our family's

---

*For more information on Jewish history in Poland see: www.sztetl.org.pl/en/cms/the-project and http://en.wikipedia.org/wiki/Synagogues_of_Kraków

** For fascinating information on property reclamation efforts, see, "The Conference on Jewish Material Claims against Germany," http://www.claimscon.org/

34. 2006: Transported to the Past

dishes and furniture. Enjoying the beautiful artwork that had hung on the walls for generations, and that I had known and loved as a child. I knew that my grandparents' valuable silver Menorah had probably been quickly buried in the garden by the new Polish residents, so that Nazis wouldn't find it and think that they were Jews. What a tragedy that countless precious artifacts of Jewish life probably remain buried throughout Europe to this day, never to be seen or returned to the families that own them.

We were determined not to let this set-back have a negative effect on our day, so we quickly crossed the street. Standing on the corner since 1862, was the beautiful, completely restored Progressive Temple. We are very lucky that even though the interiors of these synagogues had been destroyed by the Nazis, the exteriors had survived because Kraków had not been bombed by the Allies. I could feel myself becoming more emotional as we approached #23 Starowislna Street, the once proudly beautiful, but now sadly neglected, apartment where my family had once lived. This time our luck was good. The mailman just happened to be handing the mail to the current tenant. I apologized for the interruption and told him that I used to live there before the war. I asked if he would allow me and my family to view the apartment. He was kind enough to oblige us. I was shocked to see that our once beautiful and spacious apartment had been subdivided into three small, cramped, and dark units. Clearly, any Leser family belongings that might have survived the war were long gone. So while it was disappointing, at least my family was able to see part of our Kraków home.

Proceeding down Starowislna Street, we were saddened that there was absolutely no trace of my father's once thriving wine and syrup business. As we made our way across the Visla River Bridge to see the ghetto, I described

Part IV: "Zachor!"

what it had been like for our extended family to be forced out of their homes only to either starve or die there, or to be deported and then murdered in the camps. I told them that thanks to their Uncle Mechel, and his love for Lola, our immediate family had escaped to Niepolomice. Our next stop was at a grocery store to buy flowers in preparation for our visit to the Jewish cemetery in Bochnia.

During and following World War II, the Jewish cemeteries throughout Europe had been desecrated or destroyed by both the Nazis and local anti-Semites. Since Holocaust Survivors had no homes to return to in Europe, there wasn't anyone left to repair and take care of these cemeteries. So for the most part, if they exist at all today, European Jewish cemeteries are in very poor condition. Created in November 1872, Bochnia's Jewish Cemetery did not escape devastation. Unlike the others, however, it is in good condition today, thanks to the tireless efforts of its elderly Polish caretaker. Despite his advanced years this gentle man, who had lost his own mother and four brothers in the war, still welcomes the opportunity to talk about the cemetery and the people who are buried there.

When we arrived, he came out and opened up the gate for us, and gave us *Yahrzeit* candles.* As the caretaker showed us around the cemetery, we were impressed by its serenity and the many beautiful fruit and shade trees that he had lovingly tended since planting them decades ago. We stopped at Mechel's family's memorial and said *Kaddish* under the branches of an old oak tree. When we reached my parents' memorial, which also rested under the protective branches of an ancient oak, we gently placed the flowers, lit the candles, and again recited the *Kaddish*.

---

*In accordance with Jewish tradition, a *Yahrzeit*, or Memorial Candle, that burns for 24-hours, is lit in memory of the dead.

34. 2006: Transported to the Past

And then, using notes that I had carefully prepared for the occasion, I spoke to my parents in Yiddish, bringing them up to date on the family, and the purpose of our current visit. Despite the barriers of language and time, it was as if all four generations of the Leser/Lesser family sensed the comforting presence of an unbreakable, eternal bond.

From the cemetery we continued on to the Wieliczka Salt Mine, which is absolutely amazing. As one of the oldest companies in the world, it continuously produced table salt from the 13th century until 2007. Over a million tourists enjoy visiting this mine every year because it is similar to an ancient art museum. In its interior there are dozens of statues, chandeliers, an underground lake, exhibits about the history of salt-mining, and a large cathedral that was carved out of the rock salt by the miners. This cathedral, known as The Underground Salt Cathedral of Poland,* is often rented out for weddings and other celebrations.

On the way back, we stopped by the Plashov Memorial, built in honor of the victims of the notoriously brutal concentration camp near Oscar Schindler's factory. Despite personal danger, Schindler had made "friends" with many of the guards in the camp, and these relationships, along with a lot of his own money, allowed him to "employ" over 1,000 Jews as slave laborers in his factory, thereby saving their lives.

The next day, as our driver took us to Auschwitz-Birkenau, I couldn't help but wonder what his grandparents had been doing during the war. I also wondered what he was thinking about us. This was the part of the trip that I had been dreading. Without any discussion of what lay ahead, everyone's mood had changed. And as we drove along, I

---

*For more info on The Underground Salt Cathedral of Poland, see: http://whc.unesco.org/pg.cfm?cid=31&id_site=32

Part IV: "Zachor!"

could feel painful stirrings of indescribable feelings that I hadn't realized were still inside me. Suddenly, it seemed as if I was no longer a happy grandfather sightseeing with my family on a sunny summer day in 2006. Instead, I felt as if it had instantly become 1944, and I was a terrified 15-year-old prisoner in a concentration camp.

Images, smells and sounds of the past bombarded me: *brown uniforms . . . swastikas. . . sirens . . . Gestapo . . . SS . . . shiny black leather boots . . . murderous dogs . . . pistols . . . rifles . . . screams . . . shouts . . . whips . . . fire, smoke . . . ashes . . .my mother's face . . . my little brother's silent terror . . . selektions . . . mountains of skeletal corpses . . . children savagely torn from their mothers . . . furnaces . . . fire pits . . . frightened faces . . . starvation . . . gas chambers . . . barbwire . . . kapos . . . shovels . . . sledge hammers . . . standing for hours in freezing cold roll-calls . . . dying faces . . . bulging bloodshot eyes . . . typhus . . . death march . . . cattle cars . . . bunkers . . . attics . . . beatings . . . lice . . .vermin . . .latrines . . . my broken and dying cousin Isaac . . . death . . .more death . . . endless death.*

My whole body vibrated with terror, and my heart pounded so wildly that I was surprised that no one heard it. I became so dizzy that it seemed as if my head might spin right off of my neck. I closed my eyes, desperately trying to steer my thoughts away from the hideous past and back into the beautiful present. With no success. Shrieks of terror and cries of anguish filled my head, heart and soul. These were soon drowned out by the vicious, deafening Nazi shouts mercilessly hammering inside of my head: *"JUDEN RAUS, ACHTUNG!" "LOS LOS!" "RAUS SCHNELL!" "DU VERFLUCHTE JUDEN"! And the kapos yelling "ZUM APPEL!" "DIE MUTZE ABNEHMEN!" SCHWEINHUNT!"* If you don't know the meaning of any those aforementioned words, consider yourself lucky.

34. 2006: Transported to the Past

My eyes suddenly filled with visions of the gallows and I could hear the agonized cries of the Jewish prayer before dying, "*Shema Yisrael Adonai Eloheinu Adonai Ehad*" ("Hear, O Israel; the Eternal is our God, the Eternal is One"). And the closer we got, the more vivid these brutal flashbacks became. When we finally arrived at Auschwitz-Birkenau, and I saw the tracks which had led 1.5 million innocent men, women and children to the slaughter houses, my body seemed to convulse, and I almost threw up.

Knowing that my family needed me to be with them, however, I somehow managed to function normally despite the chaos that raged within me. So with determination and deliberate calm, I entered the camp right along with wide-eyed tourists and school groups — regular people who hadn't been personally touched by the horror. And in the midst of this innocence, a blind, hot anger shot through me. For the first time in all those years, the fury that I had kept so carefully locked away, seemed to explode. But no one noticed. Everyone around me was oblivious to my reality.

Was it as stunningly clear to them as it was to me that all that Hitler's "Master Race" had mastered was the industrialization of depravity and death? How strange that my dignified exterior appearance didn't show what was going on inside my mind and body. How could everything go on as usual amidst the displays of mountains of human hair that had been collected to manufacture textiles for Nazi blankets and uniforms? How could these tourists remain untouched after viewing photos of the gold teeth extracted from corpses in order to enrich the Third Reich? How could they not be affected by all the vast piles — tons — of used clothing that still waited to be recycled? Piles of shoes — tiny baby shoes . . . children shoes . . . athletic shoes . . . dainty shoes . . . heavy work- shoes . . . dancing shoes. . . women's

Part IV: "Zachor!"

shoes . . . men's shoes. Eyeglasses, brief cases, hand-bags, wallets, pens, jewelry, wristwatches, combs, toothbrushes, teddy bears . . . every kind of item that would have been possessed by a living, loving, human being. Can you imagine that the sight of a toothbrush could break your heart?

Amidst the horror of this visit to Auschwitz-Birkenau, I gained even more respect for my son-in-law Michael, who has been courageously dealing with Multiple Sclerosis* for many years, and now has lost the use of his legs. I forced myself to refrain from helping him as he awkwardly and painfully got out of his wheel-chair. He pulled himself up a flight of stairs and then down to the basement, using all the strength in his own tortured body, so that he would not miss the many exhibits. When I asked him to please take it easy, his reply was, "When I hear about the torture, starvation, pain and deaths that those poor souls had to endure, how can I not make every effort to honor their memory?"

Later that day, in Birkenau, as I gazed at the platform where the Nazis had chased us out of those cattle cars — ripping us apart forever from our loved ones — the waves of horror continued to erupt from the depths of my soul. After touring the camp we were further sickened by the marsh where the Nazis had forced Jewish inmates to dump tons of human ashes in the swampy waters. Now frogs live and thrive among the ashes of our dear departed ones. We also saw the fire pits where so many bodies — some still alive — were dumped and incinerated when the crematoriums could not "process" the bodies fast enough. Fighting nausea

---

Multiple Sclerosis is a progressively debilitating disease affecting the brain and spinal cord, and central nervous system. There is as yet no known cure. Michael has become a media spokesman for the MS Foundation. To learn more, see: http://mgerber.blogspot.com

34. 2006: Transported to the Past

and dizziness, my angry question remained crystal clear: Where was the world?

We finally completed this tour of hell, and tried to process the horror. And then we were utterly surprised and relieved to see that amidst all this anguish, there actually was one profoundly positive and healing moment. Almost as if they had been waiting for us, right in front of the new memorial there happened to be a brigade of Israeli soldiers, men and women in full dress uniform. They were conducting a memorial ceremony in Hebrew, which included reciting the *Kaddish*, and held an enormous flag of Israel. At the conclusion of the ceremony, they sang Israel's National Anthem, "*Hatikvah* (Hope)." The uncontrollable tears that flowed down our faces provided a much-needed catharsis, or release of our emotions. What a profound and perfect ending to a sad, sad day and what a perfect ending to a very meaningful and memorable trip.

Israeli Military Memorial Service
Birkenau, Poland (2006)
Lesser Family Collection

"The hope of two thousand years,
To be a free people in our land
The land of Zion and Jerusalem"
Lyrics from "HATIKVAH" based on the 1878 poem
"*Tikavatenu*" by Herz Imber (1858-1909),
Ukrainian-Jewish poet and Zionist

Part IV: "Zachor!"

ZACHOR
זכור
HOLOCAUST
Remembrance
FOUNDATION

35. 2009: ZACHOR!

> *"The souls of our dear departed ones,*
> *all six million of them, are crying out to*
> *the world in a single word:*
> *"ZACHOR —*
> *Remember"*
> Ben Lesser (1928 –),
> Polish-Jewish-American Founder
> of the ZACHOR Holocaust
> Remembrance Foundation

Since 1995, I have been telling the story of the Holocaust in schools, colleges, community, and religious groups — in fact, to anyone who will listen. In April 2002, I was deeply honored to be the Keynote Speaker for the Annual Las Vegas *Yom Ha'Shoah* Commemoration (Holocaust Remembrance Day), at Temple Beth Am in Las Vegas. And although I had dedicated the previous six years of my life to speaking publicly about the Holocaust, this audience would present a new challenge. And a new opportunity. I felt a profound sense of responsibility to do justice to this sacred occasion, so in order to prevent any "senior lapse" of memory; I prepared notes to use as necessary for reference. I especially wanted to acknowledge the dignitaries, both Jewish and non-Jewish, who would be making the time to join us.

The several hundred *Yom Ha'Shoah* Commemoration attendees who would gather together on this special night would include political and government officials, business leaders, many Survivors, and Children of Survivors. Since this audience would already be intimately aware of the horrors of the Holocaust, I would not be educating them. So instead, I decided to speak directly from my heart

Part IV: "Zachor!"

to theirs, in the hope of inspiring and supporting their efforts to preserve our history. I would tell them that it was only in 1995, at the request of my precious 10-year-old grandson, that I understood that my silence over the previous fifty years must be broken. I would tell them about my beloved, innocent family in Kraków and Munkács, knowing that the attendees would be thinking of their own lost families. I would tell them about the Death Camps, Death Marches, Death Trains, knowing many would share my memories, either first-hand or through their own relatives and friends. I would tell them that *Yom Ha'Shoah* is a permanent moral obligation to all Jewish people, and especially important when the Passover *Haggadah*, is read throughout the world.

The *Haggadah* mandates that in each generation, every Jewish individual must feel as though as he or she had truly been redeemed from slavery. It reminds us to not only recall, but to try to spiritually experience our historic deliverance from oppression. I would tell them about losing my faith at Auschwitz only to regain it with the establishment of Israel as an independent country in 1948. I would tell them about surviving the Nazi Nightmare and achieving the American Dream, knowing that many of them had also done so. And because of our combined achievements, Jewish communities now thrived all over the world. I would tell them that it remains our responsibility, and that of our children, to ensure the safe, secure, dynamic existence of Israel, so that the Jewish People would never again be victimized minorities in other people's lands. So that there would never be another *Shoah*. So that we never again would have to ask the question: "Why did the so-called rational world stand by and let it happen?"

And so, on the night of my speech, I began by telling them how blessed I was to be at the podium, speaking to such a distinguished audience. I told them that their coming

35. 2009: ZACHOR!

together on this sacred occasion to honor the six million who had been lost, made each member of the audience a "dignitary." I thanked them for their commitment to the Jewish People and to Israel. I thanked them all for coming together to remember. And then from my heart, I told them who I had once been—and with eternal thanks to God—who I am now:

My name is Ben Lesser and I am a Survivor...

The years passed and suddenly it was 2008, and at the age of 80, I was busier than ever planning, researching, organizing and making Holocaust education presentations. In addition to emotional stamina, these activities required physical stamina, because they could last up to three hours, and often involved travel to other states. So in order to make sure I stayed in shape to meet my demanding schedule, I began to work-out at the gym for two hours every morning. Some days it seemed as if my so-called "retirement" was just as busy as my years in business, and I certainly wasn't looking to add on any new adventures or responsibilities.

Well, clearly God had other plans for me, because something soon happened that gave me a new focus for my presentations. At the end of a meeting of the Las Vegas Holocaust Survivors Group, each member was presented with a very special lapel pin. This pin consisted of the Hebrew letters of the word ZACHOR, which as I've mentioned previously, means, "Remember." Despite its small size, this little gold-colored pin really struck a chord for me. It was such a simple way to represent everything I'd been trying to convey: "Remember."

I decided I would wear this pin to all of my presentations, and even brought a few extra with me to my next school presentation just in case any of the students might want one.

Part IV: "Zachor!"

After the class was over, two young students remained to ask me more questions. They wondered what the ZACHOR pin in my lapel meant. I was surprised and impressed that they'd even noticed it. I explained the meaning of the pin, and asked if they would want one. Well, you should have seen the look on their faces! They each promised that they would always cherish the pins and that they would pass them along to their own children.

After that experience, I decided to call a manufacturer to research the possibility of producing large quantities of the pins. By the end of the conversation, I had ordered 1,000 pins despite wondering if I'd ever be able to give them all way. I was delighted when they arrived in time for my next presentation, where I would be speaking to 500 teenagers. I'm always a little anxious when speaking to large groups of high-school students because I'm never sure if I will be able to keep their attention. Why would they be interested in the story of an elderly immigrant?

Well, the day of my presentation arrived, and much to my relief, all went well. The students listened attentively through my three-hour talk. At the conclusion, I explained the meaning of "the funny looking lapel pin" that I wore, and asked if anyone might want one. To my surprise, they all raised their hands! The packed auditorium looked like a forest of waving arms. And instead of stampeding out the exits, they patiently lined up and filed out, each shaking my hand or giving me a hug. And each one graciously accepted a pin. Feeling this connection with them, feeling their respect, was a very powerful moment for me. I saw that there is hope for the future.

A few weeks later, I was astonished to receive a big box containing hundreds of thank-you letters from both students and teachers. When I contacted the teacher to thank her and to ask about the pins, she responded with obvious

35. 2009: ZACHOR!

delight, "You wouldn't believe it, Mr. Lesser. The pins are everywhere. The kids are all wearing them, they have them pinned on their hats and backpacks, and are still talking about them." At that moment, I recognized the impact that this small, tangible memento could have. And once again, I realized that I'd learned as much from the students as they had learned from me! The students taught me that there was something else I needed to do.

That "something else" was, and is, to give ZACHOR Pins to speakers and providers of Holocaust education programs, so that they, in turn, can distribute them to their students and audiences. And, most importantly, these pins would be provided free of charge. I had seen for myself the power of the pin to both reinforce the learning experience and to create a tangible, physical connection with history. Well, now that I knew what had to be done, I wondered, how on earth would I obtain enough pins? After much thought and discussion, that "something" became the basis for the ZACHOR Holocaust Remembrance Foundation.* Founded In January, 2009, this non-profit educational organization could never have happened without the above-and-beyond-the-call-of-duty support of my family and many volunteers. In particular, I must express my love and endless gratitude to my daughter Gail, and her loving husband, Michael. Their long hours and dedication to the ZACHOR Holocaust Remembrance Foundation not only made it all possible, but keeps it thriving.

Much to our joyful surprise, as of spring 2011, just two years after its inception, the ZACHOR Foundation has distributed over 90,000 pins. We know that as the number of Survivors shrinks, there are fewer and fewer voices of

---

*For information about the ZACHOR Holocaust Remembrance Foundation, please see, www.zachorfoundation.org/

Part IV: "Zachor!"

truth to counteract the strident voices of those who still deny the Holocaust's existence. The consequence of this denial will be more genocide. It is only through education that the truth can overcome the lies. In our ultimately losing race with time, it becomes more and more urgent for the few of us who remain to refuse to surrender in this our last battle against man's inhumanity to man.

Helping to combat ignorance and denial is the outstanding Holocaust Studies program at Middle Tennessee State University, in Murfreesboro, Tennessee,* a town I will never forget. In October, 2009, at the age of 81, I was honored to be a panelist in their five-day long 9th Holocaust Studies Conference: THE HOLOCAUST AND WORLD WAR II: "PERSPECTIVES FROM 70 YEARS."

This event brought together many dedicated educators from around the globe for a single purpose: "Improving Holocaust Education." The sessions covered a wide range of topics, including "Crimes behind the Front Lines," and "Portraying the Holocaust in Word and Image." But none of these was more important or meaningful to me than "Survivors and Liberators," the panel on which I served. In addition to three other Survivors, our panel included two Liberators. Each of us was to recount a different aspect of our Holocaust experiences. The American Liberators, both from Tennessee, spoke first. When they were introduced, their names meant nothing to me. And along with the other

---

*The Mission of the Middle Tennessee State University Holocaust Studies Program is to provide greater understanding of and knowledge about the Holocaust from an inter-disciplinary and bi-gender perspective; as well as serving as a bulwark against the spread of Holocaust denial and antisemitism, racial, religious and ethnic hatred. This program serves to memorialize the lives, suffering and heroism of all people persecuted during the Holocaust, and to raise awareness that genocidal hate did not end in 1945. Info: http://www.mtsu.edu/holocaust_studies/

35. 2009: *ZACHOR!*

speakers and the hushed audience, I listened attentively to their presentation, while preparing mentally and emotionally for my own. They spoke calmly and humbly about what they had seen and experienced as part of the American forces that liberated Dachau in 1945.

Most people are surprised to learn that the Americans didn't come on purpose to liberate Dachau. The war was almost over, and their job had been to "occupy" Germany—a relatively routine process. They'd had no idea of the unspeakable horrors that they were about to see and experience. When they unexpectedly came across the Death Train outside of Dachau's gates, they were shocked and traumatized to see the horror within each car. As they ventured inside the camp gates and were confronted with the dead-eyed, living skeletons, any illusions of human decency they might have possessed were instantly destroyed. Even now, all these years later, their pain could still be seen on their faces.

Strangely, even though I have heard—and have told—these stories so many times, I was drawn into their particular memory as if I were an actual part of it. It seemed as if I knew each tragic detail even before it was spoken. When the speakers mentioned passing the gaping doors of the corpse-filled cattle cars that had been left stranded on the tracks outside the camp's entrance, I could smell the stench of the bodies that had died so hideously inside. I could still see those cattle cars, sitting in malevolent silence on the tracks outside the gates of Dachau. In fact, I knew every putrid inch of one of those cars all too well. Because at just 16 years of age, I had been one of the very few survivors among that tragic cargo of formerly living and loving human beings who had been dumped there just three days before. In fact, if the American Liberators had come even a few hours later, none of us would have been

Part IV: "Zachor!"

alive. This is because in addition to our near-death physical condition, the Nazis had been ordered to annihilate all the Jewish inmates of the camp by that evening. The Nazis knew that the Americans were getting closer, and they didn't want any survivors. Luckily, the Americans came at 5:30 p.m. and saved us.

The cattle cars that the panelists were now discussing, had been part of the notorious Death Train, which had shuttled around aimlessly for weeks with 2,000 sick and dying human beings trapped inside without, food, water or sanitation. My cousin, Isaac and I had been among those barely breathing prisoners who had been forced to hobble and crawl from the train into Dachau, one of the Nazis most notorious concentration camps. When the young American Liberators came through Dachau's "gates of hell," they were visibly shocked and sickened to be confronted by the sight of thousands of hideously weakened, barely conscious "walking skeletons." And I was one of those walking skeletons. Unbelievably, 64 years later, I realized that these gentlemen who shared the Middle Tennessee State University Holocaust Conference panel with me had been my liberators. They had rescued me from Dachau. They had given me my life.

From our outwardly healthy, normal appearances that soft autumn morning in 2009, no one could have imagined the horrors we panelists had shared over six decades before. In fact, seeing me today, your first impression would likely be that of an unassuming, neatly-dressed, middle-class older gentleman. It's unlikely that you would perceive the many incarnations that my life has undergone, the unimaginable—even to me, and I had lived it—reality behind the healthy, calm, exterior. And you wouldn't be alone. Because sometimes when I look at my very ordinary

35. 2009: *ZACHOR!*

reflection, I'm surprised by what I see. In fact, I'm often surprised that I'm still alive—and that I have lived a life blessed with happiness and love. When I try to see beyond the reflection, however, back to the horrors of 1939-1945, I see the face of a walking skeleton.

I realize that my first meeting with the two Americans 64 years earlier couldn't have lasted more than a few minutes. We'd had only the most basic way of communicating— never even heard each other's names. But in that one long-ago moment, we had seen across the generations, religions, nationalities and life-experiences into each other's souls—and we would never forget each other. Our mutual experience that day had become forever connected to our future lives, which we had dedicated to speaking publicly about the Holocaust. Because of the Holocaust Remembrance Conference in Tennessee, I finally learned—and will never forget—the names of these two heroic gentlemen from Tennessee: Jimmy Gentry and James Dorris. Listening to them speak, it was necessary for me to use all of my self-discipline to contain my emotions and refrain from rushing to embrace them—to thank them with all my heart for giving me my life. When their presentation was over and it was at last my turn, I was unable to speak until I had walked with shaking legs and a pounding heart to their side of the table. And as we three held each other, I thanked them for saving that barely walking, 65-pound and 99% dead, human skeleton. Without them, I wouldn't have lasted another day.

How could such a meeting happen? After so many years and such different lives, how could the three of us meet again on this stage in a small town in Tennessee? This unexpected reunion, much like the unspeakable events that brought us together in the first place, was beyond

Part IV: "Zachor!"

explanation. And as vastly different as the circumstances were, both of these unexpected meetings were tributes to the resilience of the human spirit.

36. 2010: THE MARCH OF THE LIVING

> *"As the last generation to come in contact with actual Survivors, it is our responsibility to carry on their legacy to future generations as well as to spread their message to the present one."*
>
> Student Participant
> MOTL—2010

In addition to learning, understanding and teaching about The Holocaust, it is also necessary to take action. It is for this reason, that at the age of 81, along with almost 10,000 students and Survivors, I was honored to participate in an extraordinary project: *THE MARCH OF THE LIVING* (MOTL)—2010.* This remarkable international, intergenerational education program brings teenagers and Holocaust Survivors together from all over the world every year during the week of *Yom Hashoah*—Holocaust Memorial Day. In honor of those whose lives were taken at this and other death camps, we walked together, arm in arm, out of Auschwitz. Together we provided a powerful living symbol of the victims who never were able to leave. We walked out for them. And we will continue walking for them . . . always remembering.
ZACHOR.

---

*The goal of the *MARCH OF THE LIVING* is for these young people to learn the lessons of the Holocaust and to lead the Jewish people into the future vowing Never Again. For information about this extraordinary program, see: http://www.motl.org/index.htm

Part IV: "Zachor!"

And until our last breath, we will tell the world what happened. For as Elie Weisel (1928-)* tells us,

> **"To remain silent is the greatest sin of all."**

My experience with the week-long March of the Living-2010 was nothing short of transformative. As this diverse group sat safely together in the shadow of Auschwitz, despite our different ages and backgrounds, our different personal challenges and strengths, we confronted this nightmare of hate: the *Shoah*. And by confronting it with truth and love, by working to understand it, we strengthened our determination and our ability to ensure that human beings will not be doomed to repeat it. We also spoke about the birth of the State of Israel and the necessity for the Jewish People to have their own vibrant, free, and vigilantly defended homeland. How reassuring and how encouraging it was to see in the beautiful young faces around me the resolve not just to "remember," but to take action, so that the hatred ends with us — right here, right now. It was clear that they understood that we must not let the past poison the future.

When these respectful, eager-to-learn students asked about my experiences in the concentration camps, I wasn't sure how much to tell them, how much they wanted or needed to know. But my previous experiences with talking

---

*Renowned Holocaust Survivor, Elie Weisel, is a Nobel Peace Prize winning professor at Boston University. He is also an internationally acclaimed political activist, and author of 57 books, including *Night*, based on his experiences in Auschwitz and Buchenwald Concentration Camps during WWII. The Elie Wiesel Foundation was founded in 1986 to combat indifference and intolerance through education. For information see www.eliewieselfoundation.org/homepage.aspx

36. 2010: The March of the Living

to students had taught me that they wanted to know everything. And so, gathered together at Auschwitz, I decided to tell them what they wanted and needed to know about how the eternal Jewish People managed to survive the most heinous event man has ever perpetrated on mankind. And I hoped I could tell them in way that would make sense and have meaning for them.

I started by telling them that in the spring of 1945, none of us concentration camp inmates could have known or would have believed that the Germans would surrender to the Allies. We could no longer even imagine a world without war. We could no longer imagine. And since I had been only 15 years old when I had been seized and removed from anything resembling civilization, what I especially could never have imagined was that I would be liberated. That I would regain my health, become a man, begin a new life, fall in love, marry my soul-mate, have two precious daughters and four amazing grandchildren, and a successful career. Who could have imagined that I would live to return to Auschwitz to tell this story 65 years later to hundreds of high-school students from around the world? I was amazed and touched by the depth of their understanding and ability to put their thoughts into words. For example:

> "As I promised the Survivors, it is now my responsibility to pass on their stories and experiences . . . I want to thank all the Survivors who came on this journey with us, for it is not easy for them to travel such long distances (let alone re-envision the atrocities that took place in the camps). This trip would not be complete without them. I am so blessed to be given this opportunity."

Part IV: "Zachor!"

> *"The week I spent with these incredible heroes has been life changing and inspirational...I have witnessed the horrors of the Nazi war crimes. I have smelled the awful scent of the gas chambers and crematoriums and touched the scratch marks on the walls from all their suffering. I have listened to the terrifying stories told by the survivors ... I have great respect for these brave individuals who came back to the place where their families were murdered in order to educate the rest of the world."*

On our last day in Poland, we visited the Old Jewish section of Kraków. First we went to the *Old Remuh Shul* and its ancient cemetery. Next we walked several cobblestone blocks to the newer and very beautifully decorated Reform Temple. Because it deviated from traditional Orthodox beliefs, this Temple, with its modern, Reform philosophy, had caused quite an uproar in the Jewish community when it was built in the 19th century! Well, two centuries later, we caused a completely different kind of uproar when, accompanied by a guitarist, we brought the old walls back to life. Students and Survivors spontaneously filled the Sanctuary with song and dance — and somehow I was right in the middle of it! Joyously dancing in a Temple in Kraków. In 2010!

Our next stop, the *Umschlagplatz*, instantly brought us back to earth as the students saw the staging area from where Jews were deported to their deaths. Everyone was profoundly moved by the Krakow Ghetto Memorial there. One component of it consists of 33 empty steel and cast-iron chairs in the main square, and 37 empty chairs on the edges and at bus and train stops. It represents the furniture that Jews were forced to abandon before boarding the trains to the concentration camps. It also represents the "emptiness"

36. 2010: The March of the Living

or "absence" that was created by the elimination of Krakow's Jews. Today, people often use these chairs while waiting for a train or bus.

With heavy hearts and minds, we got back on our bus and began the drive back to our dormitory. Unbeknownst to me, however, there was going to be an unexpected stop on our day's itinerary. I was surprised when I realized that our route seemed to have changed. In fact, it looked as if the bus was driving toward Bochnia, of all places.

Well, it turns out that our group had been deeply touched when I'd told them about my parents, so they got together with our group's sponsor, the Los Angeles Builders of Jewish Education Program (BJE),* and organized a surprise for me. They arranged to have our itinerary changed in order to go say *Kaddish* at the mass grave where my parents were buried. Additionally, they had pooled their spending money in order to make a generous contribution to the *ZACHOR* Foundation so that thousands of other students will receive a *ZACHOR* pin. Needless to say, I was overwhelmed by their thought-fulness and generosity.

Having last visited the cemetery in 2006, I never dreamed that I would be able to spend time with my parents again. I am so grateful to the extraordinary MOTL students and the BJE: Builders of Jewish Education Program of Los Angeles for making it possible. When we stood together at my parents' memorial, I showed the participants our few pre-Holocaust family photos and spoke about the brutally murdered, courageous, accomplished and loving people who are buried there. I could feel these beautiful young

---

*For info on the Los Angeles Builders of Jewish Education program, see: http://www.bjela.org/

Part IV: "Zachor!"

people absorbing this story into their souls and hearts. As we all said *Kaddish* together, it felt as if all the generations of Jewish history from the ancient to the present, were bridged.

It was so reassuring to look at this young generation and feel secure about their character, drive and capabilities. They are more than just our *hope* for the future. They are our *guarantee* for the future. And so this time, in the presence of these young people and other Survivors, I once again read a letter aloud to my beloved parents. I spoke to them of all the things that I've seen and done since we last spoke. Above all, I showed them that they have not been forgotten and that their spirits, values and love will live on in the hearts of all those who hear their story.

At the Jewish cemetery, I show photos of my parents to the MOTL-2010 participants
Bochnia, Poland (2010)
Lesser Family Collection

37. 2010: DEAR MAMMIKO AND TATTIKO

Old Jewish Cemetery of Bochnia, Poland
March – 2010
Dearest Mammiko and Tattiko,

It's me, Ben, your loving, and now very gray-haired, 81-year-old middle son, miraculously here with you once again. This time I am in the company of 200 amazing young people from around the world. They are participants in the 2010 March of the Living, and they are committed to learning about, and then teaching about the Holocaust. The power of their voices saying Kaddish for you, and for all the others who were lost, gives me confidence that the world will never forget. Over the past week, I have been honored to come to know these extraordinary young people and I have benefited profoundly from their insights and determination.

Even at their young ages, they understand that they belong to an eternal people. A people who are not just victims of oppression, but also heroes of the battle for human rights. They understand that they are the last generation to talk with Survivors. They know that the hopes and dreams of our silenced ancestors live on in them. And so they know that they carry a profound responsibility as the link to the future. Having met them, I know that they are up to this sacred task. They have told me that they now feel as if they know you, and that they will carry your story with them for the rest of their lives. I wish I could introduce each of them to you. Their love, energy and commitment will ensure that the souls of over six million innocent Jewish men, women and children will live on. You will be remembered. These young people are living, learning, loving, and very busy testaments to the values that you instilled in all your children, and that Lola and I were honored to pass along. They understand the responsibilities and consequneces of making personal and global choices.

Part IV: "Zachor!"

Dear Parents, I only had 14 years with you, but in the almost 70 years that have followed, I am never without you. I hope I have lived my life in a manner that honors you and would make you proud. A life that matters.
Until we meet again . . . I remember.
ZACHOR.

Rest in peace,

Your loving son,

Baynish

38. DEAR READER

A few years ago, when I started thinking seriously about writing this book, I figured that I'd organize my notes, take a few weeks and then write it all up. As usual, I'd ask my dear wife Jean to decipher my handwriting, type it up and proofread it for basic grammar and spelling. And then it would be done. Obviously, another situation where, "Man plans—God laughs."

What I didn't anticipate was that the very organizing, writing, reviewing, discussing, editing and revising of a book would, in and of itself, become an unforgettable experience. It opened a whole new world of introspection and conversations with family and friends. And just like every previous new challenge, it has provided me with a profound learning experience.

Ironically, as so often happens when we try something new, my decision to write a book unexpectedly opened another new door. And behind it was a massive project. I wasn't sure if I could undertake two huge, totally unrelated ventures at the same time. But, if not me—who? And if not now—when? So in honor of my father, and once again, with the tireless help of Jean, Gail and Michael, I decided to go ahead and hire a commercial baker to make *mandelbroyt* according to my father's recipe, in order to make it available online and through grocery stores.

Of course since my father's recipe had never been written down, this process required a lot of trial and error. I baked a batch every day for months. Fortunately for me, there was never a lack of willing tasters. And they weren't shy about giving me their opinions! I finally figured out a recipe that matched what I remember of my father's in 1943. Then we had to find and hire a commercial bakery

Part IV: "Zachor!"

that could use all natural, kosher ingredients and create the same taste in 2011. We decided to not only offer the *Original Family Recipe*, but to also provide four updated versions: *Lemon Blueberry with Poppy Seeds*; *Spicy Chipotle with Ginger and Dark Chocolate*; *Minty Dark Chocolate*; and *Chocolate Espresso Bean*! Having designed the packaging, we are now working with potential distributors to grocery stores to carry Mandelbroyt from Papa Ben's Kitchen!

I'm delighted to report that by early 2012, Papa Ben's Kitchen will distribute *mandelbroyt* online and through several major grocery stores in the western United States. We are so excited to be able to provide consumers with the opportunity to enjoy my father Lazar Leser's delicious *mandelbroyt*. Please watch for us on: www.papabenskitchen.com.

When I look back at these two enormous, emotional, and totally different projects, the book and the bakery, I'm not sure which one has been more challenging—or more difficult. I do know that each has been immensely rewarding. I was motivated to actually begin writing this book two years ago in response to the hundreds of student questions and letters I have received following my Holocaust education presentations. Initially, I thought that I would organize their questions and comments, and my book would evolve from my responses. I soon realized, however, that unlike those of us who have lived through the actual events, younger people needed a context that would allow them to understand how a Holocaust could happen. So I started to present my material in a way that would relate my experiences to a broader history.

This was quite an undertaking—and as I began to see my life through the eyes of others, my own understanding and perspective of the Holocaust deepened. I realized even more profoundly that the only way to prevent genocide

38. Dear Reader

is for each individual person to take responsibility for his and her own words and actions. To make choices that are consistent with living a life that matters. I understood more deeply the importance of actively choosing how to deal with adversity. While we can't always control what happens to us, we can try to choose effective, honorable ways to deal with even the most difficult circumstances, so that the past won't contaminate the future.

> We can choose to learn about the mistakes
> of the past so that we don't repeat them . . .
>
> We can choose to educate ourselves
> about both local and global events . . .
>
> We can choose to move ahead toward success
> instead of staying stuck in misery . . .
>
> We can choose to express respect instead of hate . . .

We can choose to Live a Life That Matters.

APPENDIX

DEAR BEN:

3/9/11

HERO

It was quite hazardous, having so many eighth-graders in one place, taken from our classes and all poured into one room. There was lethargy in the air—many didn't see the point of it all, though they were glad to get out of class—and they talked and carried on as eighth-graders do. But then, he walked in, and our voices became hushed, even the voices of those who "didn't care" became the whispers of dry crumbly paper that came from another millennia. He was dressed in gray, and when he spoke, he had a quiet authority that was tinged with a note of sorrow that made his voice curl up at the edges, a rough patch of a sea of calm.

He told his story with the strength of a prizefighter, his inflection rising and lowering in pitch with each new phrase, the slightest trace of an accent touching his syllables. And the time ticked by, two and a half hours passed by without a glance at the clock, the story spinning itself, fabricating in front of our eyes; he wove it like a master storyteller. We were enthralled; those who "didn't care" had long since forgotten their little act and, now watching him speak with attentive eyes and listening with attentive ears.

He told of life and loss, swallowing the saltwater tears that threatened to spill over the edge, telling his story with a magic that kept even the most restless of us still. WE knew that something was happening; something was changing, changing as the man in front of us brought what had previously been just text on a page to life. And it sick-

Appendix

ened me, what happened, not too long ago, sickened me that the human mind was capable of committing such atrocities, sickened me that so many had died. Horror, shock, disbelief, that they thought killing people was fun, just another game--Monopoly, perhaps, or poker. Then, relief that he survived, by luck and cunning and strength, survived on his wits and his courage. Sorrow, too, intermixed with it all; we could barely imagine six hundred, let alone six million. Sorrow, it reached deep inside of us and changed things around so that nothing would feel right for days, an unsettled stomach while his words haunted me at night.

He was strong; he was brave, and barely an adult at that. He survived, despite suffering and pain; he dared to live, with no regrets about who he was. And he was a hero — no, he is a hero.

Thank you, Ben Lesser. Thank you for everything. You are truly inspirational.

Middle School Student

Dear Ben

3/9/11

Dear Ben Lesser,

    I was one of the students who were fortunate enough to hear your story. One of the most powerful moments in your story was when you told us about being liberated by the Americans. You said that the political prisoners were jumping for joy, but the Jewish prisoners were not. You said, "What now?" I can honestly say those were the most moving words I heard from you, because the expression on your face showed your pain. You didn't have a family, a home, or a person to hug when you walked out, you didn't have a thing in the world. I can't imagine how that possibly feels. Although my words won't make a difference for the past, I am deeply sorry from the bottom of my heart for the empty feeling and the horrible things you had to go through.

    I never knew that three hours could pass by so quickly. Your story was mesmerizing from the beginning to the end. You might not remember this but while you were signing your signature on your cards, you stopped and said "When you guys go home tonight, hug your family tight, appreciate them, because that's all you have." My brother and I haven't spoken in two weeks because we were upset at one another for a ridiculous reason. That day I went home and talked to my brother. It probably seems like a small effect, but you have no idea how much that changed the way I saw the situation.

    Ben, you're a great man and there aren't any words I can possibly say to show my appreciation for the story you shared. You are a hero. If I had been in your shoes, I would have given up the day I started. You carried your cousin until liberation came; you had enough will-power

Appendix

not only to survive but to try to save your loved ones. You are one of the most amazing men I have ever met. There's only a hand-full of people like you in the world and we lose some each day. You made all of us hold each other's hand at the end and repeat, "Never Again" plenty of times—and I do promise, "Never Again!" Superman doesn't exist, but you do.

Sincerely,

Middle School Student

Dear Ben

12/5/2012

Dear Ben,

As a result of hearing your life story, my 7th-grade students have become better able to craft their own decisions about the Holocaust and its ramifications. They reflect more deeply about how their own personal choices, values, and integrity determine their futures. As you told them, "You are the last generation to hear from us . . . it's your responsibility to keep this world from acquiring amnesia."

As if you could read our minds, your book provided answers to our questions:

- How could a civilized, cultured country like Germany do this?
- Why were the Jewish people so singled out to be persecuted and exiled?
- The Nazi's believed Jews were too dirty to be considered human beings, yet their homes and belongings weren't too dirty to steal – why?
- Why is it that it is easier to believe a lie than a truth?
- How could the unimaginable become routine?
- Even if Survivors' physical strength was regained, could their stolen humanity be regained?

Your book also provides a whole new dimension for teaching about the Holocaust. In my classroom, there is a banner that reads, "There is no nobility in being better than someone else; the only nobility is being better than who you were yesterday." Living a Life that Matters," profoundly reinforces this idea. Middle school students

Appendix

need more than the core learning objectives, they need life-skills as well. Bullying, fighting, and family problems are issues that occupy more of a student's mind than a curriculum's Reading Objectives.

My first highlighted sentences in your book were:

> "I have come to understand that so much of what happens in life is the result of seemingly simple choices . . . that people do not understand that they have the power to make choices that will determine the course of their lives . . . education, more than anything else, allows us to evaluate circumstances, make good choices, and take effective action. It's our best weapon against ignorance and hate."

Students might ignore such ideas when hearing them from parents and teachers. But how could any student ignore such wisdom when it comes from a Holocaust Survivor – someone who got up every morning and did whatever he had to do to live just another hour. Someone who has "lived a life that matters" and achieved the American Dream?

Your use of quotes and explanation of historical facts make it easy for students to further relate to your story. Furthermore, your own sayings, or "Ben-isms," will undoubtedly be quoted and repeated by others. Here are some of our favorites:

- I learned that even when I had to make difficult choices, I should try to determine what the right thing to do was and then do it.
- Do everything the right way – no short cuts.
- Take responsibility for your words and actions.

Dear Ben

- Take responsibility for solving problems instead of using them as an excuse for not succeeding.
- Honor our shared humanity rather than despise our differences.

As a result of your numerous presentations at our school, I thought I knew everything about you. After reading your book, however, I realized there was so much more to your life. You did not let your life be defined by the Holocaust. Because you chose to live a meaningful life, there was love, joy, humor and success. I respected and honored you when we first met and eventually grew to love you for all that you have done to inspire my students and myself.

Ben, you've said writing this book has been immensely rewarding for you. For the rest of us, it serves as a precious gift, making us question who we are as individuals, who we can become, and how we can live meaningful lives.

With Gratitude—Zachor!
Ann T. Raskin, MS Education
Reading 7th Molasky Junior High School
Las Vegas, NV

Appendix

01/03/2012

Dear Ben,

    I could not put your book down, so I read every available moment and just finished it. Congratulations! It is well written, easy to read, and a "page turner."
    I must have read dozens of Holocaust books, covering almost every aspect of it. Your book is unique for me in the fact that you first went through the Polish Holocaust experience, and then again through the Hungarian Holocaust experience. And you survived both to live a life that matters!
    Being a child of two Hungarian Holocaust survivors, I am intimately familiar with the Shoah, and could relate to your feelings about remembering. I know all about the transports, the selection, the "Lager", the factories, etc. Your survival instincts, your quickness, your determination, your strength, your industry, your intelligence, all come through in "Living a Life that Matters" And it really matters!

M. Jacobovits
NYC

Dear Ben

12/24/2011

Dear Ben,

    Your amazing and lasting gift to humanity shines on every page of his book. You light our way from the darkest pages of a child's sudden plunge into the despairs of Nazi Germany to your stunning transformation (rebirth) to a new life in America. How did you do it? How Is it possible to survive and recreate one's life? This intimate story is a page-turner with a unique gift for every reader. You give us rare insights into how we can overcome the worst of circumstances. We live through your incredible life-and-death adventures to survive and triumph . . . In laying bare the wounds of the past, your scars are reconstituted into badges of courage.

    Your love story with soul-mate, Jean, touches our hearts and your success as a professional business man touches our minds. Hearts and Minds together, we embrace you, Ben. Your book deserves to stand as a unique testimony to the human spirit and the power of the written word.

L. Merrin
Las Vegas

Appendix

12/24/2011

Dear Ben,

I am thrilled to recommend this book to all people who might find themselves harboring any feelings of hatred or even early signs of intolerance toward another human being/group of human beings. Even if a person doesn't believe that they entertain these feelings personally, it's important to keep in mind that the forces of evil are ever present amongst humanity and remembering history, as well as understanding what led to the Holocaust, can never be forgotten or edited out of history.

Not only are the memories of innocent human beings which were sacrificed at stake. The future of mankind is at risk if we collectively forget about the "seeds of contention." We must be alert to the belief-patterns that allow the growth of extreme hatred which fueled this horrific event.

This is the first book that I've ever read which I was unable to put down. I was captivated by the story. Between my weeping and deep feelings of horror, I found myself living vicariously through your experiences as you had lived them. You have been given the talent to orchestrate the story of your life so that the reader can almost "taste" the atrocities that were thrust upon you at such a young age. It is almost impossible to even imagine how you managed to survive while maintaining the strength of human spirit. And through the strength of your spirit you were ultimately able to thrive.

While many define a "hero" as someone who does something heroic as defined by one's culture," you have shown us that the truest meaning of human heroism is not only your physical survival of the worst human cruelty in man's history, but the survival of your humanity.

Ben, it is an honor to know you personally, and it is without reservation that I strongly recommend, Living a Life that Matters: from Nazi Nightmare to American Dream as essential reading to adults of all ages everywhere. It provides the understanding that our collective tolerance for one another, amongst the family of man, may decide the fate of the human race in the near future!

Warmest regards,
Dr. S.D. Moore, DDS

Appendix

4/5/2011

Dear Ben,

 Thank you again for making time to come to our school. Although most of my students have certainly heard of the Holocaust, it is you that brings it to life for them so that they truly see it as a horrible stain in our history rather than just a story in books. Each student walks away from you a changed person, not only in themselves but with their friends, goals and families.

 As a teacher, I am so grateful that you are able to bring this experience to our students. As a human being I am amazed that not only did you survive, but, you are able to relive this story again and again. While I am never sure whether the students truly appreciate what a gift they are given at the time, I know that it is something they will carry with them for the rest of their lives.

 With the number of Survivors shrinking every year, it is important to me that I provide the opportunity to as many children as possible to hear the story directly from one who was there. Your story is shocking, amazing, horrifying and thought-provoking. What more could we ask for in an educational and human experience?

 Please accept my enclosed student letters with the reverence and honor with which they are being submitted. My students struggle to put into words the true impact of your visit because words don't seem to adequately explain the profound change you leave them with. Even as I write this letter to you, I too am frustrated that my words are not enough to express the depth to which I am grateful to you. Especially knowing that while the Holocaust was decades ago, you continue to suffer, especially during the days that surround your coming to speak to us. The gen-

Dear Ben

erosity that it takes to still bear witness is immeasurable.

Here are two quotes from you that stand out to me, my students and the other teachers with whom I shared them--and I repeat them often in my classroom:

> "Hitler did not start with weapons,
> he started with words.
> He did not start with killing,
> he started with hate."

> "Many who commit crimes
> blame their deprived childhoods
> for their actions.
> Most will agree that my childhood was deprived,
> but I came to America with nothing.
> No skills, no money—
> and I did not speak the language.
> Yet I made a success with my life,
> and so can you."

These are words every child needs to hear, and I thank you for bringing them to us. Zachor.

Sincerely,

Kristen Pohl
Las Vegas

Appendix

3/9/11

Dear Ben,

    Here are the responses my students wrote after hearing your story. I cannot begin to thank you enough for giving my students the gift of hearing your testimony. In all of my years of teaching, and there have been quite a few, I have never seen a single event have such a tremendous impact on a group of students.

    I have been teaching about the Holocaust every year in some capacity, but this is the first year that students have heard from a Holocaust Survivor. Now that I see the kind of impact, and understanding students have acquired from listening to you, I realize that I should have had you come in and talk to my students every year. You are, by far, the best Holocaust Speaker I have ever heard.

    You actually lived through everything in the Holocaust that I discuss with my students. You present it in such a clear and descriptive manner that my students can picture it in their heads. You also speak with such passion about "Never Again!" that my students feel the importance of that responsibility and take it very seriously.

    You have been a hero all of your life . . . through your actions during the Holocaust, through your perseverance and success in the U.S., And now through your retelling of your story to today's young people.

    You truly are an inspiration. I would love to make your visit to my school an annual event.

Thank you again,

J. Weinstein
Las Vegas

Dear Ben

3/9/11

Dear Mr. Lesser,

I cannot begin to share my gratitude for the time you shared with us earlier in the week. I am the young man who escorted you from the office to the library, and was very happy to do so. From right there, I could tell you were a very kind soul, and patient at that. This is something I will carry with me for the rest of my life.

There are many things that truly stuck with me as I listened to the words come from your mouth, recreating images like a painter throws himself on the canvas. I cannot fathom the pure terror of the atrocities you lived through. But you managed to make the best of your circumstances. You didn't let the controlling actions of others take over your life. Instead, you fought to survive. And after you were liberated, you fought to succeed in the world. Most people would have quit right then and there, deeming their life useless and pitying themselves. But not you, sir. Your words stuck with me:

"This is America! I believe that hard word, studying will allow you to get where you want. This allows for opportunities, and you can do what you want to do." It was almost like a game of "life-poker."

You may not have been given the best cards, but you held on to them, and raised your opponent, only to win the pot!

Another major impact you made on me was helping me to understand the value of humility and compassion. I left that discussion thinking more as a man. I thought about all did so willingly for your family—such as taking lashes for your uncle—I see your story as more than one of valor. It is a story of the true value of the human heart. It

Appendix

inspired me to really know what a man was, and that was it, acting strongly for his family. I did not hesitate all day to tell family and dear friends that I loved them, knowing that any moment could be the last opportunity to do so. I called my grandmother right before I went to sleep. At first alarmed, yet happily surprise to hear from me, she listened as I shared your words with her. I told her how important it was to harness every opportunity to make life work to its fullest. Now whenever I disagree with my mother, I just turn around and kiss her on the head.

Your story of the Holocaust and the monstrous people of it really shines a light on a problem still existing today. As awful as it was, it shows the awful tendencies that exist within mankind. Bullying is an awful thing. I now will call people out and confront them with their injustices to others. When they ask me why, I will tell them that I was the little things that blew up into the Holocaust. We must all understand that superiority because of evil is not right. And we must never be afraid to call someone out on it. "The world just stood by silently." And that was the biggest mistake of all. These lessons I will never forget. I will make it part of my life to maintain what I have learned.

Zachor—we will remember.

With Warm Regards and Many Thanks,

Middle School Student

TIMELINE

800-600 BCE:	1ˢᵗ Jewish Temple destroyed; forced expulsions/exile of Israelites from homeland then known as Judah; *Diaspora* begins.
63 BCE -70 CE:	**63 BCE:** Rome takes over Israel; **70 CE:** Roman forces defeat Jewish rebellion, destroying Jerusalem. **73 CE:** Masada falls to Rome. Hundreds of thousands of Jews were killed; thousands sold into slavery.
600-1600: *Middle Ages*	**638:** Islamic conquest of Jerusalem. **691:** First recorded Jews in England; **900-1090:** Golden Age of Jewish Culture in Spain; **1095-1258:** Christian Crusades at war with Islam in Palestine; capture Jerusalem. Hundreds of thousands of Jews are killed by Crusaders throughout Europe & Middle East. **1290:** King Edward I expels Jews from England; **1385:** Jewish District of Kraków Founded; **1306:** Jews expelled from France. **1385-6**: German Emperor expels Jews of Strassburg; **1463-92:** The *Inquisition*, a tribunal whose courts were held throughout Europe, is started by Roman Catholic Pope Innocent III to punish heresy. Torture and death were common. The Accused had no rights. Led by Father Tomas de Torquemanda, Spain expelled entire Jewish population (over 200,000); **1492:** Instead of reaching India,

321

Appendix

	Christopher Columbus lands in America; **1496:** Portuguese Jews either forcibly converted or expelled. **1516:** Jewish Quarter in Venice, Italy becomes known as the "Geto Nuovo (New Foundry)" which later became the basis for the word, "Ghetto."
1534-1585:	First Yiddish book is published in Krakow, Poland; Ivan the Terrible expels Jews from Russia; Jewish Ghetto instituted in Rome. **1585:** First known Jew arrives in the American colonies.
1791-1917	90% of Russian Jews are expelled to the Pale of Settlement.
April 20, 1889	Adolf Hitler is born in Braunau am Inn, Austria.
1914-1918	Austrian Archduke Francis Ferdinand's assassination in Sarajevo starts WWI (1914-1918), which formally ends with the Versailles Treaty (1919); **1917:** Russian Revolution breaks out; over 2000 pogroms took place, claiming the lives 200,000 Jews.
1925-1926	Hitler writes *Mein Kampf* while in prison.
1928	**October:** *Ben Leser born in Krakow, Poland*
1929	US Stock Market Crash causes world-wide economic disaster: The decade-long Great Depression begins.

Timeline

1933-1936	Hitler appointed Germany's Chancellor; anti-Jewish boycotts begin; Dachau Concentration Camp opens; German Parliament gives Hitler dictatorial powers; Hitler becomes Führer; **1935**: Nuremberg Race Laws against Jews decreed; Olympic Games begin in Berlin.
1938	Nazis take over Austria; League of Nations convenes with delegates from 32 countries refusing to accept Jews fleeing Hitler's regime; Nazis occupy the Sudetenland; Nazis arrest 17,000 Polish Jews living in Germany, expelling them to Poland, which refuses them entry. Ernst vom Rath, of the German Embassy in Paris, is shot by Herscyhel Grynszpan, the angry 17-year-old son of deported Polish Jews. Rath's death allegedly ignites Kristallnacht: **November 9-10**.
1939-1940	*September: Nazis invade Poland; 11-year-old Ben's world changes forever.*
	The *SS St. Louis*, with 930 Jewish refugees, is turned away by Cuba, the US and other countries, returning to Europe, where many perish in concentration camps. Great Britain and France declare war on Germany; Soviet troops invade eastern Poland; yellow stars are required to be worn by Polish Jews over age 10. Oswiecim (Auschwitz) near Krakow, chosen as the site of a new concentration camp. Poland's Łódź Ghetto, with 230,000

Appendix

	Jews, the Krakow Ghetto, containing 70,000 Jews and the Warsaw Ghetto, containing over 400,000 Jews, are sealed off. Nazis occupy Paris; France signs armistice with Hitler.
1941	**March:** *Ben and family leave Krakow for Niepolomice.*
	SS murder squads (*Einsatzgruppen*) begin operations in Poland; Japanese attack US at Pearl Harbor; US/Great Britain declare war on Japan; Hitler declares war on US. The *SS Struma* leaves Romania for Palestine carrying 769 Jews but British deny permission for the passengers to disembark. It sails back into the Black Sea and is sunk by a Russian submarine as an "enemy target"; mass killings of Jews using Zyklon-B gas begin at Auschwitz-Birkenau with the bodies being buried in mass graves in a nearby meadow.
1942	*Leser family escapes to Bochnia in the middle of the night.*
	The *New York Times* reports that Nazis have machine-gunned over 100,000 Jews in Baltic states, 100,000 in Poland and twice as many in western Russia; *London Daily Telegraph* reports that over 1,000,000 Jews have already been killed by Nazis; Swiss representatives of World Jewish Congress pass information to London and Washington regarding Nazi plan to exterminate all Jews; open-pit burning of Jews begins at Auschwitz.

Timeline

1943

February: The Romanian government receives no response from offers to Britain and the US to transfer 70,000 Jews to Palestine; **March:** American Jews hold mass rally at NYC's Madison Square Garden pressuring US government to help the Jews of Europe; Krakow Ghetto is liquidated; newly-built gas chamber/crematory IV opens at Auschwitz for arriving Hungarian Jews; Warsaw Ghetto Uprising; **April**: At Bermuda Conference, US and British representatives discuss problem of refugees from Nazi-occupied countries; no action results; Nazis declare Berlin to be *Judenfrei* (cleansed of Jews); US Congress holds hearings about State Department's inaction on European Jews despite mounting reports of mass exterminations.

November: *Ben and brother Tuli transported to boarder in bottom of truck, meet Uncle Baruch at bottom of forest ravine; reunited with Lola and Mechel in Budapest; reunited with Munkács family.*

1944

January: Responding to political pressure to help Jews under Nazi control, President Roosevelt creates the War Refugee Board; **March 19:** Germans occupy Hungary; President Roosevelt issues a statement condemning German and Japanese ongoing "crimes against humanity." **May 15:** Beginning of deportation of Jews from Hungary to Auschwitz.

Appendix

> **May:** *Ben and entire family are forced to leave their homes and are crowded into cattle cars for deportation to Auschwitz-Birkenau.*
> **June:** *Ben is sent to the Durnhau Labor Camp.*

June 6, "D-Day": Allies land in Normandy, France. **July:** Swedish diplomat Raoul Wallenberg saves nearly 33,000 Hungarian Jews. **August:** Anne Frank and family are arrested in Amsterdam, and sent to Auschwitz. **October:** Auschwitz-Birkenau *Sonderkommandos* (Jewish slave laborers) revolt, destroying Crematory IV. **November:** Nazis force 25,000 Jews to walk over 100 miles in rain and snow from Budapest to the Austrian border, followed by a second forced-march of 50,000 persons, ending at Mauthausen; Oskar Schindler saves 1200 Jews.

1945

> **February-March:** *Ben and Cousin Isaac survive Death March to Buchenwald, and then Death Train to Dachau.*
> **April:** *They are liberated at Dachau. Isaac dies in Ben's arms. Ben loses consciousness, waking up four months later in St. Ottilien hospital in Germany. Joins young Zionists in Feldafing, Germany.*
> **December:** *Reunites with Lola and Mechel.*

April 30: Hitler commits suicide in Berlin bunker. **May 8:** War ends with Germany's unconditional surrender. **November:** *Nuremberg War Crimes Trials* begin.

Timeline

1946 — January: *Ben's nephew Heshi is born;* March: *Ben moves into apartment in Munich, Germany with Lola, Mechel and Heshi.*

1947 — **September 21:** *Ben arrives in the USA via the SS Ernie Pyle. Moves into Brooklyn, NY apartment with Lola, Mechel and Heshi; attends night-school and peddles hosiery on Delancey Street.*

1948 — May 14: British Mandate ends in Palestine. Declaration of Independence of the State of Israel; Arab armies invade Israel. Israel wins the Arab-Israeli war.

1949 — *Ben takes bus from New York to Los Angeles.*

1950 - 1953 — Korean War.

June 17, 1950: *Ben and Jean Singer marry in Los Angeles.*
1952: Ben and Jean's daughter, Sherry, is born.
1953: Ben becomes a US citizen.

1957 — *Ben and Jean's daughter, Gail, is born.*

1967 — June 5-10: Israel wins Arab-Israeli War (Six-Day War) between Israel and the United Arab Republic.

1970s — *1973: Ben and Jean's granddaughter, Robyn, is born. 1978: Ben Lesser & Associates is established in Los Angeles.*

1980s

1980: Daughter Gail Marries Michael Gerber.
1982: Granddaughter Jenica born.
1983: Daughter Sherry marries Larry Kramer.
1984: Grandson Adam born. 1987: Granddaughter Cindy born.

1990s

1995: Ben speaks about the Holocaust publicly for the first time at grandson Adam's school; Ben and Jean retire and move to Las Vegas, Nevada.
1996: Ben and Jean visit Ben's parents' memorial in the Bochnia, Poland Jewish Cemetery.

2000s

2006: Ben visits his parents' memorial in the Bochnia, Poland Jewish Cemetery.
2009: Ben founds the ZACHOR Holocaust Remembrance Foundation; Ben speaks at the Tennessee State University Holocaust Education Conference.
2010: March: Ben participates in the March of the Living at Auschwitz-Birkenau. Ben and 200 other participants visit his parents' memorial in the Bochnia Jewish Cemetery.
June: Ben and Jean celebrate their 60th wedding anniversary.
October: Ben celebrates his 83rd birthday by being an honored guest speaker at the Tennessee State University Holocaust Education Conference; Ben establishes "Papa Ben's Kitchen."
November: Lesser family celebrates wedding of granddaughter Robyn Kramer to Chad Weber.
2011: Ben's book, LIVING A LIFE THAT MATTERS: from Nazi Nightmare to American Dream" is published.
2012: Joshua Weber, 1st Great Grandchild, Born May 2, 2012
Adam Gerber, Grandson married Abby Lane, June 24, 2012
2015: Ethan Weber, 2nd Great Grandchild, July 7, 2015

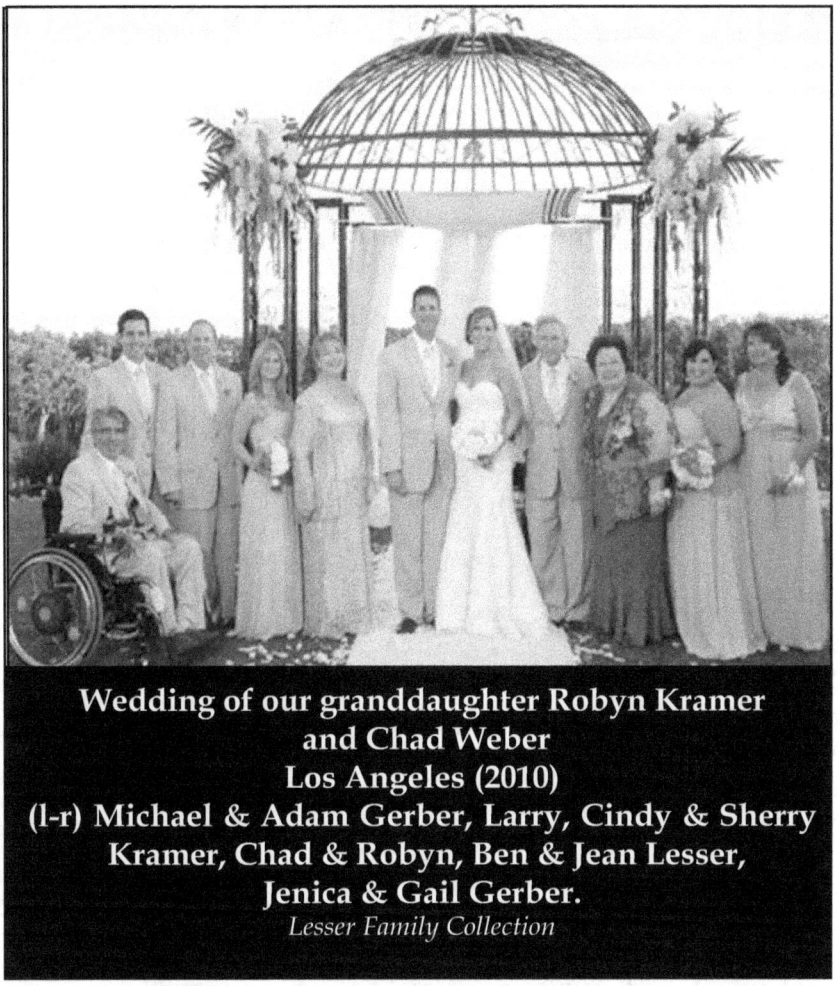

Wedding of our granddaughter Robyn Kramer
and Chad Weber
Los Angeles (2010)
(l-r) Michael & Adam Gerber, Larry, Cindy & Sherry
Kramer, Chad & Robyn, Ben & Jean Lesser,
Jenica & Gail Gerber.
Lesser Family Collection

As you might expect, Ben Lesser continues to
"live a life that matters."
Please check his websites for the latest updates!

www.I-Shout-Out.org
www.ZachorFoundation.org

Appendix

MAJOR NAZI CONCENTRATION CAMPS*

AUSTRIA:
    Mauthausen

CZECH REPUBLIC:
    Theresienstadt

FRANCE:
    Drancy
    Gurs
    Natzweiler-Struthof

GERMANY:
    Bergen-Belsen
    Buchenwald
    Dachau
    Flossenbürg
    Neuengamme
    Ravensbruck
    Sachsenhausen

LATVIA:
    Vaivara

POLAND:
    Auschwitz/Birkenau
    Belzec
    Chelmno
    Gross-Rosen
    Majdanek
    Plaszow
    Sobibor
    Stutthof
    Treblinka

THE NETHERLANDS:
    Vught
    Westerbork

---

*Source: United States Holocaust Memorial Museum

*READERS AND DISCUSSION GUIDE**

1. Before you read this memoir, what did you know about The Holocaust, and from what sources had you acquired this information?

2. What do you think is meant by, "a life that matters"?

3. Describe someone you know who was directly/indirectly affected by The Holocaust.

4. Who are "Holocaust Deniers," and why do they deny this historic event?

5. Are there genocides taking place in the world today?

6. What is "The American Dream"?

7. Do you know anyone who has achieved "The American Dream"? How did they do it?

8. How might the Albert Camus quotation, "Life is the sum of all your choices," apply to everyday life as well as The Holocaust?

9. Describe the most influential person in your life, and describe the impact that he/she has had on you.

10. In what way are you choosing to live "a life that matters?"

*A comprehensive *READERS AND DISCUSSION Guide* is available online through the ZACHOR Holocaust Remembrance Foundation's website: www.ZachorFoundation.org

Appendix

SELECTED VOCABULARY

During the course of reading "Living a Life That Matters: from Nazi Nightmare to American Dream," there have been opportunities to learn or refresh your memory about many word/phrase meanings, historic events/eras, religious and ethnic holidays, concepts, and important people. How many of the following do you know?

1. ***Adolph Hitler***: Known as *Der Fuhrer*, or Dictator, he became Chancellor of Germany in 1934. He and his Nazi Party embarked upon a murderous campaign known as the "Final Solution" with the goal of eliminating the Jewish People of Europe.

2. ***Anti-Semitism***: the hatred of Jewish People based on nothing more than their ethnicity.

3. ***"Arbeit Macht Frei"***: written on the sign over the entrance gate to Auschwitz, these words ironically say that, "Work Makes Man Free."

4. ***Aryan Master Race:*** Hitler believed that only people of Northern European descent should rule the world.

5. ***Blitzkrieg:*** the strategic, lightning-fast coordination of all mobilized military equipment in order to break through borders and quickly overwhelm the enemy.

6. ***The British Mandate:*** Britain's legal control over Palestine from 1922 to 1948.

7. ***Chanukah (Hanukkah):*** the Jewish Festival of Lights, lasting 8 days and celebrates two "miracles": 1. the rededication of the Temple after it had been defiled by

Selected Vocabulary

Syrians; and 2. The small amount of sacred oil that burned for 8 days instead of just one.

8. ***Chalutzim:*** the Zionist pioneers from many European countries whose goal was to create the independent Jewish country of Israel.

9. ***Concentration Camps:*** Hitler's brutal, often deadly prisons for Jews and others he considered undesirable. There were labor camps where prisoners were worked to death, and death camps, where prisoners were murdered in massive gas chambers and then burned in crematoriums.

10. ***Death Marches:*** When the Germans saw that they would soon lose the war, in an effort to hide evidence of the camps, they evacuated prisoners to more centralized camps by marching them for weeks at a time. Thousands of these died from starvation, thirst, exposure, disease, or were murdered by the guards during forced marches from one camp to another. They were left where they fell and died.

11. ***Death Trains:*** Stuffed into over-crowded, filthy cattle-cars that were devoid of sanitary facilities, 1,000s of prisoners were provided neither food nor water. The trains sometimes just went back and forth without stopping or unloading their "cargo." When liberated, sometimes 2 or 3 prisoners would climb out from under the pile of corpses with whom they'd been "traveling" for weeks.

12. ***Diaspora:*** The 6th century BCE exile of the Jewish People from Judah, the area that is now the State of Israel.

13. ***Final Solution to the Jewish Problem:*** Phrase coined by Hitler to describe his plan to exterminate the Jewish People of Europe.

Appendix

14. *Exodus:* The 2nd book of the Bible tells the story of the Israelites escape from Egypt; the name of the ship that tried to carry Jewish refugees to Palestine in 1947, but was seized by the British and sent back to Europe.

15. *Genocide:* Geno = race of people/cide = murder. The deliberate, systematic, government- sponsored annihilation of a people. The term was first coined by Raphael Lemkin at the Nuremberg Trials following WWII.

16. *Gestapo:* Hitler's secret police. Another branch of his military was his ruthless personal body guard unit that was called the "SS" (Schutzstaffel).

17. *Ghetto:* A section of a town where Jews were forced to live in crowded, squalid conditions.

18. *Great Depression:* Caused by the 1929 American Stock Market Crash, this world-wide economic disaster lasted until 1939.

19. *Hamantashen:* three-cornered filled pastries traditionally eaten during Purim, that are said to resemble the ears, hats or pockets of dead Haman, the vicious enemy of the Jewish People.

20. *Holocaust:* Means totally consumed by fire, and usually refers to Hitler's systematic campaign to exterminate the Jewish People of Europe.

21. *Israel:* The independent Jewish country founded in 1948 as a homeland for all Jews.

22. *Jude (Juden, plural):* A Jewish person.

Selected Vocabulary

23. *Kaddish:* Jewish mourners' prayer for the dead

24. *Kapos:* Ghetto residents or concentration camp inmates appointed by Nazis to positions of authority over other residents or inmates.

25. *Kibbutz:* A collective farm/settlement in modern Israel.

26. *Kristallnacht:* The "Night of Broken Glass" November 9- 10, 1938, was a massive government-sponsored series of anti-Jewish pogroms throughout Germany and Austria. Its goal was to terrorize the Jewish People by smashing the windows and burning Jewish homes and businesses, beating and murdering Jews and taking 30,000 Jewish men to concentration camps.

27. *Mandelbroyt (Mandelbrot):* This crispy, rich, traditionally twice-baked Jewish biscuit-shaped cookie or "Almond Bread," originally contained chopped almonds, but in modern times can also include different nuts, dried fruit, and chocolate chips.

28. *Mein Kampf (My Struggle*): Written in 1925-6 by Adolph Hitler during the time he was in prison for treason, this 2-volume book describes Hitler's plan to exterminate the Jewish People of Europe.

29. *Nazis:* Hitler's fascist National Socialist Party based on the belief that Germans were part of the Aryan Master Race and therefore should rule the world. They demonized the Jewish People as being a threat to Aryan supremacy.

30. *Nuremberg Laws:* These brutally anti-Semitic laws were established in Germany in 1935, depriving Jewish residents of Germany their basic human rights including citizenship, employment, and property ownership.

Appendix

31. **Nuremberg Trials:** A series of post WWII military trials held in Nuremberg, Germany and conducted by the Allies to prosecute Nazi War Criminals

32. **Orthodox Judaism:** A traditional interpretation of the Torah (The first 5 books of Moses in the sacred Jewish scriptures) that stresses strict adherence to religious rules.

33. **Passover:** A Jewish holiday commemorating the Exodus of the ancient Israelites when they were freed from slavery in Egypt and journeyed across the desert to Jerusalem. The flat, unleavened Matzo made of flour and water is one of the traditional foods of Passover.

34. **Pogrom/Aktion:** A violent, usually deadly, often Government-sanctioned, riot directed against a specific ethnic/religious group.

35. **Purim:** This joyous Jewish holiday celebrates the deliverance, arranged by Queen Esther, of the Jewish People from the murderous plans of the evil Haman. It includes masquerades, festivals, special gifts and delicacies.

36. **Rabbi:** A teacher of Torah, and the leader of the Jewish congregation. A Cantor assists the Rabbi by singing and leading the congregation in sacred songs.

37. **Righteous Gentiles:** In Israel, non-Jews who risked their own lives to help to save Jewish people during the Holocaust are known as "Righteous Gentiles."

38. **Shoah:** The Hebrew word for The Holocaust; *Yom Ha'Shoah:* Holocaust Remembrance Day.

39. **Shtetls:** Jewish villages in Central and Eastern Europe

Selected Vocabulary

(this area was known as The Pale of Settlement) that were originally settled by Yiddish-speaking Jews who had been expelled from Russia.

40. ***Star of David:*** The 6-pointed Jewish Star, also known as the Shield of David (Mogen David).

41. ***Swastika:*** The twisted cross symbol of Nazi Germany.

42. ***Torah:*** According to the Jewish religion, Moses received the Torah from God on Mt. Sinai. Thus, it is considered to beJudaism's most sacred Jewish book.

43. ***Talmud:*** The Talmud was written around 70 AD, and contains rabbinical interpretations and commentaries on the Torah.

44. ***Third Reich:*** The German government under Adolph Hitler from 1933-1945.

45. ***Yad Vashem:*** Established in 1953, the Holocaust Martyrs' and Heroes' Remembrance Authority's living memorial to the Holocaust safeguards the memory of the past, and transmits its meaning to current and future generations. It is the world center for documentation, research, education and commemoration of the Holocaust.

46. ***Yarmulke:*** Small, round skull cap traditionally worn to Temple by religious Jewish men.

47. ***Yiddish:*** This Jewish language, originally spoken since the 10th century by Eastern European (Ashkenazi) Jews, is a fusion of several languages and dialects including: German, Slavic, Hebrew, and Aramaic. Today, it is spoken throughout the world.

Appendix

48. ***ZACHOR:*** Remember.

49. ***Zionism:*** The Jewish political movement that supports the self-determination and defense of the Jewish people in Israel, the Jewish national homeland.

50. ***Zyklon B:*** The cyanide-based pesticide used by the Nazis to kill human beings in the gas chambers of extermination camps during the Holocaust.

A THANK YOU TO MOTL—2010

**Along with MOTL—2010 participants,
I visit the Majdanek Dome of Ashes**
Lublin, Poland (2010)
Lesser Family Collection

It was a great privilege to take part in the International March of the Living—2010. This outstanding educational program brings students and Holocaust Survivors together in Poland on Yom Ha'Shoah (Holocaust Memorial Day) in order to march out of Auschwitz-Birkenau, the largest concentration camp complex built during World War II. The program's participants also visit Israel to observe Yom HaZikaron (Israel Memorial Day) and Yom Ha'Atzmaut (Israel Independence Day). This year almost 10,000 teens from around the world participated in the event. I was part of the Los Angeles contingent, a group of about 160 teens and six other Holocaust Survivors. Our group also visited the Warsaw Ghetto area, Treblinka, the Jewish ar-

Appendix

eas of Krakow, Bochnia, Lublin, Majdanek and the Zbilagovska Gora Forest, where 800 children were brutally clubbed to death.

While this event was one of the most important and meaningful events that I have ever experienced, there is also no question that this was a life-altering event for the students and other Survivors. I feel truly blessed and privileged to have made this trip with all of you. The entire March of the Living experience is so moving, profound and important, that it is deeply etched into our hearts and memories and will always be remembered . . . ZACHOR!

Each member of the staff did an outstanding job of organizing and coordinating every aspect of this trip. The travel, meals, sites and activities were meticulously timed, and contributed to a profound impact on all of us. Monice Newman, you are remarkable. In addition to being a great administrator, you have a wonderful heart, treated all of us as family, and added a level of emotion to everything we did that touched us all. Much of the meaning and purpose of this trip was enhanced because of you and who you are. Even though the words, "Thank you" are not enough, I thank you for making this trip so special for all of us.

Ronnie Mink, you are a true historian. Your stories came to life by your knowledge and understanding of these horrible events. We have not only learned from you, but will remember it because of you. You are a great teacher and a great friend to me on this journey.

Our extraordinary tour guide, Victor Kuptel, went beyond the call of duty in organizing a surprise side-trip to Bochnia, taking five busloads of tourists — along with a police escort — to visit my parents' gravesite. I know that the students will long remember this visit, and I will always be grateful to you for having arranged it.

A Thank You to MOTL-2010

A special "Thank you" must go to the parents of the students. Please know that by allowing your children to participate in the March of the Living, you have given them a life-altering experience. You have connected them to our people and past generations in a way that will last throughout their lifetimes. This may be one of the greatest gifts you could bestow upon them. I am extremely grateful to you for having done this.

Dear students, remembering the past is the greatest method we have of preventing the tragedies of history from recurring. We Survivors have remembered, shared and shown you all that we can, with the hopes that you will understand and remember these lessons. Together we laughed, cried, ate, danced, and witnessed (or re-witnessed) those places where many of the world's greatest atrocities took place. And in this process, we Survivors also learned profound lessons from you.

You are the last generation to be able to make this trip with Survivors. It is now up to you to tell your children that you went to these camps with a Survivor; that this is what you heard, and this is what you learned. I cannot stress enough the importance of remembering . . . ZACHOR.

I hope you have also learned about the importance of family and to take nothing for granted, because someday, you may no longer have that which is most precious to you. Gratitude is the opposite of taking things for granted. Be grateful for your parents and siblings. Be grateful for each day that you are blessed with. They are all gifts from *Hashem*.

To my own children, grandchildren and much of our extended family, I am known as "Papa Ben." I am sure that our other Survivors also have special names such as, Bubbie, Safta and Saba, and that all of us would be honored to be called these names by any of you. Through this trip and process we have bonded in a way that few others will ever know. We are all a part of a bigger family, an eternal people, a strong link between generations. The hopes and dreams of our silenced ancestors live on in you. Accept that responsibility with pride. Always be proud that you are a Jew. You have made this trip one of my life's fondest memories. "*Dayenu* — it would have been enough. But you went even further and surprised me with a gift that I never anticipated and that moved me to tears. Your generous donation to the Zachor Holocaust Remembrance Foundation is a true mitzvah. Because of you, thousands of others will receive this tangible memento of what they learn about the Holocaust.

This heartfelt gesture makes me even prouder to know you and to be considered as "your Papa."

I really do love each and every one of you.

Ben Lesser (a.k.a. "Papa Ben")

Appendix

Lola and I at family dinner celebrating Jean's and my 55th wedding anniversary.
Alaska (2005)
Lesser Family Collection

ABOUT LOLA

To say that my late sister Lola was my hero, mentor, and inspiration, would be an understatement. From confronting Nazis in an effort to save our father's books, to creating an underground forgery operation to save some of Bochnia, Poland's Jews, to finding me in a Displaced Persons' Camp, bringing me to her in St. Ottilien after the war, then providing me a home in Munich, and ultimately the United States, she was more than a good sister. She was a guardian angel for me and many others too numerous to count. Her passionate commitment to her family, religion, and the Jewish community was unstinting, even as the challenges and infirmities of old-age took their toll. Lola truly lived a life that mattered.

Until her early 90s, Lola stayed busy speaking at schools about the Holocaust. She also continued her work as a fine artist and the busy owner of Lola's Gallery in the heart of Chassidic Borough Park, Brooklyn. Her work has been exhibited in many art galleries throughout the United States, and is in the permanent collection of the San Francisco Museum of Art. Her paintings are also in a number of private collections as well as in the Yad Vashem archive in Jerusalem. Lola was often commissioned to paint portraits. Her paintings encompass a range of styles from traditional and impressionistic, to modern. I thank her for graciously allowing me to include paintings from her Bochnia Series in this book.

While Lola's memoir, A World After This: A Memoir of Loss & Redemption, includes her terrifying experiences during the Holocaust when she was on the run from the Nazis for six years, it is also a love story: love for her family, her beloved first husband, Mechel Lieber, and her religion. At the risk of sounding like an adoring brother, I have to say that her book is wonderful! The experience of reading about my own family's experiences through Lola's eyes was very powerful, and she provided invaluable encouragement and assistance in the writing of my own memoir.

To the great sorrow of her large family and many friends, our beloved Lola Leser Lieber passed away, at the age of 91, on November 2, 2014. Of special note is that this was the 48th anniversary of Mechel Lieber's death.

RESOURCES

A Film Unfinished: http://www.flixster.com/movie/a-film-unfinished

"Aliyah Bet," *Zionism and Israel Encyclopedic Dictionary*, see: http://www.zionism-israel.com/dic/Aliya_Bet.htm

A Man from Munkacs: Gypsy Klezmer (2005): http://www.yalestrom.com/films.html

Auschwitz-Birkenau Memorial and Museum: http://en.auschwitz.org.pl/m/

A WORLD AFTER THIS: A Memoir of Loss and Redemption, Lola Lieber Schwartz, DEVORA Publishing: 2010. http://lolalieber.com/index.html

"Bach in Auschwitz and Birkenau": http://www.cympm.com/orkest.html

Ben Lesser: www.benlesser.com/

Belzec Death Camp: http://www.chgs.umn.edu/museum/memorials/belzec/

Bochnia Jewish Cemetery: http://www.lostfamily.info/cemetery.html

Buchenwald Memorial: http://www.ushmm.org/wlc/en/article.php?ModuleId=10005198

Building Jewish Education/The Jewish Federation of Los Angeles: www.bjela.org/

Appendix

Dachau 29 April 1945: The Rainbow Liberation Memoirs, Sam Dann, Editor; Publisher: Texas Tech University Press; 1998

Dachau: http://www.kz-gedenkstaette-dachau.de/index-e.html

Generations of the Shoah International (GSI) http://www.genshoah.org

"Goethe's Tree": http://www.bbc.co.uk/programmes/b00swq96

Hebrew Immigrant Aid Society (HIAS): http://www.hias.org/

Hillel: The Foundation for Jewish Campus Life: http://www.hillel.org/index

The International Raoul Wallenberg Foundation, www.raoulwallenberg.net/

Jewish Family Service of Las Vegas: http://www.jfsalv.org/

Jewish History in Poland: www.sztetl.org.pl/en/cms/the-project

Jewish Material Claims Against Germany: http://www.claimscon.org/.

Jewish Federation of Las Vegas: http://www.jewishlasvegas.com/

Jewish Virtual Library: http://www.jewishvirtuallibrary.org/jsource/Holocaust/cclist.html

Resources

The Manischevitz Company: http://www.rabfoodgroup.com/contact/index.php

March of the Living International (MOTL): http://www.motl.org/

Middle Tennessee State University Holocaust Studies Program: http://www.mtsu.edu/holocaust_studies/

Multiple Sclerosis info: http://mgerber.blogspot.com

Outwitting History: The Amazing Adventures of a Man Who Rescued a Million Yiddish Books, Aaron Lansky, Algonquin Books: 2005.   http://www.yiddishbookcenter.org/people

Papa Ben's Kitchen: www.PapaBensKitchen.com

Rabbi Eli A. Bohnen and Dachau Liberation, Virtual Jewish Library: http://www.jewishvirtuallibrary.org/jsource/Holocaust/GI22

"Yad Vashem — Righteous Gentiles," http://www1.yadvashem.org/righteous_new/index.html

The Survivors of the Shoah Visual History Foundation (Shoah Foundation): www.dornsife.usc.edu/vhi/

Synagogues in Poland: http://en.wikipedia.org/wiki/Synagogues of Kraków

The Tenement Museum: http://www.tenement.org/

Timeline of Jewish Los Angeles: http://www.jgsla2010.com/hotel-los-angeles/timeline-of-jewish-history-in-los-angeles/

Appendix

Underground Salt Cathedral of Poland: http://whc.unesco.org/pg.cfm?cid=31&id_site=32

United States Holocaust Memorial Museum (USHMM): www.ushmm.org/

Elie Wiesel Foundation: www.eliewieselfoundation.org/homepage.aspx

Wikipedia: www.Wikipedia.org

Yad Vashem Archive: http://www1.yadvashem.org/yv/en/about/archive/index.asp

Zachor Holocaust Remembrance Foundation: www.zachorfoundation.org

CPSIA information can be obtained
at www.ICGtesting.com
Printed in the USA
BVHW041835020519
547222BV00015B/179/P